SEA SALT
Memories & Essays

STAN WATERMAN

New World Publications
Jacksonville, Florida

PUBLISHER'S CATALOGING-IN-PUBLICATION DATA

Waterman, Stan.
  Sea salt : memories & essays / Stan Waterman; [foreword, Peter Benchley; foreword, Howard Hall]
— 1st ed.

  p. : ill.; cm.
  ISBN: 1-87834-8-40-X

1. Waterman, Stan. 2. Cinematographers—United States—Biography. 3. Underwater cinematography.
I. Benchley, Peter. II. Hall, Howard, 1949- III. Title.

TR849.W38 W38 2005
778/.598/577/092

First Edition: 2005
ISBN# 1-878348-40-X
Copyright ©New World Publications, Inc. 2005
Published by New World Publications, Inc., 1861 Cornell Road, Jacksonville, FL 32207
(904) 737-6558, www.fishid.com, eric@fishid.com.

For my wife of fifty-four years, Susy,
who always encouraged my travels and adventures
and welcomed me home with love and family.

CONTENTS

FOREWORD

Peter Benchley

Ladies and gentlemen, are you in for a treat! You are about to make the acquaintance of one of the most extraordinary gentlemen of this or any recent age. And not just a gentleman but a filmmaker, an adventurer, an explorer, a daredevil, a gallant, a poet, an intimate of creatures as exquisitely exotic as the leafy sea dragon and the sloe-eyed cuttlefish and – this above all – a true pioneer in the discovery of our last frontier, the sea.

Stan Waterman has spent more than half a century in, on and under the sea, and in these pages he takes you with him on the amazing ride he calls his life. There is excitement enough in his encounters with wild animals and weird people to fill a hundred lives and all their fantasies. To cite just one example, have you ever wondered what it would be like to dive in the open ocean with a huge school of certifiably anthropophagous sharks as they gorge on the carcass of a whale ... at night? Probably not. But hang on, because when Stan recounts scenes from the filming of the classic 1971 documentary feature film, *Blue Water, White Death*, you'll be there beside him, and astonished that anyone lived to tell the tale.

Stan is on intimate terms with many of the seas' most formidable denizens, including that ultimate marine predator, the great white shark, and he writes wonderfully about the contradictions inherent in this magnificent creature: the incomparable natural beauty, the perfection of function, all manifest in the creature's capacity as a killing machine.

Sea Salt is far more, however, than just a catalogue of critters and close calls. Stan has a profound rapport with the sea, and his command of language and literature eloquently conveys the depth of his feeling. The thoughtful, graceful writing sets the book a full step above most memoirs about the sea; not only does Stan appreciate good writing – you'll be pleased to encounter an occasional quote from Joseph Conrad or Henry Beston – but he'll often turn a phrase or craft a paragraph that could well have come from the pen of a master.

Born in Montclair, New Jersey, one of two sons of a cigar manufacturer, Stan served in the Navy during the last days of World War II and then graduated from Dartmouth College. He was a blueberry farmer in Maine for a while, and tried his hand as a charter-boat captain in the Bahamas. Scuba diving was in its infancy back then, but as soon as Stan discovered that there was a way for him to be able to both see and breathe underwater, he was hooked. Soon he added a movie camera to his kit, and thus was born a career that would lead to five Emmy Awards and would inspire the next two generations of underwater filmmakers.

Today, this gentle man still leads dive tours all over the world, and he is equally at home pursuing schools of whale sharks and sitting at home by a fire on a blustery autumn evening, re-reading "Hamlet" for the twentieth time.

I've had the privilege of knowing Stan since 1974, and I must admit that, like many of Stan's friends, I take a tiny measure of pride in the publication of *Sea Salt*. For at least the last couple of decades, we've been urging him to commit himself to paper because we felt it was important that his vast archive of memories not be permitted simply to evanesce.

As you enjoy each grain of *Sea Salt*, I hope that your richest reward will be a sense of comradeship with the very special man who's sharing with you the story of his utterly beguiling journey.

FOREWORD

Howard Hall

I last dived with Stan Waterman in the Tiputa Pass of the Rangiroa Atoll. On an incoming tide, a dozen of us slipped off a large aluminum skiff and began dropping into the cobalt-blue water just outside the lagoon. All were exceptionally experienced divers including Australian superstars, Ron and Valerie Taylor, and acclaimed author, Peter Benchley. As we fell, Stan rolled onto his back, raised his video camera, and shot a silhouette of our group descending.

We hit bottom at about one hundred and twenty feet, and began drifting into the pass with the current. Gray reef sharks glided past by the dozen and seaward we could see legions more silhouetted against the dark water where the mouth of the pass plummets into the abyss.

The current increased dramatically further into the pass as the bottom rose and the channel narrowed concentrating the current into a raging undersea river. Soon the bottom was hurtling past us as the current approached a velocity of nearly five knots. Five knots may not sound like a great deal of current, but to a diver it's a hurricane force. Even if a diver could hold to a rock in a five-knot current, his diving equipment would be ripped from his body and his arms would soon dislocate at the shoulders. Drifting with a five-knot current, however, can be absolutely delightful, providing one can avoid being swept miles out to sea and lost. To avoid this unpleasant consequence, we would all have to end our dive by moving laterally across the pass and into an eddy created by the reef just inside the lagoon. The timing of this move is somewhat critical and the effort it takes to move through the current, even laterally, is considerable, especially when carrying a bulky camera.

As we drifted through the pass I held to the side so that when the time came I could more easily move across and into the eddy. Sharks, however, tend to stay in the deepest water at the center of the pass. The current was at its peak when I noticed a dozen gray reef sharks hovering. Then, upstream, I noticed a column of bubbles racing toward the sharks. Stan Waterman was deep in the channel and poised to film the sharks as he hurtled through the center of the pass. If he stayed there too long he would never make it across the pass and into the eddy before being swept far into the lagoon where for miles the lagoon surface was a nightmarish fury of six-foot standing waves; conditions that would make surface rescue difficult.

Stan triggered his video camera as he flew through the center of the school of sharks and as he rushed into them the predators scattered like an exploding grenade. The shot recorded on video tape, Stan then made his move across current at the last possible moment kicking ferociously and using his free hand to help pull himself laterally across the pass. For a minute or two I was afraid he wouldn't make it. But his timing had been perfect and soon he joined the rest of the group decompressing in the calm eddy behind the reef. As he swam up to me and the others, Stan, filled with enthusiasm, pumped his fist, rolled his eyes and yelled "Wow!" loudly through his regulator mouthpiece.

And that is how Stan Waterman celebrated his 80th birthday.

In a sport that celebrates big-game hunters who arm themselves with underwater cameras, Stan Waterman is a legend. He is one of the extraordinary few who, compelled by adventure at the dawn of a new sport, cast-off the security of ordinary life and set out to pioneer a new and dangerous wilderness. In those early years there were no dive instructors, no dive resorts, no live-aboard dive boats, no dive guides, no rules, and no articles in dive magazines that might have allowed Stan to predict what he might find on his next dive. There was nothing but the unknown and every dive was an adventure filled with uncertainty and the possibility of life-threatening danger. Today it's hard to imagine what it must have been like to dive at night, swim with whales, or leave a shark cage when no one had ever done it before.

I was studying biology in college when I saw *Blue Water, White Death* playing in the movie theater. Even then, many years after Stan had become a veteran diver and noted underwater cinematographer, leaving a shark cage was considered insanity. I remember watching Stan and his companions open the doors to cages surrounded by ten-foot sharks, then swim out among the monsters to what seemed like certain death. I was thunderstruck. Today it's something you can see almost any night on the Discovery Channel, but back in 1970 leaving the cage was simply unthinkable.

Years later, and by wonderful circumstance, I had the privilege of meeting Stan, working with him, and becoming his friend. As is the nature of such relationships, the protégé benefits from the friendship far more than does the mentor. Certainly, no one in this business has been more influential or more instrumental in the development of my career. His uninhibited gifts of wisdom and opportunity are debts that can never be repaid. But sharing hundreds of dives with Stan is the gift I most cherish. Stan dives with an almost childlike enthusiasm that has never dulled. And the more challenging and dangerous the dive, the more Stan seems to relish it. Though he often tells hilarious stories about acts of foolish bravado by screwball divers who "know not the meaning of fear," I suspect that he has never been truly afraid himself. Many times I have dived with Stan in situations that, at the time, seemed dire and sometimes life-threatening. Yet he always led these dives without reservation or hesitation and often without even serious consideration. If in the following pages one senses a lack of reverence for the dangers this man has faced over his long diving career, it may simply be that he does not describe fear well because he really doesn't experience the emotion as most of us do. I once saw Stan paralyzed from the chest down by decompression sickness. Then only hours later, after what can only be described as a miraculous recovery, he was eager to dive again as if nothing had happened.

The following pages are filled with stories culled from a lifetime of diving adventure written by the man who pioneered exploration under the sea and the art of capturing this exotic and often dangerous wilderness on film. And the adventure continues. As I write this, two years after our dive together in the Rangiroa Atoll, Stan has future diving expeditions scheduled to Palau, Truk Lagoon, Grand Cayman, Cocos Island, Sulawesi, Tonga, the Galapagos, and to Guadalupe Island, Mexico, to once again, confront the great white shark. For Stan, each dive continues to be a great adventure.

PREFACE

"I shall be telling this with a sigh ages and ages hence,
Two roads diverged in a yellow woods and I, I took
The one less traveled by and that has made all the difference."
— *Robert Frost*

As I totter into my eighty-third year I am reminded that an age, or at least a lifetime, has passed since I took to the sea. I might have stayed with blueberry farming in Maine, a viable but boring business. I recall Robert Frost writing about a man staggering around lost in the woods who "…lets death descend upon him where he is, with nothing done to evil, no important triumph won more than if life had never been begun." I didn't really have triumphs in mind but I did want some real adventure in my life. The exploits of Hans Hass and Jacques Cousteau fired resolve to seek my future under the sea. I was already inclining in that direction: the ocean that had been my summer playground as a boy and almost surrounded our house in Maine was a potent force in shaping my dreams. This coupled with an adequate income from my father's generous legacy enabled me to take a chance. I built the *Zingaro*, a Maine Coast lobster boat modified for diving, abandoned the blueberries and cast my lot with the sea. That was the fork in the road. I never turned back.

My love affair with the sea came as easily as a little boy might be drawn to the pretty girl next door. The sea became a wonderful and exciting part of my life from the time I could walk and – soon after – swim. During my school years I spent half of my summer days with a gang of surf and beach brats on the Delaware shore. With the exuberance of sea otters, we were in and out of the water, defying riptides and undertows, body surfing on great storm waves that would have broken older, less supple bodies. At day's end we grudgingly turned our backs on the sea and headed home, wrinkled like prunes and burnt umber from the sun.

The other half of summer was spent on the Maine coast. My father's house was at the end of a point. From porches on three sides you could throw a stone into the sea. The air was deliciously rich with the smells of low tide clam flats and weed-wigged rocks, mingled with spruce and pine. Overseas during the war, I used to have three-dimensional olfactory dreams of Maine. I remember awakening on foggy mornings and listening to the sounds that the great pulpwood schooners made as they groped through the pea soup fog of Eggemoggin Reach, less than a football field away. The staccato bark of their one-lunger, make-and-break yawl boat engines bounced like pistol shots in the echo chamber of the fog. Their foghorns, lung-powered or hand-cranked, called to one another like lovesick cows. We were in and out of boats, fishing in the cove, and sailing the gaff-rigged sloop in 40-knot winds. On picnic days that took us an hour's run to Marshall's Island – with nothing between it and Spain but open Atlantic – we would set a 500-hook trawl. When I was old and strong enough, I helped with the great silver harvest of cod, haddock, and dogfish and occasionally a halibut as big as a barn door.

So for me, by circumstance of birth, the sea was a vital, forming part of my growing years. I was wedded to it and took it for granted without even realizing that I had succumbed to a siren song and a love affair that would last for life. Before television would create a race – as Milton Berle once said, "With eyes as big as cantaloupes and no brains at all," – we read. The exploits of Commander Ellsberg and Colonel John Craig were illuminated by flashlight under the covers after "Lights out." Jules Verne, Victor Hugo, Jack London, Conrad, and many others who filled the sea with romance, monsters and red-blooded adventure provided the stuff for dreams of the ultimate adventure. That was, of course, diving into the submarine world. It was virtually unattainable in the 1930s. Hardhat divers were a breed as far removed from a boy growing up in a middle-class eastern suburb as cowboys and Bengal Lancers.

Then came a second honeymoon. On a Florida holiday with my family I was presented with a curiosity from Japan. It was a handcrafted facemask, used by the female Ama pearl divers. The year was 1936 and I was 13 years old. That mask, which still hangs on the wall near my desk, preceded the arrival of today's common skin diver's mask by almost five years. With the mask pressed tightly to my face, I entered the water along a stone jetty, opened my eyes, and beheld. Landing on the moon could not have been as electrifying as was that first clear vision of the remote world that had only existed in my fantasies. That truly set the hook. When the first skin-diving equipment appeared in the early 1940s and the first Aqualung at the end of that decade, I was as ready as Tom Jones was for the favors of Sophie Weston.

My love affair is so inextricably wound into my origins that I could not avoid it. A lifetime has already passed. Thanks to my wife's hectoring about a high-fiber diet and moderation in my passion for cheese, I still succumb to the siren song. I still enter the sea with a sense of adventure and enthusiasm. Because almost every dive is a learning experience, it has become an ongoing affair in which I come to know this beautiful mistress in her infinite variety better and better. I am reminded of a line from Shakespeare's *Antony and Cleopatra* in which the speaker describes Cleopatra: "Other women cloy the appetites they feed, but she makes hungry where most she satisfies." The sea has given me that love and shares with my family the very fabric and heart of my life.

There were many catalysts and supports for my turning to the sea and staying the course through the years. Susy, my wife of more than 50 years, backed and encouraged me all the way. She was virtually a single mother as I went off on expeditions and film productions for months at a time. The G.I. Bill of Rights provided by our government for service men and women after World War II paid for an Ivy League college that I could not otherwise have afforded.

Throughout the 1990s, the publishers of *Ocean Realm* magazine, Charlene deJori and Cheryl Schorp, encouraged me to write and accepted my essays for each of their quarterly publications. My family laughs easily. We share a sense of humor that feeds on itself and makes our regular reunions happy occasions. Dive journals are not strong on jesting. Their subjects are usually taken very seriously. However, I discovered during my lecture years that diving audiences very much appreciated humor. So I have made much use of it in my writing. The *Ocean Realm* ladies, who were themselves witty and urbane, encouraged and applauded my sense of humor.

The heart of my writing was penned during that happy decade-long relationship in a column entitled "Sea Salt." The remaining selected writings and letters presented here were drawn from both published and private materials in my files. Although my life of adventure at sea deeply defines who I am, I chose to center my personal story around the Punch Bowl, my previous and rapidly rising new summer home on the shores of Maine.

Memories

The death of objects can release a grief even more bewildering than the death of a loved person. People are supposed to die, hard as that is to keep in mind. Whether one lived with boring prudence or courted death, the end is the same, inevitable. But objects as durable and as ancient as antique vases, especially such objects, which have survived so many centuries, offer a promise of immortality. Part of why we become attached to them, collect them, is that it is not inevitable that they will some day be subtracted from the world. And when that promise is broken, by accident or negligence, our protestations seem pointless. Our grief a mite indecent. But the mourning, which amplifies grief and thereby eases it, still needs to be done.

— *Susan Sontag* THE VOLCANO LOVER

I

THE PUNCH BOWL

The coast of Maine in the summer months is about as close to heaven as one may come in these United States. At least, so it seems to those who are blessed to grow up there in the summertime. It took days to drive there in the early 1930s. Roads north of Boston were dirt. The summer trek was a real odyssey. From Montclair, New Jersey, where we lived, I remember the endless three-day journey, stopping overnight in Deerfield, Massachusetts, then in Rockland, well down the Maine coast from our summer home, and finally way down east to the northern shore of Penobscot Bay. The air changed as we approached the sea. A particular aroma, compounded of spruce and pine, mingled with the pungent low tide flat, all in a matrix of salt vapor from the waves of the sea that beat itself against the granite coast. Tangy and clean and promising, it freshened the memories of the last summer.

My father, who worked in a cigar factory in Boston, first went to Maine as a young man in the 1880s. He and his two brothers and his sister, my Aunt Alice, traveled by boat, the Eastern Steamship Line. The fast packet took them overnight from Boston to Rockland. There they changed to the local, a smaller ship that stopped all along the coast at little villages that had steam boat wharves – Camden, Belfast, Castine, Cape Rosier, Bucks Harbor, Sargentville and on eastward to Blue Hill. They disembarked at Cape Rosier and could walk from the wharf to the boarding house where they would stay for their holiday. From all these village stops small steam launches would transport summer visitors to the many islands in the bay that had summer hotels.

From Cape Rosier, Dad, Uncles George and Charl, Aunt Alice and other guests would hire a day sailer, usually a Friendship sloop with a local captain, and sail as the wind allowed to one of many favorite islands or coves along the coast for a picnic. An hour's sail from Cape Rosier was a cove called the Punch Bowl that was a favorite picnic place. The peninsula that formed the cove was heavily wooded with spruce and pine and several great oaks on the point. The cove was sheltered on all sides by an evergreen forest. At the head of the cove were the ruins of two massive granite wharves, all that remained of a great ice works that prospered before the invention of refrigeration. Great four- and five-masted schooners took the blocks of ice into their holds, packed sawdust around them for insulation and sailed away for the Bahamian and Caribbean markets. On the point itself, there was a shallow hole under a great pine. Legend imputed its origin to being the hole from which Captain Kidd removed a treasure chest. This was substantiated – or so we believed – by men still alive in my father's day who actually witnessed from concealment in the woods a sailing ship entering the cove and a long boat carrying the chest out to the ship. My father, who continually inspired us with wild and wonderful tales, further averred that the men made their way to the point after the ship had departed and found the hole with the imprint of a chest in the fresh dirt. Saplings laid down like rails from hole to shore were scraped free of their bark by "something heavy" that had been slid along the rails. We children had no doubt about the nature of that "something." So the Punch Bowl was richly imbued with the romance of real and imagined history.

My father, Will Waterman, worked hard, was enterprising and in time owned the cigar company where he worked. He never finished high school, but his ship came in as it did for Horatio Alger. He remembered the Punch Bowl, found that the property was for sale and purchased 150 acres of land that included the peninsula and the great forest that surrounded the cove and extended beyond the monumental ice wharves. The property included almost a half mile of shore. In 1929, on the eve of the Great Depression, he commenced the building of a house.

The property is in the village of Sargentville, hard by what is today the Deer Isle Bridge. I am told that more than 100 men from Sargentville and neighboring villages were employed to push through the building of the house and clearing of the property in a single winter so that it would be ready for summer use. The house would be the capstone in the career of a young Blue Hill builder named Herrick. It had five bedrooms in the main wing and three more in the servants' wing. There were three fireplaces to which my wife, Susy, and I added another in an expanded kitchen. Two porches faced the ocean and the beautiful passage called Eggemoggin Reach that separated Deer Isle and Little Deer Isle from the mainland. A third porch faced the cove itself from the back of the house. That was for the servants (in the last of the upstairs downstairs Victorian era, Dad was an enlightened employer). In the generation that followed my father, that is my own generation, Susy came to love that back porch. It was in a warm lee and even when a nippy wind blew off the Reach on the other side of the house the sun flooded in the porch. She often served tea there for friends and her family when they stopped by.

Mom and Dad were divorced soon after I was born. In the pampered cocoon of the third-floor nursery, attended by a German governess and doting servants, the world passed me by. I knew nothing of social fractures. When I was old enough to make some sense out of life in general I learned that my father had married late in life, having worked hard and climbed the ladder to the presidency of a successful cigar company. Although he was a newly-minted millionaire by then, he had no social pretensions. When he finally had time to think about marriage he met my mother at a tea dance, or what would today be called a "swingles bar." Vulgarians would identify it as a "meat market." Mom was beautiful, young and right out of a convent school. Dad was ready. The scenario was a familiar one and often a prelude to social disaster.

Used to a blue-collar home of near tenement dimensions, Mom was propelled into a world of servants, a huge manor house in Montclair, New Jersey and life with a conservative older man. She was gay and vibrant and entered into the Roaring Twenties and its speakeasies and post-World War I frenzy with exuberance. I remember Dad telling me that when he first returned to the site of the Punch Bowl, intending to build on the magnificent, wild and isolated shore, Mom was with him. As the story goes she viewed the unbroken forest and coastline on which no other houses appeared and turning to the real estate agent and asked, "But where are the night clubs?"

The end was foreseeable. She was hit on by a gigolo named Mervin Lafferty, who played the piano and golf – sounds like a soap opera, doesn't it – and soon announced her intention to divorce Dad and marry Mervin. Dad sent her on a round-the-world cruise to give her time to think it over. When she returned she said, "You lose, Will." And that's how I came to spend half of each summer at Rehoboth Beach. Dad bought her a house and settled her there with enough support to live comfortably and support Mervin.

II

REHOBOTH DAYS

Rehoboth was the weekend and holiday shore point for Baltimore, Washington and Philadelphia. It had no social distinction. Life focused on the magnificent beach, a long boardwalk and the tawdry, honky-tonk town, the main street of which terminated in the ocean. The Silver Dollar dance hall and the Top Hat nightclub and liquor store were Mom's nightly haunts. Mervin danced divinely.

My brother Bill, four years my senior, was dashing and handsome and ran with a teenage crowd. Both of us spent our days at the beach. Burnt black by the sun, we body surfed in the great Atlantic breakers. I had a bunch I hung out with who were my own age and all from good middle-class families. We put our beach towels down near the lifeguard stand and, as regulars, prided ourselves in recognition by that godlike figure enthroned under an umbrella at the top of his high wooden stand. It was a healthy life by the sea. We burned off enormous reservoirs of energy, charged home at noon on our bikes to wash down peanut butter sandwiches with quarts of milk and raced back to the beach again. This was the part of my Rehoboth activity that Dad envisioned when he allowed Mom to have me for half of the summer. And indeed, I was delivered back to Maine brown and lean and healthy.

Dad knew nothing about the flip side of the Rehoboth experience. Our having referred to "Uncle Wally" having coffee with Mom in the morning no doubt disturbed him, but not enough to challenge Mom's qualifications for having my brother and me with her part of every summer. "Uncle Wally" was a bookie. He took Mom's racetrack bets at what served as breakfast for her. By the time she got up, Bill and I had already gone through a pound of bacon and a half dozen fried eggs and were off to the beach. If we did linger past breakfast, which happened on rainy days, we would hear Mom routinely throwing up in her bathroom. When she emerged, appearing deathly pale and martyred, she refused to talk or even acknowledge us. Alice Wiggins, our cook, had her coffee ready, or else! Mom had long ago established the morning ground rules: "I will not talk until I've had my coffee." By the time Wally arrived she was wired for the day.

Both Bill and I cut loose after dark. Bill had his own peer group. I never saw him in the evening. I dressed fit-to-kill: white Palm Beach suit, dark blue shirt, yellow tie and two-tone shoes – a perfect junior hood. I would hit the boardwalk, stride the half mile into town, and go to the movies. Today I can never smell the pungent aroma of french fries and broiling hot dogs and the sickening sweet smell of salt water taffy without returning sensually to Rehoboth on the midway in the evening.

Nothing bad happened. There were no drugs back then. We weren't even tempted with liquor, because it tasted so bad. After the movies I would meet some of my bunch, ride the Bump'm Cars in the arcade, perhaps spend a dime in pennies on the Pitch' N Toss suckers' game, and climb the wall in the alley behind the Silver Dollar Dance Hall to spy on the dancers and drinkers inside. Mom was often there. When we broke up – and I was often the last one since I had no time restrictions – I would head for home down the boardwalk. The house would always be locked; so I would climb the roof of the shed by the back door and from there onto the roof and let myself in through the dormer window of my bedroom. The time might be ten or 11 in the evening. My gang for the most part had responsible parents. My fellow boardwalk cowboys (and girls) had to be home at a reasonable time. I was the only loose cannon and too young to do a solo adventure. So I was generally tucked in and hard into charging my batteries when a warm body slipped into bed with me.

It happened more than once, but I will cover the wee-hour-of-the-morning visits with just one recollection. The time was probably about two a.m. A party was going full-blast in the living room below me, the piano – ill-tuned in that humid climate – pounded on by Uncle Mervin, laughter and shouting fracturing the night. I would have slept through it all and never knew how many times I did. But the introduction of a body into my bed and the stale, sweet smell of gin breath on my face woke me up pretty fast. I remember a slurred voice telling me her name was Ginger, or it might have been Dawn or Laverne or another name. Whatever name, the body was sure to have originated at the Top Hat Night Club, the hottest and sleaziest nightery in town. Mom, a regular there, frequently brought the entire establishment home to keep the party going.

Now understand, all this happened in the early thirties. I was about ten or 11, old enough to be interested in girls and to scatter my seed upon the bottom sheet every night with a wet dream. It may seem inconceivable in this day of full-blown, hardcore porn no further away than the video tube and the Internet or, perhaps, the magazines under the shirts in your older brother's drawer. But, I was so innocent that I had never seen a vagina, had no idea what was down there, hadn't the least concept of how babies were created, and nonetheless woke up with a murderous hard-on each morning.

The body of the wretched, thoroughly smashed bar maid felt good and warm and – without defining the sensation – erotic enough to produce the first hard-on of the morning. And nothing happened. I was initiated into the wild kissing then known as French kissing, something I had never experienced with my German governess. A tongue was thrust into my mouth without a by-your-leave, and despite the whisky/gin flavor that came with the insert, I recall it being rather pleasant.

The curious thing about all that, as I look back upon it, is that the girl (or woman), coming from the lowest order of promiscuous environment, did not molest me any further. She wouldn't have discovered much if she had. And they all must have crashed and started snoring before the groping started. Even though I was fully awake by then I never got around to launching an exploration of my own. Either I was witless or so impacted by the Victorian restraints that smothered my growing up years in my father's household that I dared not make the move. Some few years later, when I was packed away to boarding school and erupting with the post-pubescent urges of a young teenager, I fantasized about those nocturnal visits. Alas the time had passed. In that prison-like dormitory, I would gladly have abused a warthog had it climbed into the bunk with me.

The second half of the summer was by decree spent with Dad at the Punch Bowl. The difference in social climate couldn't have been more dramatic. I never told Dad what went on at Rehoboth. I did have enough sense to keep that to myself. He would not have been amused.

Mom loved her two kids, especially me as the youngest. It was a maudlin kind of love, but it was real. She was a kind-hearted person, meant well and did the best her own background and family environment allowed her to do. I was her "Little Angel." She borrowed respect for herself by showing off the fabric of manners I learned at home – holding doors for elders and chairs for ladies, shaking hands, courteous replies, and so forth. We seemed to Mom's friends to be from another world, and indeed we were.

Mom died in 1942 of alcohol-related diseases. Her last stand was a cheap apartment on a side street in Miami. Her only friends were the owners of the tavern where she bellied up to the bar about mid-day every day and passed time. I can only recall a line from Shakespeare's *Richard II* spoken by the king as he was taken to his death: "I wasted time, and now doth time waste me."

I don't want to dwell too long on some of the odd things that happened in my upbringing. Surely the comparison between my divided holidays, half mom and half dad, presented a wild dichotomy. None of us, writing about ourselves, are apt to admit to any weirdness; and – certainly – I turned out reasonably stable. In hindsight, I probably had a more realistic learning experience with Mom and her libidinous social environment than I did in Dad's Victorian household, where I was raised for the majority of the year.

Dad's was an upstairs/downstairs household. At the huge brick house in Montclair, New Jersey we at times had two cooks, three maids, a governess, a gardener and a chauffeur. The first governess I remember – and probably the first I had – became mother to me, since Mom departed for the pleasures of the flapper and speakeasy era when I was two. Her name was Fraulein Krum. The language in the third-floor nursery was the language of the governess. Apparently it was all the vogue then to have children raised by foreign nannies. Until the age of five I was raised speaking German. Dad spoke no German. So – I am told – I was trucked out from time to time to stand before the great god, my father, scrubbed and brushed and awe-struck, say something polite that I had been coached to say (in German, of course) and then swifted off to the nursery. I was about five before Dad decided it was time for some communication with his own son and sent me off to kindergarten.

I am certain that Fraulein loved me and cared for me in her Teutonic way. In Germany generations of children were raised under the rod. Harsh, swift discipline was illustrated in picture books depicting death and mutilation for the child that disobeyed. I had a primer entitled *Strubelpater*. The cartoon-like drawings, accompanied by short verses that lamented the terminal fate suffered by the child who strayed from the true course, showed – in one two-page sequence – a child playing with matches, catching fire, burned to a crisp and, in the final panel, a pile of smoldering ashes on the floor. Another series of panels illustrated a child sucking on his thumb, admonished by a parent, and threatened with what would happen if he did it again. In the next panel the child is thumb-sucking again. A dreadful man with scissors darts out from behind the curtain and cuts off both thumbs. In the final panel the horror-struck reader may meditate on the picture of the chastised child, holding up his thumb-less hands spurting blood. So I was raised in an atmosphere of fear that regularly impinged on genuine affection that Fraulein could soothe me with.

That my sex life turned out to be normal and robust enough for me to produce a healthy family may testify to the resilience of children growing up. If you think the circumstance of the bimbos climbing into the bunk with me was disruptive, Fraulein's remedy for any aberrant, libidinous behavior I might slip into as a child might well have unhinged a more sensitive nipper and ruined his sex life forever.

One day, when I was probably about six or seven, I was sitting on the pot, playing with my weenie and absorbed in the phenomenon of its response to stimulation. Fraulein suddenly appeared, yanked me off the pot, boxed my ears (a favorite punishment) and directed my attention to the large laundry hamper that stood opposite the pot. Her voice, no doubt anticipating the shrill, animal-like roars that would accompany Hitler's broadcasts, let me know that if I ever touched my weenie again a horrid man would spring out of the hamper with scissors, cut off the offending organ and sew it onto the middle of my back so that I could never reach it again. No wonder that on the occasion of my first initiation into the rites of intercourse (with a gentle and wise New York City prostitute, who became a friend and lover for almost a year while I was in boarding school) I approached the dark deed with my back forward.

III

INHERITANCE

My father died in 1943 from natural causes. I was in the service. When I returned at the end of the war the Punch Bowl had been unoccupied for three years, looked after by our caretaker, John McCabe. He was an avuncular, loquacious Irishman, a former chauffeur for the family, and had been my gentle mentor as a child. Dad built a cottage for him and his wife at the head of the road. He lived out his life caretaking for the Punch Bowl and a neighbor's property.

The property was left to my brother, Bill, and me. He is four years my senior. Our relationship was no better or worse than may be normal for younger and older brothers. I resented his superiority, especially since he had achieved Captain rank in the Army and I had been a sailor. He barely tolerated my immaturity. Had we continued spending our summers there together, one of us would have surely murdered the other. At the time neither of us could see owning such a great summer estate. We put the entire property up for sale at $52,000. There were no takers. Remember, in 1946, as we emerged from the war, we were also just emerging from the Great Depression. $52,000 was a big poke then; $1 million could have bought the Taj Mahal. Bill and I both had some liquid assets in one of the trusts that Dad had left equally to each of us. As the magic of the Punch Bowl again invaded my heart and soul, I determined not to lose it. Bill was set on going into farming. Fortunately for us both he was mature and prudent enough to know that a great summer estate was economically foolish if he was to earn his keep farming; and he wanted to farm. His wife Ali's sister was married to the manager of a big farm estate in Virginia. Bill and Ali found the country squire life that prevailed in that part of the country appealing and had the means to support it with income from stock raising. On the other hand, I was about to return to college on the G.I. Bill of Rights and had no need other than a home for the summers ahead. He sold it to me for $10,000 – the whole enchilada, 150 acres of ocean-front land, the great house on the magnificent point, shaded by tall oaks and outbuildings that included two boat houses. He never regretted it. I look back upon it as one of the happiest circumstances in my life. Bill and Ali never had children and created a pleasant, active life for themselves. They raised Angus cattle and Southdown sheep for breeding, joined the horsy set and, indeed, had the life of the country squire with plenty of hard work on the land and with the animals to make it succeed.

I took over the Punch Bowl, realizing one of my dearest fantasies. I was laird of a manor, pursued adventures with my boats and, in turn, became part of a young group of summer kids that were about my age, perhaps a little younger. Summers were (and still are) filled with boats, picnics and working on my own land with axe and chain saw to keep the beautiful point trim. My only social life was with my young friends in the village. Inevitably my eye was filled with the image of a handsome, blond, blue-eyed laughing and energetic girl who summered in the village with her family. And because I was really without family, they took me in. Her name was Susanna Peck. She went to Bennington College, which was about an hour across the mountains from me at Dartmouth. I pursued. She acquiesced. We were married in January 1950, just weeks after my off-term graduation from Dartmouth.

In the more than 50 years since that time, the house was filled with our three children and then their five children and artifacts – things – that caught my eye as I traveled each year, and often several times a year, to far parts of the world on film productions. Gradually the house took on the appearance of an eclectic mini-Smithsonian. Very little was left from Dad's time. The most spectacular items were the two Bengal tiger skins that dominated the great hall. They set the rather exotic tone for the whole house: they and the beautiful stained-glass window over the landing at the bottom of the two stairs. There were weapons that ranged from flintlocks to cap and ball to contemporary assault rifles. Susy hated these last, which were given to me by Peter Benchley. We kept them out of sight. There were swords, great double-handed crusaders' broad swords, Navy cutlasses, Scottish claymores, a two thousand-year-old amphora that I raised from the Turkish coast, the cannon from an 18th century privateer, ships' models, insects in cases and on and on with a few thousand books wherever we could find space for them.

We all worked hard and lovingly to keep the house shining. I called it "pulling on the oars to keep the boat afloat." In Dad's time the house had three to four servants inside and three groundsmen/boatmen outside, the latter year round. We ran it ourselves and loved it even more for our labors. In time we put most of the land into an environmental trust and ultimately gave ownership of the entire property to the children. The house might have gone on for generations past ours. It was solidly set on granite and built with the skill and care and strength that is almost a lost art in carpentry and house building today.

The terrible thing happened mid-October 1994. The specter of fire had always haunted us. With four fireplaces, two of which were in use daily, and old wiring through walls that were squirrel warrens, and a house that was all wood and shingle, fire was both the joy and hospitality of crackling logs in the fireplaces and a potential horror. I was away at the time, returning from New Guinea. Susy, who loved the quiet of the late fall months, always stayed on by herself, visited by a few friends, until she was practically frozen out. She returned from the morning trip to the village post office to find a fire raging in the kitchen wing and already out-of-control. A fresh northwest wind, the kind we most loved for sailing and wind surfing, fanned the flames. Before the village pumper and the modest equipment from two surrounding villages could even reach the ocean with their hoses, the house was gone. Only the chimneys remained, and they, too, were beyond reconstruction. I am glad I did not see it happen. Susy will be haunted by the image of all we loved and nurtured in that splendid house being reduced to ashes. She still wakes up crying in the night. The land remains. The point is still one of the finest locations on the coast. We are building again. But we know that an era, a grand style, passed and can never be duplicated. Thank God we knew what we had and used it well. We appreciated every nuance of it and passed that awareness on to our children.

Now, while I can recall in detail every collector's piece that I brought to that house and the experiences and adventures that attended the acquisitions, I will use my mind's eye to scan each room and recall the origin of those pieces. There may be some good storytelling there. I intend to enjoy the telling.

IV

"FIRE AND ICE"

To the right of the desk on the wall hangs a framed letter from Robert Frost to my uncle, Dr. George Waterman. Uncle George was one of the prominent residents of Palm Beach, Florida. He was elected the first president of the Society of the Four Arts, a cultural forum to which Robert Frost was invited as a guest speaker. He stayed with Uncle George and Aunt Claire. Frost loved Uncle George but fell afoul of my redoubtable Aunt Claire, for whom punctual attendance to social hours by guests gave no quarter to any deviation, no matter how famous he or she might be. Frost was late to dinners or failed to show up at all. He did not retire with the household but wandered afield along the oceanfront at all hours of the night. He used the house phone to conduct long distance phone calls to his current girlfriend. Aunt Claire could not control him and it pissed her off. He returned the feelings. The letter was a warm expression of thanks to Uncle George without a single reference to his acerbic hostess. Remember, it was Frost who wrote in his short poem, "Fire And Ice":

> Some say the world will end in fire;
> Some say in ice.
> From what I've tasted of desire
> I hold with those who favor fire.
> But if I were to perish twice,
> I think I know enough of hate
> To know that for destruction ice
> Is also great
> And would suffice.

When I was a senior at Dartmouth College majoring in English, I took part in a competition that offered a limited number of English majors the privilege of attending a seminar with Robert Frost. It was to be held in the

Rare Books room of the Baker Library twice a week for one semester. Of course, every one in the English department wanted in. Sixteen students out of perhaps 150 applicants would be the lucky winners based on a short essay on "Why I Want to Sit with Robert Frost." There were so many bright students in the department that I knew I didn't have a chance. I hit on one desperate – and slightly despicable – approach. I submitted my essay, which said, in short: "I know that you behaved very badly when you stayed with my Uncle George and Aunt Claire in Palm Beach and I think you owe it to me." It was brash and rude, and I still look back upon it with wonder at my cheek. But it worked. I was ushered into the office of the great man. He didn't look up when I took a seat by his desk and appeared to be reading my wretched essay. Then he looked up and fixed a pair of penetrating eyes upon me. They were light blue and they were sharp but not unkind. He studied me for a moment. Then, with something akin to the proverbial twinkle, he spoke: "So you're Dr. Waterman's nephew? That wife of his is a real gorgon, isn't she?" I happened to agree with him and let him know. With that we talked a little while about Uncle George, who was, indeed an almost hypnotically charming, erudite, delightful gentleman. And I was in.

We lucky ones met by the fireplace in the Rare Books room each evening of the seminars. Frost sat in a great wingback chair. We sprawled on the carpet. He talked about anything that came to his head or recited lines from a poem he was working on. We listened. There were no questions or notes. I think we were all aware that we were having a rare, privileged live contact with literary history and one of the great poets of the time. I could not know that I would so enjoy Frost's poetry that it would provide a precious tool for a vocation that then lay many years over the horizon. On the long drives south from Hanover to Boston or New York or for holidays with my brother in Virginia I would double space write out poems that I loved and memorize them. In those days, the late forties, there were no in-car cassette players (today I am addicted to recorded books for long drives) and the radio had little to offer. So I entertained myself by reviewing what I had learned and practicing the vocal delivery of the poems. Years later, when I started to earn my bread as a platform speaker, those lines from Frost were recalled and dropped into the talks effectively. The memory of his white-thatched, puffy brown face with the bushy eyebrows and riveting eyes returned to me often when I glanced toward that letter on the wall.

V

NELLI B.

I let my eye drift around the living room on a leftward swing, past the great fireplace with its mantelpiece collection. Two handsome antique Chinese tobacco jars stood to the right. They were almost the only artifacts of value that remained from my father's day, and I have no idea where they came from. A handsome watercolor by Sessions hung in a place of honor over the fireplace, entitled "Driving Home to Gloucester." I acquired it while I was still at Dartmouth and it hung in my room there. I loved it, having read the story of the Gloucester fishermen, the men who sailed to the Grand Banks in the great topsail schooners that were designed by Herreshoff. In order to beat their rivals back to market with a hold full of cod and haddock they carried full sail in heavy blows to the perilous point of capsizing or losing their top masts. It was a great era in North American sailing. The watercolor depicted one of the 120-foot schooners at deck level driving to windward on a beam reach, lee rail under and topsails set. Two of the crew in oilskins and boots lounged easily against the stacked dories, smoking their pipes, heedless of the green seas that reached up the slanted deck to their very boot ends.

The painting had a rather special meaning for me. A serendipitous trip and a willingness to take a chance had led me to join the crew aboard one of those Grand Banks dory schooners. During the summer of 1949, my last year at Dartmouth, Susy and I became engaged. With an impecunious indulgence I had blown a part of my inheritance on the car of my dreams, a beautiful gray Cadillac convertible. With the pleasure of summer driving as a lure I induced Susy and her mother to take a road trip with me to Nova Scotia. Remember, a chaperon for such overnight adventures was *de rigeur* back then. Furthermore, Susy's mom was my friend and the best of company.

As we progressed down the west coast of Nova Scotia, we came to the famous fishing port of Yarmouth from where many of the Grand Banks schooners had sailed. From the main street and looking toward the docks

I saw two heavy masts that stood out above the other shipping. I knew it had to be a schooner – a big one – and I was drawn to it with force, thrilled to encounter one that had survived. The ladies went shopping. I headed for the docks and found my way to the side of a fine old, 115-foot Grand Banks schooner.

There was a bustle of activity on deck, supplies being loaded aboard. This was obviously a working ship, but not at her old trade. She had been modified: her topmasts were gone, the spars were no longer gaff-rigged with sails and a 15 foot-long harpooning pulpit projected from her bow. There were three nested dories and a raised pilothouse astern. The graceful lines of the hull were still there, but she no longer sailed. She was diesel-powered and modified for the hunt. She had become a swordfisherman. In tarnished gold leaf the name *Nelli B.* was carved on her bow rail.

I called down to a grizzled, weather-worn man who was watching the loading and asked for permission to come aboard. I asked some questions about the origin of the ship, all of which he courteously answered, and finally asked if I might meet the captain. "You're looking at him, son," he answered, not unkindly. I learned that he had been with the ship as mate and then captain when she still sailed to the Banks. They were heading out on the morrow at dawn, bound for the Brown Banks to hunt swordfish. This was irresistible adventure. This was the stuff that my dreams were made of. I identified myself as a college student and may very well have blurted out some cock-and-bull story about my doing an article for *National Geographic* (I wouldn't put it beyond me). I truly don't remember what I said. But I said I wanted very much to sail with them, would work in any way that I could learn to be useful to them, and had no communicable diseases. To my amazement, he did not throw me off the ship right then and there. Instead, I remember him looking shrewdly at me for a few moments and then saying, "I'll ask the crew." And forthwith he did. I could hardly believe my wild gambit had gotten this far. I pretended great interest in the rigging and tried to look amiable and more adult that I really felt; and out of the corner of my eye, I could see him talking with a knot of hardy, weathered-looking men who had gathered around him. When he returned he said, "There'll be no shares, but you can bunk forward and mess with the crew. They'll have you. You'd better get some oil skins and boots and be aboard when we cast off at four in the morning." I was in.

My future wife had no intimation that she might be tied to a man who would leave her for months at a time through much of a married life, the prospect of which was still clothed in romance. Susy and her mom took the news as if they expected it, and said they would continue their trip with my car and drive it back to Sargentville. I would have to find my own way home when I returned. We stopped by a ship's chandler, a low-ceilinged, antique wooden building half-perched precariously on pilings in the harbor so that dories could come right under it at high tide and load gear through trap doors. The air was redolent with the smell of tar and varnish. The ceiling was festooned with blocks of every dimension, and there were wooden tubs filled to the top with neatly coiled marline. I purchased the oil skins, boots and other things I would need, and next morning Susy and her mother waved me off as the ship slid away from the wharf and moved out into the stream. The adventure had begun, setting the pattern for what I would be doing with the rest of my life.

It was Susy and her mom who had introduced me to Kenneth Graham's The *Wind In The Willows*. I may have thought then, as I watched their figures diminish in the distance, still waving, of the words of the Wayfaring Rat as he cast his spell over the sedentary Water Rat, "Tis but a banging of the door behind you, a blithesome step forward, and you're out of the old life and into the new."

The captain, the engineer, and the harpooner bunked aft in the main cabin. The rest of the crew bunked forward in the fo'c's'le. Bunks on either side were three high. I was shown to a middle bunk, just high enough to slide into. The mess table extended between the bunks along the center line. At the aft end of the table, where the hull's width increased, was the galley, a great wood-burning stove under a canopy of pots and pans. Food supplies on shelves and in bins flanked it. A heavy iron triangle hung over the stove. The fo'c's'le had an aroma as thick as a forcefield. As I descended the ladder into that dark hole, I was enveloped in a pungent smell that almost stopped me. It was a blend of old fish, damp clothing, stove fat, sweat, and tobacco smoke. When I first slipped sideways into my bunk, I discovered the source of the fish smell. Under the mattress of the bunk above me was a slab of salt pollack. There was one under every mattress except mine. These fishy bed mates provided snacks for the crew. In their bunks they could at any time lift the mattress and slice off a sliver of salt fish to chew on.

I also learned why the captain had consulted the crew about my joining them. They all had a share in the voyage. Proportional to each one's share, he chipped in on the provisioning of the ship. So they had a say in everything. Life aboard a swordfishing schooner was hard and almost entirely devoid of any material amenities. One that they allowed themselves was food. They didn't stint on it. It was hardy, plentiful, tasty, and a cholesterol catastrophe. But that was before the days of cholesterol awareness, not that it would have mattered one whit. There was big meat and potatoes and gravy daily. The cook baked fresh pies twice a day. A crewman could stop by the galley for a mug up and slice of pie any time that he pleased. And I observed in good time that no one took gross advantage of this freedom to shirk, not when each and every man had a stake in the outcome of the hunt – a piece of the profit.

We had hardly cleared the harbor and stowed the lines when the triangle reverberated through the whole ship as the cook beat it with an iron rod announcing CHOW DOWN! And what a breakfast! Sausage, eggs and pancakes along with a huge pot of strong coffee were in reach of every man. The meal was topped off with pie.

Missing at our forward mess were the masters of the pecking order. The captain, the harpooner (called the striker) and the engineer had their meals in the wheelhouse and bunked there as well. All treated the striker, who became my friend during the trip, with great deference. His name was Ted, a big man, weathered and fit and surprisingly soft-spoken. On his skill with the harpoon rested the fortunes of the ship.

Our weather was fair and before noon we had reached the cruising grounds. The crew was aloft and I with them. The routine, that would be unchanged through the days ahead, had started. The main mast had been rigged with two cross spars. On a square-rigged ship they might have supported square sails. Now they provided stations for four crewmen, halfway out on each side of each spar. Another crewman sat in a crow's nest at the top of the mast. We were the eyes of the ship. As the ship cruised the banks at a steady six to eight knots, all five pairs of eyes scanned the sea in the sectors of their vision. I joined the watch on the lower starboard spar where I met Orville. We would become dorymates. This first day I would be checked out aloft to see if I could handle the height. Stays and braces were rigged so that there was something to hold onto either standing or sitting. With rough weather – and we would have some – the ship could wallow in a beam sea. The mast would transcribe a 20-degree arc. I held on for dear life to the unending amusement of my mates. Their practiced sense of balance would have well served Ben Hur in his chariot race.

During the summer months the swordfish cruise the surface, enjoying the short-lived sun-warmed layer there. Their dorsal and great crescent-shaped caudal (tail) fins break the surface. That small body of black is what my companions looked for. If the sea was calm, and it was for most of our first week, the trained eye could spot that black speck 200 yards away. All eyes but mine were as keen as an osprey's. I never acquired the skill, but wished that just once I could be the successful spotter. It never happened. I put in my time up there with decreasing pleasure, especially when the sun warmed and the ship rolled easy over long, gentle swells.

The spotting of a fin was announced with a cry, "Fin at two o'clock." If it wasn't the masthead man who had made the spot he would scan the sector, and confirm the sighting, "I'm on it." A button in the crows nest would signal the wheelhouse, one long buzz for contact, one short buzz for starboard, two short ones for port and three short ones for steady on course. Thus the masthead man could steer the ship onto the prey. Shorter signals would fine-tune the course as the range closed.

Half of the time the alarm proved false, usually from sharks cutting surface. Their dorsal fins looked much like the swordfish, but the movement of the caudal fin as it swished back and forth was shark distinctive. Another signal would announce the false alarm and the boat would continue on its way. In fact, our speed never varied. The great diesel pushed the massive wooden hull along at a steady six knots.

If on approach the target proved right, four of the crew would go to action stations. Ted, the striker, a powerful, heavyset man with face burned to the color of a Maduro cigar, his skill so critical to the success of the hunt that he was equal to the captain in shares, would make his unhurried way to the pulpit at the end of the long bowsprit. He would knock out his pipe, methodically put it in his pocket, and unlash his 12-foot lance from the railing of the pulpit. I never tired of watching the calm, unhurried assurance with which he made his preparations. A barbed bronze dart crowning the end would detach on impact. It was secured by a leader to a barrel with 50 fathoms of half-inch manila at the ready. The line, wound around the barrel, would unwind as the creature sounded for the bottom hundreds of feet below, and the barrel would mark the location of the fish.

Now the cook would appear, wiping his hands on his apron, check out the day and take his station by the barrel attached to the dart. The engineer would emerge from his oil and noise-saturated cave, loosen one of the three dories towing astern and pull it amidships on the starboard side. At the same time the watchman aloft whose turn it was for dory duty would slide down a shroud with the ease of an acrobat, land on the deck with a thump and perhaps take a quick leak over the side before climbing into the dory. All these movements were smoothly accomplished as the ship closed on the basking swordfish. With the pulpit almost over the great fish, Ted leaned over the rail and placed the dart on the broad back. The swordfish would dive with a convulsive flail. The boat would sweep past. The cook would heave over the barrel and the dory would be cast off.

I watched this dramatic and well choreographed action many dozen times over the days and could never understand why the swordfish was never alerted by the thrum of the engine and the body of the ship approaching. The mother ship continued on as the dory fell astern. It would continue the search on a long circular course that would bring it back to the dory within two hours. On the way – and with luck – two more dories might be dropped off. On our second day out I learned what happened as the dory and boat lost sight of one another. My new friend aloft, Orville, agreed to take me with him as dorymate observer.

He gave me a wink and said, "We're on" then disappeared down the stay. I used the shroud with the rope footholds. As fast as I dared, I grabbed a sweatshirt from my bunk and climbed into the dory as it banged and splashed against the ship's hull. The painter was heaved after us and home afloat was away to the southwest. Orville took charge. "You just sit in the stern. I'll let you know if you can help," he said. He never did need help; it was a one-man task. He had a very rapt, energized audience as I watched the routine progress.

The barrel was in sight, spinning like a top as the giant fish at the other end of the line sounded all the way to the bottom almost 300 feet below. Orville rowed us over to the barrel, waited until the animal had finished its run and brought the barrel aboard. Into a socket in the dory's gunnel, he secured a single-wheel pulley, looped the slack from the barrel over it, spat on his ungloved hands and set to work.

Hand-over-hand the line came in with a rhythmic, seemingly effortless swing of his body. "We've got a big one," he grunted and shifted his feet, never stepping within the mass of line now building next to him in the bow. "If he runs there's no way I can check him. I'll let him have it all back and I don't want a foot caught in that line going out and me with it."

The great billfish, still far out of sight below us, turned out to be the third largest taken during our three weeks out. He was close to 500 pounds. So Orville was pulling up that enormous weight attached to the line at the middle of its body by a dart no larger than a hand. It might as well have been a barn door flat side up. It was the most ponderous, exhausting version of handlining imaginable. Orville had to feel the tension on the line and let the animal run if it wished. Overstrain could pull the iron out.

A half hour passed with no pause in the hauling rhythm. My dorymate, his sleeves rolled up, displayed forearms like hams. He worked smoothly, his body tuned to this unique exercise. His breathing was regular. I took note of all this, knowing that I could not have sustained five minutes of this arduous exercise myself.

A gaggle of gulls had arrived and comfortably floated on the easy swells. The *Nelli B.* was already hull down over the horizon. Save for the gulls, our 16-foot cockleshell and a monster now not too far below us we had the vast expanse of ocean to ourselves. The day had warmed. Orville's face was streaked with rivulets of sweat.

"We should see him soon," he said. I looked over the side, searching far down along the sun shafts that lanced into the darkening blue and I did see him…or thought I did. His black back so merged with the background of deeper water under him that the outlines of the form were barely defined. He was huge. It seemed impossible. I was so excited that I probably cried out something like, "Oh shit! I can't believe what I see." Orville laughed and, almost at the same time, the giant below us must have seen or sensed the dory at the surface. It happened with instant drama. Orville released the line and quickly stepped away from the pile that hissed over the side with a high-pitched whine. "He's running for the bottom," Orville said. There was no surprise in his voice. "They'll almost always take off with their first sight of the dory. There's no stopping him until he bottoms out. He'll come up easier now; he won't be so fulla beans."

The line soon went slack. Orville set to work again taking the loss of the first round with complete equanimity. The big animal was still a dead weight, but the odds in this battle seemed to have changed. The line was won back more easily. Another 25 or 30 minutes and the leader clicked over the gunnel. There was no need to peer into the depths. Like a submarine surfacing and shedding water from its hull, Leviathan rose beside the dory. The top of his crescent tail stood higher than our dory and his bill reached beyond the bow. It was monster size. It could also stove in the dory in a last explosion of rage. I was told that many times big swordfish had powered up upon seeing the boat and driven their bills through the two-inch-thick bottom of the dories.

"Now hang on!" Orville yelled. "He may kick up a might and decide to run again." As he shouted this warning a four-foot lance with a rusty knife blade appeared in his hand. Still holding the leader he made two powerful thrusts into the pulsing gills of the giant, which reacted with one convulsive lash of its tail that sent water over me and into the dory. As the blood streamed, life ebbed from the great fish. In my dreams I can see the eye, large as a billiard ball, bent upon us accusingly. The conquest was wildly dramatic, in its way heroic and ineffably sad. Later I remembered a Shakespeare piece, "And Man, brave man…plays such tricks before High Heaven as makes the angels weep."

Orville was not ready for a break. We changed places in the stern and he secured a loop of stout hawser rope around the muscular ridge that joins the fish's tail to its body. The other end of the rope dressed with another loop was secured to the boat. The bill was similarly secured and the dart was cut away from the back.

Thus the magnificent creature joined our side. Only then did Orville relax, light his pipe and listen quietly to my babble about what I had witnessed.

I had not noticed that the *Nelli B.* was now clearly hull up and steaming for us. Years later I would meet the great white sharks off South Australia and dive with the humpback whales off Maui. But the sight of that magnificent oceanic hunter surfacing by the side of the dory would remain in my mind's eye as the most exciting moment.

Orville prepared me for the rather frantic action that would very soon take place as the *Nelli B.* bore down upon us. She had not – and would not – diminish speed. As the ship closed, he cast loose the line that secured the bill and maneuvered our prize forward to the bow. "They'll not slow down for us," he called as the throb of the engine came closer. The seagulls scattered and were circling, having transferred their attentions to the big ship. Their plaintive cries were a chorus of expectation, "I'll heave the painter and as we warp into the side I'll feed the tail loop to a hook they'll have ready. It will all happen fast. You scramble out. There'll be a hand to help you."

And then the ship was upon us. The dory was slammed along side, two hands practically lifted me aboard, and as I scrambled for my balance Orville followed. The fish was smoothly hoisted and lowered to the deck. Another hand ran the painter astern where the dory fetched up in tow with one other. The third was still far ahead in the big circle. In the euphoria of being safely aboard and not having disgraced myself in the scramble I almost hugged Orville. Probably with some sense of control I shook his hand vigorously instead. He was almost surely embarrassed.

The beat went on. *Nelli B.* continued on her course. The watch crew that had descended for the recovery sawed off the tail and bill of our now fallen and maimed warrior. He was gutted with a surgeon's skill and lowered into the ice-filled hold. Two men packed his body cavity with ice and then buried him with shovels. The viscera went over the side falling astern and battled over by the screaming gulls. No ceremony celebrated the conquest, death and burial of this once truly great champion. Among the top ranks of predators in the oceans of the world he had been a king.

Orville and I enjoyed what I assumed was a traditional break. In the galley Cook produced generous wedges of the current pie. With steaming cups of coffee we sat for an accepted few minutes on deck in the sun, quietly consuming our reward before taking our places aloft. I would not trade a dinner in the most expensive restaurant in New York for that coffee and pie at that time in my life.

During the remaining two-and-a-half weeks of the trip I only went out in the dory three more times. Orville always scored, but never matched our big one so early in the game. Most swordfish averaged 200 to 300 pounds. We guessed the prize take was close to 500 pounds.

I was accepted by the crew and became well adjusted to the routine as the days unwound. I had with me a Leica camera with a half dozen 36-exposure rolls of color film. The drama in this arcane mode of fishing was so evident that I realized there was an opportunity for an article when I returned home. I shot every part of the activity. As I became adept at balancing aloft on the spar I got some splendid shots of Ted making his strike. With the morning sun behind us the swordfish were visibly sharp at the surface just before the pulpit. Like Frost's woodsman who turned to fresh tasks and never got around to splitting the wood he had cut and left it to "…the slow, smokeless burning of decay." I never got around to writing the article. My pictures, printed as slides and stored with many hundred others, vanished in the Punch Bowl fire, so only memory fuels this account.

Some days all three dories were working at the same time in the big circle. Occasionally a dory would return with no fish. The doryman would take a good-natured ribbing from the crew. There was no sense of blame. All had their measure of lost fish. It was a well-run, happy ship. There was no alcohol. The pipe smoke in the fo'c's'le was at times as thick as a pea-soup fog. We were all part of the bunkroom aroma. I ceased even noticing it.

I wakened in my half sleep each morning as the aroma of frying bacon and brewing coffee permeated the recesses of our bunks. At 4:30 a.m., Cooky would sound the breakfast bell, which was also the wake-up alarm, by whanging away at the iron triangle that hung in the galley. Nearly all of the crew would have turned in with most of their clothes on, leaving their boots under the benches that lined the mess table and their oilskins on pegs. Before the vibration of the abused triangle had subsided, the crew would have slipped out of their bunks, taken their seats at the table and in one fluid motion – from bunk to pancakes and sausages – have started their breakfasts.

Their ablutions, when and if there were any, came after breakfast. The heads were aft on either side of the transom with open access to the sea and a bucket with a lanyard for flushing. A small copper sink with a pump for cold water was attached to the bulkhead near the stove. There was a mirror for shaving along with hot water from the stove. Beards were cultivated; teeth pretty well neglected.

The weather held fair with only three or four days of seas heavy enough to make the spotting difficult and the watch aloft miserable. The Gulf of Maine is at its kindest in August. I often sat in the sun with Ted when action was slow. For a half-day and more there might be no contacts at all. Ted taught me knots and told me stories about growing up in Yarmouth and going out with the dorymen when he was a teenager. I sat with the skipper in the wheelhouse often enough for the stories to unfold from his experiences on the Grand Banks. As a doryman with his mate, hauling their trawls in winter weather, they filled the dory almost to swamping with big cod and haddock and halibut. He had risen in his long time at sea to master of the *Nelli B*. They belonged together: He had survived a passing era by adapting to changing times and she was a survivor from the age of sail.

On invitation I frequently had the evening meal with the skipper, Ted and the engineer in the wheelhouse. I was by no means a full working part of the forward crew. I ate and slept there. I liked them all and was pleased and honored to be accepted by them. I believe they sensed that. They reciprocated. We got on well. They were pleased as they realized that I was learning from them and held in high regard their skill and courage in that rough life.

The days passed with the speed of Thomas Mann's *The Magic Mountain*. Weather, the ultimate master of the mariner, cut our cruise short. The radio brought news of an early hurricane with seas that could reach to Northeast Maine and Canada; it crackled with talk from other boats in the area, all friends or good acquaintances of the skipper. All were apprehensive. Some intended to try their luck a day or two longer. We all gathered in the wheelhouse, listened to the radio and to the skipper. He advised heading home for port and put the move to a vote. His decision would set the course but the crew's real share in the cost and profit from the trip created an impressive measure of democracy. All were in favor of a prudent return.

So two-and-a-half weeks out we headed home. The hold was not full. I never did learn if the trip proved profitable. Back at Yarmouth, I would leave the ship early in the morning to catch a bus to Ellsworth, Maine. From shore I had called the Punch Bowl and warmed to the shriek of my engaged lady, "You're home!" She would pick me up in Ellsworth, no chaperone needed.

The truck was already at dockside, the catch unloading and the crew busy in the hold and with the blocks and tackle. I had said my good-byes. Shaking hands with everyone I had felt a heart-warming sense of *esprit* with each one. We had shared that time and adventure together. Our lives were worlds apart, but they had accepted me into theirs. I had guessed that I would never see any of them again, and so it proved.

VI

CORSICAN HONEYMOON

That would bring my visual sweep to the corner of the living room, next to one of the French doors. Sitting at my desk I could, of a morning, look out through the open door and watch the lobsterman pulling his pots by the ledge in front of the house. The mornings were so still, especially when the Reach was shrouded with fog, that I could hear the sound of his power winch and the splash of the trap when he rebaited and pushed it back over the side followed by the staccato blat of his engine as he headed off for the next pot.

But as I was saying, before I was carried away with my thoughts of the lobsterman through the open door: another picture hung in the corner just beyond the Frost letter. This was an enlargement of a Kodachrome transparency. I had taken the picture in 1950 when I was hiking around the island of Corsica by myself. Toward sunset I had climbed upward through ancient olive groves to gain high ground so that I could look out over the sea. The inland mountains of Corsica rose before me. As I crested one of the foothills a deep valley unfolded before me. And nestled in the curve of the valley was a mountain village bathed in gold from the low western sun that shone full upon it. It nestled snugly in the curve, so small that only one dirt street bisected it, following the curve of the mountain. The topography was such that I looked down upon it. There was no movement in the village. A church bell tolled, surprisingly loud in the hot, still air. It was not musical. It clanked rather than rang as if the bell dome were being held as the clapper struck it. The moment was frozen in time, the village ageless. The camera, an old Leica, had a fine lens. The old Kodachrome, ASA 12, was fine-grained. The picture remains perhaps the best composed and most evocative of any photographic memoirs I have.

What was I doing in Corsica? I was having an adventure. The year was 1950 and I was on my honeymoon. What was I doing hiking alone if I was on a honeymoon? Therein lies a cue to an urge for independence that would sorely try my marriage and demand patience and adaptability on the part of my wife, above and beyond anything a chauvinist male might expect these days. We had a protracted honeymoon. It lasted almost nine months, during which we traveled all around western Europe.

We were married just weeks after my mid-year graduation from Dartmouth. I cradle-snatched Susy out of Bennington College in her sophomore year. She was 19. I was six years older, having delayed my college education with three years in the war-time Navy. I had enough of a poke from my father's estate to see us through an extended honeymoon and no real plans or prospects for getting to work. By the time we reached Monte Carlo we were about four months along on living together. We were having a splendid time. But I was ready for a little of my own space and the adventure of lone travel. So I left Susy in a comfortable little pension in Monte Carlo, where we had been staying for several days, and booked passage on one of the daily ships making the run to Corsica. I carried my mask, fins and speargun with me plus my backpack. It was my intention to be gone for a week. During that time I envisioned hitch-hiking along the coast from town to town, diving and spearfishing wherever I could conveniently reach the sea. Susy, bless her forgiving soul and generous supporting nature, urged me to have my adventure. Over more than 50 years of marriage she has never withdrawn that support and encouragement.

I landed at Calvi on the northwestern side of Corsica and put up at a pension for the first night, having in the late afternoon the experience with the walk into the hills that I described. The next morning I set out on foot along the west coast. My *Guide Bleu* indicated a road that followed the coast to the south, all the way to Ajaccio. There were no suburbs to Calvi. As was so often the case with European towns, the boundaries of the town ended abruptly. This stemmed from a time when towns hung tightly together for security and cities were walled.

I intended to hitch a ride. It was a cloudless day that soon became a hot day. The narrow dirt road hugged the coast. The sea was seldom out of sight, but far below my narrow dirt road, which followed the meandering turns of the steep coast. The measured crash of great ocean swells was muted by the distance. On the inland side of the road was the Corsican *maqui*, stunted scrub set off by grotesque, warped boulders, sloping upward into foothills that rose to the mountains. The road was deserted. Nothing moved in either direction. My own footsteps on the dirt road, the surf far below and a buzz of insects from the *maqui* mingled, unbroken by the sound of any vehicle approaching from either direction. I walked on at a good pace for over two hours, listening for and expecting to hear an engine sound. There was no shade other than one skinny, fruitless olive tree that appeared at a turn of the road. I broke off my hike there, sat down on a stone, took a swig from my water bottle and dug my *Guide Bleu* out of my backpack. I searched for a description of the area I was in. I found it and a reference to the very road I was on. It said: "This picturesque but seldom-traveled road...etc. etc." Seldom-traveled turned out to be no exaggeration. I walked the morning without encounter with any human being, in or out of a vehicle. The western coast of Corsica was mine, alone.

About noon the road dipped down to the sea. A stone jetty extended out from the shore about 50 yards, at the end of which was a beacon atop a cement pylon. This was the first sign of human activity I had encountered in a half a day on the road. So there were life forms on this planet after all. I was hot and covered with dust from the dry dirt road. The sea looked cool and clean. I was ready for it. I changed to my swim trunks and entered the Mediterranean with mask, fins, snorkel and Arbalete speargun, my first dive on the old world side of the Atlantic. The recollection is so clear that it might as well have been yesterday.

I was immediately surrounded by a great school of silver jacks. They flashed in the sun as they turned in unison, circling around me. They were friendly, curious, beautiful ambassadors of the Mediterranean world. And how did I greet them? I fired into the middle of the school, wounding one and frightening away the entire lot. And such was my fear of sharks and the unknown in the deep blue water beyond my reach that I nervously swam for the jetty and scrambled out of the water, happy to have escaped alive from this daring adventure. There was no shame in having violated that peaceful world into which I had intruded. I was rather proud of myself for having at least winged a fish. Yet the memory of that violent, thoughtless act still evokes an unpleasant sense of shame today.

There is more to the story. Late in the day as shadows lengthened and I had long since started wondering if I would find darkness upon me in this wild, empty place, the road curved inland away from the sea and the terrain somewhat flattened. I rounded a bend and there before me, on the other side of a bridge that spanned a small stream, was a single stone and plaster, two-story building. In letters that covered one entire side it said: HOTEL. There were no other buildings. The road at the end of the bridge forked to the right, following the stream and then turned out of sight. A cement road marker gave the name of a village that apparently existed five kilometers up that road. Darkness would be soon upon me. The left fork led to the hotel and beyond. I turned left.

There was nothing friendly about the building. It was plain with small window frames that were fitted with shutters. I pushed open a heavy, much scarred wooden door and entered a main room with a hard-packed dirt floor. There were perhaps a dozen men sitting at tables with glasses of the milky, licorice-flavored drink favored all along the Mediterranean coast. Conversation stopped dead when I entered. All eyes were directed toward me. The scene was right out of a classic western. The stranger enters the saloon. When my eyes had adjusted to the smoky gloom, I saw that there was a raised wooden platform at the rear of the room which supported a great stove and other kitchen things. It also supported a broad bottomed woman with her hands on her hips. She wore a black dress, no stockings and rough sandals. Her face was unsmiling. As formidable as she appeared, I thought her more hospitable than the glowering men. I made my way to her and, with my pathetic little French that provoked a hint of a smile, requested a room for the night. Following her I ascended rough stairs on one side of the room and was led to a clean, airy bedchamber. It wasn't the Hyatt Regency, but it looked like heaven to me. There was a big double bed with a rough cloth feather comforter on it. A chair, a stand with pitcher and washbasin and a chamber pot completed the furnishings. She opened the twin shutters to let in the setting sun and looked to me to see if I wanted the room. I nodded vigorously. Had it been $200 a night instead of $2.00 I still would have taken it.

The happiest surprise awaited my return to the room below. While I had been settling in a young British couple had arrived and already secured the only other room. Our meeting had all the drama and relief of Stanley and Livingston's historic meeting. They had been bicycling along the coast from the other direction and would easily have traversed my deserted road between Ajaccio and Calvi in one day, but one of the bikes had a flat. They had no repair kit and so reached the hotel on foot with a sense of relief as intense as mine. They both spoke fluent French and were urbane continental travelers. For me they were saviors. They were also delightful company. We made common cause.

They determined that we might have lamb or trout for dinner and that the trout would be fresh. We opted for the trout. They also learned that if we wanted to bathe, we should take our towels and bathing suits across the road. Out of sight around a rocky outcropping we descended to a clear pool with a pebble bottom. The pool was refreshed by the small stream that ran through it. We submerged our travel-worn, dust-powdered bodies in the clear, cool water and literally moaned with ecstasy. I think it was the most wonderful bath I have ever had. We soaped and rinsed and scrubbed away the day's travel and sharpened our appetites. My own spirits had risen from near zero to about nine on the scale. When we met for our own glasses of anisette the scale topped ten. We were accepted by the men almost all of whom were dressed in rough corduroy trousers and jackets. My new friends, the Alexanders – I've long since forgotten their first names – told me these were shepherds from the hills and that almost the entire economy in this region pivoted around the raising and tending of goat flocks.

When we were ready for our dinners we were beckoned to the kitchen by our hostess. She lifted a trap door in the middle of the raised wooden floor and we found ourselves looking into a clear pool, fed by a brook that ran right under the building. The pool was alive with fat trout. We made our selections. She netted them, gutted them and within three minutes they were sizzling in a giant skillet on the stove.

The next morning the Alexanders fixed the bad tire and continued their trip to Ajaccio. They determined for me through the landlady that a truck collecting goat cheese along the route I had traveled the day before, would give me a ride back to Ajaccio; and so it happened. My ride was an ancient vintage machine with the general shape of a pickup truck that made periodic stops where shepherds had come out of the *maqui* to wait by the roadside with their boxes of goat cheese. I sat on boxes of goat cheese that had already been collected before the two bandits in the front picked me up. The black, oily exhaust that was sucked back into my face and over the cargo and the chronic objections of the motor suggested that fuel some grade below black market regular was being fed the sick beast.

We were headed back to Ajaccio. That was enough for me. I had had a surfeit of all-day walking on deserted roads. The looks of my two cheese traders belied their generosity in taking me aboard. At the same time their appearances epitomized the world image of Corsica as an island of brigands, murderers, cutthroats and assassins much occupied with frightful acts of revenge. They were swarthy, short and muscular. Both were heavy with faces uncreased by smiling. On being introduced to them as a traveler needing a lift they had examined me with beady little pig eyes and a grudging nod toward the truck.

Our stops were frequent. The shepherds, invisible to me along this stretch of road the previous day, were awaiting the truck almost every ten or 15 minutes. The transactions between seller and buyer were not smoothly or quietly conducted. I did not become used to the scene even though I watched it two dozen times or more before we reached Ajaccio.

My two rogues and the shepherds were pretty much dressed alike: rough, baggy corduroy trousers, equally baggy and probably home-knit sweaters, shapeless caps and sandals. Many of the shepherds were barefoot. Greetings with small geniality were exchanged as the tripod legs for the rusty scale were set up. Boxes with layers of goat cheese in square blocks were set on the scale and tallied. That done my chief thug would add up the take, set a price and announce it. There was no pantomime of incredulity by the seller Middle East bazaar style. A fierce shouting match ensued. Faces with yellow teeth bared almost touched. Hands fingered knives – big knives – visible on the belts of either side. Maiming, if not murder, was obviously just one more insult away when the hostility abruptly stopped. Hands were shaken and my pair produced a bottle of what I presume was raki. The bottle was passed – but not to me – and we were off in a cloud of dust.

The exhibition was repeated at every stop. I understood none of the language, relying on the body language for the entertaining intervals. So the day ran its course. There was no stop for lunch. My ride did not include refreshment, although the bottle probably passed back and forth in the front seat as we rattled along. I dozed or watched the road through the open canopy at back. No other vehicle, person or mule appeared the entire day.

Toward evening we arrived at the outskirts of Ajaccio. Soon there was busy traffic. As we passed I saw a lamplighter with his ladder, took interest in the passing scene and a return of civilization. Perhaps I was going to survive this adventure after all without being robbed or even murdered. Our truck stopped to let its load of cheese and a body-aching passenger in steerage off right in front of the little hotel I had stayed at two nights previously. Both rogues got out to meet me as I clambered out of the back. I had already extracted my cache of French francs from the bottom of my backpack and had ready a little fold that amounted to about 20 U.S. dollars. As I shook hands with the driver and handed him the bills with the other hand he appraised them, then actually smiled. He pumped my hand with pleasure. Fellow bad chap joined in (another smile) and they were off with a last blat of oily exhaust.

There was a most happy postscript. I had planned to meet the Alexanders at the hotel. They had arrived earlier that day, their bicycles having held up. We met for dinner on a lovely outside garden terrace of the hotel. Warmed by the friendship that grew by having shared the adventure, we demolished two bottles of wine. On parting they gave me a card with their London address and phone number and were genuine in their urging to call them when Susy and I finally got to London. Surprisingly we did. We met at a delightful restaurant they suggested. Both Susy and I in our very travel-worn clothes were acutely aware of the differences. The Alexanders were now London people with the affluence and professional level of their lives apparent. But the open pleasure of the reunion bridged the gap easily. Susy was delighted with them and with their mock-serious admonishment to me, "How could you have left this lovely girl behind?"

It was years before we returned to London and then we only passed through on our way to Scotland. I had lost their address, but I can still see them in my mind's eye. They were the best of the English breed, I thought: urbane, humorous, well educated and sophisticated without pretension – the sort who take their holidays with real adventures.

VII

The Gumshoe Circuit

As my visual cruise around the Punch Bowl living room continued to the left I would come across three items that were related to my lecture years.

When I started charter boating in the Bahamas with my own boat, the *Zingaro*, I had with me the first 16mm underwater movie camera on the market. The year was 1954. The Fenjohn Company of Ardmore, Pennsylvania was a sideline of the Fenimore Johnson Foundation, that worthy having been the inventor of the Victor Talking Machine. His son and grandson were both keen on diving and filming underwater. They were early wholesalers for the first scuba equipment and also came out with a line of underwater cameras. When I built *Zingaro* and prepared to take it to the Bahamas to try my luck as a dive guide with my own dive boat, I purchased my stock of scuba and diving equipment from them. I also talked them into lending me one of their 16mm cameras, convincing them that my customers might be interested in buying one. My first films were made with that system. The camera was a military surplus 16mm Bell & Howell gun camera. The housing was terrific for the time. It had a flat port, a surprisingly good and ahead-of-its-time inside changeable filter, variable speed control and a spring-wind drive that provided about 25 seconds of running time. The limitations of the unit were serious and became very apparent as I started work with it. The camera only took a 50-foot magazine load affording just one-and-a-half minutes of shooting time. It also had a consumer Kodak 12.5mm lens. So this remarkably engineered housing was built for a cheap camera system. I learned to work with it.

By the end of my third season in Nassau I had enough Kodachrome footage to put together a 90-minute film. One of my diving customers was Herman Kitchen, a senior editor for CBS. He became a good friend and, with unreserved generosity, gave me his time and expertise in learning how to edit. I'm not really sure where the term "gumshoe" came from. It may have characterized detectives and their propensity for sneaking up on bad chaps. During the McCarthy hearings, the senator's two youthful Myrmidons, Cohn and Schine, were wryly referred to as "gumshoes." Whatever the origin, I was fond of referring to my film lecture activities in the sixties and early seventies as "gumshoeing through the Bible Belt."

For a maker of underwater documentary films way back in the early 1960s, the game was to hit the road for a series of personal appearances with one's 16mm films. Mind you, television had not yet invaded the American living room. The neighborhood and small town movie theaters dominated entertainment. Tinseltown was in its heyday. So was the film lecture, a personally presented version of the travelogue. They provided wholesome family entertainment. The series were often sponsored by Kiwanis Clubs, Audubon Societies, or church groups and were called "Armchair Adventures." The late Colonel John *Danger Is My Business* Craig and I were the only speakers with underwater films. The general fare presented such riveting titles as *The Four Seasons of Scandinavia; Russia, Land of Contrast*; and *Exotic Hawaii*. In hindsight, the entertainment was pretty vapid, mine included, but the series brought the outside world to small towns across the U.S. Impresarios in big cities could fill a 3,000-seat auditorium with the best of the speakers. For me and many of the other speakers, the activity provided a way to amortize the cost of traveling in the summer with our Bolex 16mm cameras.

Thank god for television. It emancipated me from the relentless traveling to fill as many as 90 dates in the short fall/winter/spring season, night after night in a different small town, three weeks at a time. I felt like Professor Harold Hill in *The Music Man* without the demonic drive. I did see America; I spent weeks in the land of Sinclair Lewis – Ohio, Iowa – and more weeks traveling the far western states. The lecture dates were as disparate as Calgary, Alberta, The Parker Ranch on the big island of Hawaii, Seventh Day Adventist Colleges, and the Anthropo Piscatorial of Yale University.

Film lecturing was just what the title implies. The speaker spoke live from stage while his film was projected on the screen. If you wanted to make your presentation a little slicker, you accompanied the film with music from a tape recorder that you punched on and off at the lectern. I did that and was scorned by the purists. The programs were two-reelers with an intermission – 90 minutes of film. Question and answer times were expected with the small town shows. Deadly receptions after the shows, organized by the sponsors and their friends, required attendance by the speaker. The refreshments were cholesterol catastrophes. I was thoroughly briefed on corn, wheat, pigs, cattle, and any local farming economy.

All I wanted (desperately) was to return to my motel, have a great slug of vodka, and crash. It was all an educational, bone-wearying experience, but it paid for my early life of adventure.

My first attempt at riveting an audience with my eloquence and underwater shooting plummeted into the abyss of disaster before it even reached the visuals. I had roughly edited my first film, *Water World*. I thought the title infinitely clever. A friend of the family, a museum director in Scranton, Pennsylvania, had seen the film in the living room of my wife's family in that capitol of the anthracite world. With generous intent, he suggested that I could charge a fee for showing the film and talking about the underwater world. At that time any pictures from that newly-opening world beneath the sea were an innovation. I agreed. Billy Graham eat your heart out. Here comes a golden-tongued competitor for the mass market. My kind family friend arranged for me to entertain a meeting of doctors at a country club just a few miles upstate. Here was the break. How to make a million from your hobby with scuba and a 16mm projector.

The doctors were a great bunch. They were keen for the entertainment. They plied me with a good dinner, cocktails, and wine. I needed courage from the bottle. I was as nervous as a tick at the prospect of standing up before these arbiters of life and death. I had prepared a clever introduction. I would liken penetrating the surface of the water to Alice through the looking glass. The simile would immediately reveal my acquaintance with literature and my superior education. I had it nailed down. I had practiced it in the men's room just before the show was to begin. I stood up before them, straight and strong, the sophisticated, confident entertainer, and started my spiel. I managed to unload the first sentence, grasped for the next line, failed to find it, felt myself plunging into the dark abyss, and fainted. The doctors in the front row saw it coming (eyeballs rolling up, face turning to chalk), grabbed me before I hit the deck, and supported me to a chair.

I did recover. There must be genes from a vaudevillian ancestor in me somewhere. The show must go on. I got up, bagged the clever intro, and talked off the top of my head about why I loved diving and what I was seeing. In short, enthusiasm about sharing what was then a hobby replaced the stilted, show-off prep. The show was a fine success. They loved it. Today it wouldn't cut the mustard. My shooting was green. Some splices parted, but the old Kodachrome film original was at times gorgeous, and, most of all, the subject was mint-new. I would never be so lucky again. A short month of lecture dates generated by a mailing to boarding schools in the east, provided my first professional tour. For $125 a shot, I did 12 schools. Overnight hospitality was the only perk. A lecture agent got wind of it and signed me on for an extended tour the following season. Many of the dates were far enough afield to require air travel and rental cars. The contract was princely. My fee was $150 per date less 30 percent to the agent. All travel expenses were mine. I had aligned myself with a predator who made a great white shark look like a parrotfish. Even though my wife and three children were camped at the door of the Alms House, I was in business with my films – a real professional; also a thoroughly skinned chump.

Other agents followed. Prosperity from a viable profit was a stubborn fantasy that faded forever with the final accounting each season proving that I was not very good at math. In time a good and decent man from an agency in Boston liked my act, signed me up and negotiated fees that at least saved me from returning to blueberry farming. Thus evolved the block bookings, 21 evenings in three weeks on the road. They were often in a single state, one small town after another with a rental car and rural hotels and motels. I did get to see America's heartland.

On one such block booking in a small town in western Iowa, I came a cropper from the monotony of showing my same film night after night. Among audiences who would rather see Alaska, Land of the Future than a new world of eels and sharks and groupers bigger than any local bass pond offered, the audience in this town was uniquely unreceptive. This was a Dutch Reformed Church community. Their religion placed strictures on expression of human emotions. Laughing, clapping, shouting were all off limits. Two hundred faces as immobile as Ben Turpin's stared back at me from the reflection of the screen. (I had come to look for and expect some expression of pleasure and interest from an audience, some indication that I was reaching them. Zero came back from that varnish-scented high school gymnasium audience.)

At that occasion I was screening the story of my year in French Polynesia with my family, a film that was later picked up by *National Geographic* for an hour special. To enliven an audience I had shot a sequence of my wife and children all swimming out of the hatch of a sunken PBY (amphibious airplane used during World War II), carrying their tote bags. It was corny, but it always got a laugh. This time it totally bombed.

Not a sound. I carried on, hoping I could evoke some measure of energy in my delivery. Now understand that after narrating the 90-minute film live repeatedly like a long run of a play, I had pretty well memorized the whole narration. It hardly deviated by a word even though the narration had never been scripted.

It happened one evening halfway through the first reel. I was narrating from a lectern on the stage, half watching the screen, my other half to the audience, spinning out my blather to the stone silent pit. Suddenly I felt myself falling. I had dozed off standing at the lectern, even while I was narrating. I fell into the orchestra pit and landed on a batch of folding chairs. It was a catastrophe for me. It was an epiphany for the spectral audience. I heard genuine screams and shouts. The lights came on. Hardy farmers, fast to respond, jumped up to help me. Women stood up and craned to see, clucking with horror. If I hadn't hurt so bad from a couple of cracked ribs, I might have exulted at finally winning an eruption of emotion. The show did go on, and I had a legitimate excuse for not attending the reception afterward.

On the road evening after evening I soon developed a need to fortify myself before my shows and by doing so, generate some measure of enthusiasm in my delivery. The mute audiences had little if any rapport with the marine world I had embraced. So I carried with me a flask, well charged with vodka martinis. I had my cocktail before supper when I was on the road.

One year my gumshoe tour took me through Nebraska, a dry state at the time. In the small towns, abstinence was a moral force. The "mullahs" of the Southern Baptist Church saw to that. So my flask was my shield and buckler.

At a restaurant in Scarlet, Nebraska – the only one in town – I ordered my dinner before my show. And since my show was also the only game in town, many of my forthcoming audience members were making a night of it with their families. My entry into the restaurant was as marked as the arrival of Gary Cooper at the saloon's swinging doors in a hostile town. A waitress attended me for my order. I requested a glass with ice. She pursed her thin lips and stepped back as if facing a hooded cobra. However, she reluctantly did the bidding of the devil. Eyes followed her progress back to the table with the damning, ice-filled glass.

Fortified by my imagined Ivy League, northeastern corridor, sophisticated superiority, I made a bold show of snapping open my briefcase, extracting my Dunhill flask, and conspicuously filling my glass with the maddening fluid. As I returned the cap to the flask I purposely looked up to challenge the stares of the diners. I was gratified to see them quickly evade my bold defiance. Rattling the ice in the glass, I raised it to my sinful lips and tilted back for the first satisfying pull. The fickle finger of fate poked me right in the eye. The ice shifted in the glass. The martini avalanched down my shirt. I caught a horrified glimpse of parents turning their children away from the sight. I shrank into a shell of shame and kept my eyes discreetly down for the remaining dinner. And I determined not to fall off the stage. I hoped the show would be cancelled. It wasn't. I slunk out of town before dawn next morning.

VIII

AEGEAN TREASURE

The amphora stood upright in a special wrought-iron stand I had made for it. It was almost 2,000 years old and was still covered with the skeletons of marine worms and encrusting coral. The story about how I came by this amphora covers one of the most memorable diving experiences I ever had and certainly the most interesting and productive of the cruises I took with my old friend, Drayton Cochran.

It started in the Bahamas and ended up in the Aegean. That is the way chance meetings may evolve and way lead on to way. He came aboard my dive boat when I was a charter boatman in the Bahamas. That was 1954; but I can still vividly recall my impressions of the man. He walked with a rolling gait. His face was weathered, brown and the corners of his eyes creased from long hours on watch in wind and sun. This man was a mariner. His name was Drayton Cochran.

On the way back to Nassau from the day's diving he joined me on the flying bridge of the old *Zingaro* and we talked all the way as I steered our course back along Rose Island, picking up Hog Islands on the final leg into Nassau Yacht Haven. I learned that Drayton owned a 71-foot motor sailor, the *Little Vigilant*, which he kept in the Mediterranean/Aegean part of the world, his cruising ground every summer. He took my measure, gauging my vulnerability to a suggested adventure, spun a yarn of cruising the Aegean Islands on wine-dark seas, balmy evenings ashore at open cabarets, sipping the golden retsina with dusky maidens and – most compelling of all – diving in the graveyards of ancient ships. I was nearly hypnotized, caught body and soul by the spell of his talk. I was breathing heavily and so tuned to adventure that I overshot my slip at the Yacht Haven, tangled my pulpit with that of the sport fisherman in the neighboring berth and thoroughly disgraced myself in view of a man I would later learn was one of the most respected mariners in the international yachting community.

Drayton and his friends were with me three more days. By the end of that time a friendship had incubated and hatched. He asked if I would be interested in crewing with him the following fall, helping him and his permanent crew get the *Little Vigilant* ready for sea and take her for a two-month cruise of the Aegean Islands. I did not decline.

And that is how I found myself painting and scraping and chipping and yielding to the orders of my new friend, who had become a tyrannical bo'sun. The previous year Drayton had hauled the boat out at a small yard on the island of Spetsai, which is part of the Dodecanese group in the Greek part of the Aegean. Drayton's son John, his girl Susy Phipps, a young and muscular school friend, John Righter and I were the deck hands. There was also Willie, the cook, and Gert, a professional crewman. Drayton was, of course, the skipper and also the engineer. He pitched into all the dirtiest work and was by experience a real marlin spike seaman. But his prime focus was on the engine, which he could totally assemble in his sleep, and the navigation of the boat when we were under way.

I am rather ahead of my story. Drayton had indicated that he intended to make his way eastward and then cruise the Turkish coast. He further suggested that he would be happy to have some sort of constructive purpose to the cruise, a *modus operandi*. I had correctly surmised from this that he was not only interested in my willingness to scrub decks and polish brass. He hoped I would come up with some sort of diving agenda; and I did. I learned about a young underwater archaeologist named Peter Throckmorton, who had been living and working with the Turkish sponge divers. Through his contact with the hard-hat divers he had already located a number of wreck sites. We met in New York City. To say the least he was enthusiastic about the availability of a boat with which he might carry out a first search for ancient wreck sites along the Turkish coast south of Bodrum. His plan: to examine wrecks already located by his friends, the sponge divers of Bodrum, identify them as far as possible and accurately locate them on a chart of the coast. We could thus create an index of sites for future development by archaeological expeditions. I liked the idea; so did Drayton. With that purpose he installed a fine Bauer compressor in the engine room of the *Little Vigilant*. The U.S. Divers Company came up with all the scuba equipment required and – the cherry on the sundae – Rolex pitched in with watches for the team. I might add, that was the start of a long and fruitful association with both companies.

I belonged to the Explorers Club. Carrying their flag on expedition was both a privilege and an honor. Byrd, Amundson, Perry, Lowell Thomas and many other great names in exploration had carried their flag. I was awarded one by the Club to carry on this trip. It lent prestige to our modest expedition. At the same time it imposed on us the onus of accomplishing something of worth. Thus armed with prestige (so far unearned), well equipped and poised on the starting line of a great adventure, we motored to the harbor entrance. A gaggle of island folk waved from the shore. *Little Vigilant* was freshly painted, polished and sparkling like a maiden on her first date. Once outside, we bent on the sails. She rose easily to the great green swells and leaned into the fresh 25-knot wind that the seasonal Meltemi had given the ancient mariners for more than 3000 years. Her mizzen, main and jibs pulled evenly. We pointed east. I was too excited and young then to make a poetic reference to the occasion. In hindsight I recall the wonderful line from Ernle Bradford's book, *Ulysses Found*: "One night they slid the black ship into the sea and unloosed the mooring rope from the pierced stone. They turned the eyes of the ship toward the west and, sitting all in order, they smote the gray sea waters."

Bodrum, a small town and the sponge diving center for that part of the coast, had known greatness. As Halicarnassus it had once been a great capital of the ancient province of Caria. In the year 352 B.C. a king named Mausolus had a tomb built for himself that was so huge it became one of the Seven Wonders of the Ancient World. The word mausoleum derives from that great work. Stones from the wondrous structure went into the building of the crusaders' fortress that still dominates the harbor at Bodrum. Peter Throckmorton awaited us here and joined the ship with a porcine and somewhat bewildered representative of the Turkish government, one Haki Bey, and two young Turks who proved to be fine divers and durable companions.

Amphorae were the jerry cans of the ancient world. In many different shapes and sizes, they carried bulk cargoes like wine, olive oil, and grain. They were ubiquitous on docks and in warehouses as well as in homes, and they dominated the cargo holds of the merchant ships. Those that carried wine were coated on the inside with resin to improve the seal. Thus the wine of the ancients carried with it a taste of resin. The descendant of these wines is today's retsina, the wine of the Aegean people. When I first tasted it I could only think of turpentine and was thoroughly revolted. However, it is an acquired taste as is the licorice-flavored ouzo and raki. In a surprisingly short time my taste adjusted to both spirits and I held happy union with countless legions of landsmen and mariners who had tippled before me in this part of the world. And that tippling by captain and crew alike in the ancient merchant ships, aided and abetted by treacherous winds and the unforgiving ledges that bare their teeth all along the major trade routes, sent literally thousands of ships to watery graves. In Melville's words: "They have swallowed full many a midnight ship and all her shrieking crew." It is usually amphorae, mounds of them on the bottom, that mark the wreck sites.

The approaches to Bodrum from the west are guarded by as mean and ill-placed a collection of low-lying islands and ledges as any mariner might hope to escape. The main island is called Yassi Ada. Peter had dived there and found the bottom littered with the shards of amphorae. At varying depths down to 60 feet were mounds of unbroken jars. He deduced that these mounds marked individual wreck sites. He was right. On our first dive we descended through fields of ceramic rubble, following a sand and grass slope into the cool depths of the ancient sea. The first whole cargo was magnificent, a classic picture of graceful, double-handled amphorae strewn about and on top of one another. Some projected upright from the sand even as they were stored almost 2,000 years ago in the sand floor of the cargo hold. The ship had struck the island, springing the planks of its wooden hull, then drifted away into deeper water before it settled to the bottom at 60 feet. It may have burst its seams on impact with the bottom, releasing its cargo of amphora. Those on top tumbled down the steep slope, spreading out fanlike as a river will when it reaches a delta. There were hundreds of them visible and probably many hundred more beneath the sand.

To raise them we would upend each one, shake the sediment out of it and let air into it, just as one would with a lift bag, and send it rocketing to the surface. Divers needing surface time would receive them at the top and relay them to the dinghy. It was heady business. We thought we were archaeologists and enjoyed ourselves enormously, looting the cargo at will. In fact, trained archaeologists cringe when they hear about this sort of thing. Fortunately our aim was truly to sample the cargo of the wrecks we found and so reveal artifacts that would identify the shipwreck. The fact that one amphora would have done the trick does neither dismay nor shame me at this distance from the event.

We explored deeper along the slope, the cool depths still well-lit by the hard Aegean sun. We also fanned out in our search. I remember the anxiety I felt when I glanced at my depth gauge and found I was just passing the 100-foot mark. Back then we had 72 cubic-foot standard tanks with 2,300 p.s.i. maximum fills. There wasn't much leeway when you fooled around beyond 100 feet. If ever there were a temptation to woo a diver away from prudence, it was the expectation of coming upon another one of those amphorae mounds – and I did. It was as close to the ultimate rush that a treasure-hunter might have. I reached the first amphora at 115-feet. Its small neck and finger-purchase handles thrust up out of the sand. It was glorious! It was also no more than a shard. I tugged at the handles and up came the neck and just the upper quarter of a globular-shaped jar. Another, just three feet away, was half-buried, the graceful curve of its side visible above the sand. I carefully loosened it from the sand and pulled it out. It was whole. It was also filled with sand and heavy, and a quick glance at my pressure gauge shocked me into releasing it and starting up without delay. My gauge showed 200 pounds. Buoyancy control vests hadn't been developed yet. We didn't even have the original horse collars. The surface was a long way up, even without the impediment of a sand-filled amphora.

At that time the leading authority on amphorae in the world was Dr. Virginia Grace from the American School of Classical Studies in Athens. From pictures that we sent to her she identified the first group of amphorae as Rhodian from the first century A.D. They brought with them echoes of another wonder, the great Colossus of Rhodes, a massive giant hewn from stone and said to have spanned the harbor entrance to the City of Rhodes with his giant legs. He, too, was one of the Seven Wonders of the Ancient World. Triremes rowed by a thousand slaves passed under those legs. Shakespeare knew that bit of history when he wrote in *Julius Caesar*:

> *"Why, man, he doth bestride the narrow world*
> *Like a Colossus; and we petty men*
> *Walk under his huge legs, and peep about*
> *To find ourselves dishonorable graves."*

Those from the deeper wreck were Byzantine from the tenth century A.D. When they settled to the bottom ten centuries ago the Maya nation in Central America was in its ascendancy and the western world was ruled from the city of Byzantium.

All the Aegean is volcanic. The islands and ledges drop off into hundreds of feet of water close to their edges. Ships that drifted away from their point of impact for just a few minutes would often sink into depths no sponge diver could reach. One may guess that the wrecks of Roman ships that were carrying the looted art treasures of Greece had laid undisturbed, unseen, but not in perpetual rest. One of the dreams of Bob Ballard, the discoverer of the *Titanic*, is to explore such wreck sites with deep ROV's and then raise their cargoes from a thousand feet and deeper with a manned submersible like Alvin. It is thought that the works of the greatest sculptors of the Classic Greek period, Praxiteles and Phidias, may well be awaiting discovery in such deep graves.

By far the most exciting find we would make in our summer's survey was still ahead of us. We would follow a clue that Peter had picked up as he drank with the Bodrum sponge divers in a harborside cantina. It was the word BRONZE that had caught his ear as he half listened to the babble of talk over raki and dominoes at the neighboring table. He knew the captain who had spoken the word, stood him and his companions to a round and had the story retold. It seems that the captain and crew of his sponge boat had worked far south, ever seeking better harvests. Off a point of land called Gelidonya Burnu on the charts and next to a small rock island they had brought up scraps of bronze and an intact bronze box. These had been found in 90 feet of water and a swift current close by the island. The depth was close to the outer reach in which the hard-hat divers could work. They had returned with the bronze and sold it to a metal worker to be melted down. That was the whole story. They had not returned to that dangerous depth for more of the metal.

To Peter bronze could mean Bronze Age; and if, indeed, those scraps marked the position of a Bronze Age wreck, it might very well prove to be the oldest shipwreck ever found. So we started a progress down the coast toward a still distant point on the marine chart. Searching for such a needle on a deep ocean bottom was a long shot. For better or worse the search there would mark the end of our expedition. We were almost into September. The seasonal Meltemi would be upon us, leaving us to work on a lee shore. We would have to move along, our course now set south and then southeast for that point on the charts, marked Cape Gelidonya.

As we cruised down the coast we stopped at Rhodes and hiked up a long and winding dirt road that led to the ruins of a crusader's castle on a high headland. It is said that the place at which St. Paul wrecked on the coast of Rhodes was directly below the castle. Who am I to gainsay any who wish to believe it. En route eastward we landed at the site of an ancient city that thrived 2,500 years ago when the Achaean Greeks colonized that part of the Mediterranean. Patara and Myra were its great cities. During the rein of Ramses II the Lycians were allied with the Hittites. Lycia was frequently mentioned by Homer in mythology. This had been a powerful, civilized state in the mainstream of history. That stream had dried up. No habitation was to be seen among the ruins. Scattered gnarled and ancient olive trees offered a little shelter to a half dozen goats. A line from a long-forgotten poem kept passing through my mind: "…and we, who pass like foam, like dust blown through the streets of Rome." There were two thousand and more years of ghosts in this place.

A fine stone amphitheater, cut into the side of the mountain that overlooked the city, could still have supported players and an audience. *Little Vigilant* was a black toy speck of a boat in the empty harbor far below. It took little imagination to evoke the ancient past in one's mind and I did just that as I sat apart on one of the tiered stone seats. I could almost see the chorus chanting the prelude to the play as the audience, filling that great crescent, quieted in anticipation. Before we sailed on we wandered through a necropolis, a veritable city of tombs, which must have been close by the outskirts of the city. What may have been grand avenues and streets were lined with sarcophagi. Their massive stone lids were tipped off and half-buried in the grass. We separated as we walked through that ancient place of the dead, each wishing to be left quietly with his own thoughts. I remember the harsh, white click of light on the olive branches and the sense of eternal stillness. There was no wind. Only the rising and falling thrum of an insect chorus broke the quiet. The sea had risen to cover that part of the burial ground that had been closest to the shore. I snorkeled around the submerged tombs and in one found the shards of two amphorae. Only the necks remained and one still had four finger-wide handles just under the lip of the opening. I brought them home with me, and they had found a place on the hearth of the hall fireplace.

So doing a progress along the coast we ultimately reached the headland called Cape Gelidonya. A quarter mile off the point a barren rock thrust its jagged mass out of the sea. It was made for wrecking the ships of the ancient mariners. By the description of the rock off which the Bodrum sponge divers had found the scraps of bronze, Peter knew this had to be the place. We had arrived. After anchoring in 90 feet of water, we watched with some dismay the fast-moving current that stretched our anchor chain as taut as a bowstring. Drayton was anxious to wrap up the cruise and start the return trip. And, indeed, the summer had run its course. We had rounded from September into October, the time of the Meltemi, the gale-force winds that had driven the ancient mariners onto rocks and lee shores all along this timeworn coast. The skippers gave us three days, four at the most, to find what we were looking for. And we didn't really know what we were looking for. Our first three days of diving revealed a boulder and crevasse-strewn bottom with wreckage of the ages strewn about, mostly anchors. The bottom shelved off into deep water very quickly. We would frequently find ourselves at 150 feet, 160 feet and having to fight our way back to our anchor line by pulling ourselves from rock to rock. It was dark and treacherous and nonproductive.

The break came on the third day. Because we had come up with nothing of significance, Drayton announced that would be our last day. And on the last dive of the last day, Susy Phipps saw something that looked interesting. Without fanfare she called to John Cochran to come down with her and see what he might make of it. They weren't at all sure about what they had found, but it was unusual enough for Susy and John to urge us all down for another dive. At 75 feet an object shaped roughly like an animal skin barely revealed its outlines. It lay atop a hardpan outcropping that was continually scoured by the racing tides. The object was overgrown with the algae and weed that covered the bottom. I would never have spotted it. When we tried to lift it we found it firmly cemented to the bottom. At that time we dove only with the slack tide twice a day; and now darkness and tide were upon us. Drayton's interest was piqued enough to postpone departure. We had another day in which to explore the area.

The following morning we dove with crowbars and hammers. The object was pried loose, attached to a down line and hauled up to the boat. Under it was another. When that was pried up we discovered a packet of sand under the lime accretion in which the object had settled. Fanning through the sand we hit a recognizable jackpot. In quick succession a bronze dagger blade emerged from the sand, followed by a bronze double-bitted axe head and a farm tool, like a hoe, and also of bronze. Three more of the animal skin-shaped objects were pried loose and raised to the boat. There was nothing else to be seen. The sand pocket bottomed out. The rest of the immediate area was lime-hardened rock; and our time had run out.

Not until we arrived back in Bodrum to leave off our Turkish companions did we learn that the large objects were ingots of copper. They were, in fact, called "cow hides" and were made in open molds in the sand. They almost certainly came from the copper mines in Cyprus, mines that are still worked today and have been continuously worked since biblical times. The extended parts on the four corners provided handles for carrying the ingots. Many weeks later, when I had returned home to Princeton, I spent some time researching the history of copper and came across an Egyptian tomb drawing that showed slaves carrying the cow hides of copper as part of the tribute to their master, an important government official during the reign of Tutankhamen around 1350 B.C. One of the advantages of living in a university town is the availability of experts in many fields. It so happened that Professor Erich Scherquist was the country's foremost authority on Cypriot bronzes. We had – I am somewhat embarrassed to admit after all these years – smuggled back with us the dagger blade and axe head. These, when I unwrapped them before the learned gentleman, popped his eyeballs out and elicited a wild exclamation: "Where did these come from? How did you find them?" He identified them within a half century as being from the Late Bronze Age, about 1,300 B.C. Further, they were of Cypriot workmanship. And most exciting to all of us who had taken part in that amateur expedition, that would make our shipwreck – at least at that time – the oldest ever found.

In hindsight I am glad we did not try to do more. Archaeologically, the wreck site was, needless to say, extremely valuable. Our crude way of attacking it would have destroyed its integrity and much of its value as a unique find. However, we did accomplish something by locating and identifying the wreck. That was enough for the University of Pennsylvania Museum to fund an expedition the following summer. A young doctoral candidate, George Bass, spent much of the summer opening up the wreck with professional care and later published a definitive report on the expedition. His conclusion: the ship was a trader from Cyprus, carrying raw copper and what turned out to be zinc. There was a forge on the ship and baskets of broken and used bronze tools and weapons. The ship was probably trading along the coast, forging new tools and weapons and buying scrap. That opening experience was for George Bass the start of a career. He would ultimately achieve a reputation as the leading underwater archeologist in North America, if not the world. George is one of the founders of the Institute for Nautical Archaeology, which is located in Austin, Texas, and today serves on their Executive Committee.

IX

CRUISES ON THE *LITTLE VIGILANT*

There were other splendid experiences cruising with Drayton Cochran on the *Little Vigilant*. During the fall of 1959 I joined Drayton and his crew at a little shipyard south of Bremen, Germany. The yard of Abeking & Rasmussen had built *Little Vigilant* and was making it ready for a cruise all the way to the Mediterranean via the canals and rivers of Germany and France. That turned out to be one of the most pleasant and beautiful experiences I would ever have.

We worked our way down the Weser River, through the industrial Ruhr on the Rhine-Ruhr Canal, entering the Rhine at Duisberg on a monstrous elevator like a giant swimming pool that lowered the entire ship down into the Rhine. On that great thoroughfare, in company with the barges and the paddle wheel steam tugs, called *Schnelldampfers*, we made our way south and up-river to Strasbourg, then south by the Rhine-Rhone canal system, ascending and descending a ladder of canals that carried us over the foothills of the Alps, then through the wine country of the Loire to Besancon. There we made a side trip to Dijon for Lucullian gastronomic excesses. Stuffed, like Strasbourg geese, we continued down the Saone to Lyon; and there we ran out of water. The Rhone was so low for lack of rain that the *Little Vigilant* had to be laid up at Lyon for the winter. The Mediterranean would have to wait until the following summer.

It is not easy to recall which part of that inland trip was most enchanting. Through the German part we had been ushered in and out of the locks by crisply uniformed officers in glass towers. All was order and precision. It was very German. In the locks we often found ourselves in company with steam tugs. Draytie loved engines and was himself a skilled engineer. He delighted the engineers of the tugs by clambering aboard to have a look at the steam engines with their polished copper and brass valves and conduits and hissing pistons. The engine rooms were spotless; the simplicity of the harnessed steam power was beautiful; and the engineers and captains almost squirmed with delight at being asked about their machinery and fulsomely complimented and admired by the American yachtsman.

Late in the afternoon the locks would close, ending the day's travel. We would secure the *Little Vigilant* fore and aft to a couple of convenient trees on the bank and put down a gangplank. Two bicycles were nested behind the wheelhouse. Draytie and I would roll ashore and set off along any nearby country road. Sooner or later we'd reach a village; and every village had a *Stubli* or *Wirtshaus* where we could have a stein of that wonderful German beer and a wurst. As evening came on we would peddle back through the countryside, the low mists beginning to rise from the fields. The boat was often almost obscured by the mist that spilled over the edge of the canal like dry ice in a beaker. Topping off the day, Willy, the cook, would have dinner on the table as he heard the bikes clatter up the gangplank.

The passage up the Rhine was a combination of a Wagnerian stage set and a scenario for the revels of a student prince. Great Teutonic castles dominated every bend of the river. One evening, before we reached the ancient city of Koln, once a bastion of the Roman Empire, we stopped for the night at the little river town of Boppard. The waterfront was hung with colored lights and the crowds of students and apparent visitors promenading along the quay more than hinted at a festival of some sort. And indeed, it was their annual wine gala letting loose all the stops over a long weekend of carousing. Before dinner we stretched our legs with a walk up a cobblestone street that led us to the town square. The entire square was set with long trestle tables and benches. At the center under an open bandstand were three enormous barrels large enough to be called tuns. Each had three or four spigots, and we had no doubt that with the coming of night and the arrival of the band, the spigots would flow continuously.

Back in the cabin of *Little Vigilant* we had settled down to dinner and reached whatever dessert Willy had for us when we heard the oomph-paa-paaing of big brass approaching from up-river. As we emerged onto the deck the first of a glorious display of rockets and fireworks started up from the opposite shore. At the same time a barge drifted by in mid-stream with a military band punishing the tubas and horns and drums. On the pier side the entire village had turned out to watch the show. As we settled in a pair of deck chairs, Willy appeared from below with a flaming platter of crepes, a pot of coffee, cups, plates and silver. A moan went up from the crowd pressed no more than eight feet from where we sat. It was half sigh, half groan and accompanied by considerable scuffling as the crowd pushed in to ogle these plutocrats pigging out on their deluxe tucker from the front-row seats of their yacht. Actually, the crowd was entirely good-natured. We didn't feel intimidated at all and raised our wine glasses to them. Perhaps I should explain that in Boppard a yacht with a Liberian flag and nabobs on-deck sipping wine had not been seen since mad King Ludwig tied up there with his swan boat in the last century.

The wine binge was going full blast when we walked back to the square. Several hundred red-faced revelers, old and young, had bellied up to the tables and were tossing off beaker after beaker of the maddening fluids. One table was all young students. The boys, many in *lederhosen* with the distinctive caps of their universities and the girls, most in *dirndls*, made room for us. We soon found ourselves clanking our tankards on the table to the rhythm of the band with all the rest, linking arms, swaying right and left and singing with the loudest, knowing nothing about the words. That's all I remember…or all I care to tell you about in this remembrance.

When we entered the French canal system at Strasbourg we found ourselves in a very different world from the Germany we left behind. There were no glass control towers and uniforms at the locks. Most of the time there were no lock keepers either. Hand-operated capstans replaced the precision electric machinery of the German locks. The system we now handed ourselves through had not changed since the time of Napoleon. The weather was glorious. The land basked in the sun. Fields with graz-ing cattle bordered the canals, the horizon of our view broken only by distant villages or tight compounds of farm buildings. We passed old men and women fishing with long poles, their bicycles on the ground behind them. They waved and called greetings to us: "Where are you from? Where are you going?" The passing of the strange yacht with the hull of a North Sea herring boat would be the prime topic in their villages that evening.

At times, when we arrived at the locks and sounded the horn, a broad, strong woman wiping her hands on her apron, would appear from the lock keeper's house, stare incredulously at the boat and then put her back to the capstan, flooding or emptying the lock as the case might be. We pitched in, making good sport of it and always leaving something with the lady of the house. And soon we took turns on the bicycle, peddling ahead from lock to lock on the paths that always bordered the canals, arriving at the next lock before the boat to start the capstan working. More often than not there was no one at the lock keeper's house. We worked the locks ourselves and enjoyed the exercise and the spirit of the game. As I think back on those golden days, I believe there could be no more enchanting, delightful way to do a progress through the old world, and especially the fertile, green, somnambulant countryside of Southern France.

The following spring Draytie started south again from Lyon with the *Little Vigilant*. The winter snows had replenished the Rhone so that he had clear passage all the way to the Mediterranean, entering that ancient arena of naval battles at Port St. Louis. I joined the boat at Villefranche on the Riviera at an antique shipyard that, like the locks, was virtually unchanged since Napoleon's time. We cruised south along the coast of Corsica. It was 11 years since I had hiked on that deserted road along the western coast. At the southern tip of Corsica we entered a narrow passage between high cliffs and wound our way through a meandering defile into the little land-locked harbor of Bonifacio. Ernle Bradford, in his book, *Ulysses Found*, which traced the voyage of Ulysses home from Troy as celebrated in Homer's Odyssey, postulated that it was from the high cliffs that commanded the narrow entrance to the harbor that the defenders hurled great rocks down upon Ulysses and his men in an attempt to destroy them. At the quiet waterfront cafes, even though it was early morning when we dropped anchor in the harbor, the old men were already sitting at the tables, sipping their glasses of milky-white Pernod and concentrating on their games of dominoes.

We traversed the Straits of Medelaine, finding the bottom littered with the shards of amphorae whenever we paused to dive, and continued down the east coast of Sardinia, and on to Tunis where we wandered among the ruins of the ancient Carthaginian Empire. While we were there I made my way into the heart of the Medina, a maze of alleys bordered by bazaars. Their awnings covered the alleys so that one moved through shaded tunnels marked by laser-like shafts of sun breaking through here and there. I had in mind to purchase a *burnoose* and finally arrived at a bazaar that was festooned with beautiful, heavy, lanolin-rich *burnooses* hanging from overhead racks. I saw one that I liked very well. Mindful of my western vulnerability in matters of trading with these people, I assumed a careless, nonchalant air as I pointed to the *burnoose* and asked, "How much?" I should have known by their grasp of English that they were well experienced with the occasional western customer. Determined to play their game, I shrank back with the announcement of the price, shook my head in disbelief, looked to heaven for strength to contain my incredulity and making great show of reexamining the garment, shrugged and offered them half. To my consternation and confusion they shook their heads and with self-deprecating smiles stuck to their price. At that point I knew the right maneuver was to throw up my hands in resignation, turn and walk away. In that scenario the next move, of course, was for one of the men to run after me, urge me back to reconsider and perhaps ply me with mint tea to soften the bargaining. I strode down the alley, pausing to glance into another stall and allow time for their surrender. No one came. I continued around a corner and stopped to consider. I wanted that *burnoose*. I was humiliated to even think of returning with my tail between my legs. I knew that they knew that I knew that they knew I lusted after that *burnoose*. I returned, threw down my money ungraciously and departed with the *burnoose*. To my unending relief, no one even snickered.

That night, snug in my bunk and actually quite pleased with my possession of that heavy, beautifully designed, handcrafted garment, I reflected on the cunning of my adversaries in the bazaar. Like sharks, millions of years old in their predatory senses, those descendants of two thousand years of traders easily sensed the vulnerability of their target. I was an easy mark. If anything, the victors must have experienced some disappointment at having been denied the usual keenly contested game.

From Tunis our course took us eastward to Malta, stopping at the volcanic island of Pantelleria and Malta's neighboring island of Gozo.

I found the island so fascinating and all of its parts so wonderfully accessible through Draytie's local friends, that I stayed on for two weeks after the *Little Vigilant* pushed on northeastward past the boot of Italy and up its eastern coast to Bari. There she was laid up for the winter.

Draytie's friends were the Laycocks. Major General Sir Robert Laycock was at that time the governor of Malta. He and his beautiful wife, Angie, had known Draytie and his family since childhood. At that time Malta was still British. Not long after our visit the islanders would agitate for independence, win it, and England would lose another jewel in her dwindling crown of empire. But then it was still thoroughly British. The harbor, with its massive fortifications, was – and still is – one of the finest harbors in the world. It was full of warships and could, indeed, hold the entire British Mediterranean fleet and more. Bob Laycock arranged for me to tour the harbor in the admiral's gig, one of the last steam launches still in use. It had a brass smokestack that gleamed like gold and an open bridge on which the bos'n and deck hand stood squeaky-trim in dress whites and conducted me through the ranks of destroyers, corvettes and a battleship and past the impregnable ramparts that frowned over the harbor. In their chauffeured Daimler, Angie took me on a tour of the Stone Age ruins. We picnicked on a high bluff, sitting on the stones of a miniature Stonehenge and peered into the honeycomb dwellings that had been quarried out of the limestone escarpments and in which a Runic people had lived in pre-Roman times.

There was much more that kept me fascinated during my two weeks there. I took a room at the Hotel Malta. The ashtray by my reading chair at the Punch Bowl was slipped into my pocket at the dining room one breakfast. I hired a car and, with directions from the Laycocks and at times with a guide, absorbed the island. I dined each evening with Bob and Angie at the Palace at Valetta, and those evenings are most cherished in my memory.

We dined in a vaulted hall in the palace that had been built by the Grand Knights of Malta in the 14th century. There were seldom fewer than ten to

16 guests at the table, many of them visitors like me, but there were also government dignitaries passing through, who, by protocol, had to be entertained. The long table was set with massive silver candelabra that provided the only light used in the great stone chamber. Floor to ceiling portraits of the Grand Masters lined the walls on either side. Places were set with three to four wine glasses and more silver than I knew how to use.

I had been told that coat and tie were not required for these "home" dinners, but was nonetheless surprised to find the guests in sport shirts and slacks when I arrived for cocktails. Bob wore military dress trousers with a scarlet cummerbund and loose white shirt. He was ramrod straight, fit, with perfect military bearing and as handsome as a whisky ad in *Esquire* magazine. Angie was agonizingly beautiful, tanned and healthy. They were the epitome of gracious, congenial hosts, and the table conversation was as cosmopolitan, challenging and – at times – brilliant as I have ever been treated to. Servants moved noiselessly in the darkness behind the chairs. Wine glasses were refilled until you chose to proceed to the next vintage. The eyes and stern faces of the Grand Masters seemed in the flickering backlight of the candelabras to be watching us. As I refreshed myself not wisely but too well with the copious wine, I became convinced that a pair of those glowering eyes were watching me.

The timeworn ritual of the Stilton and Port and nuts was observed. Angie excused herself and the ladies to await us in the drawing room. We gentlemen filled the chairs at the end of the table by Sir Robert. The brandy and cigars were passed and I found myself living the Victorian era and the social world of British custom that I had always loved reading about.

Some years later, when Susy and I were living in Princeton, I came across an obituary for Bob Laycock in *The New York Times*. I did not know at the time of my visit to Malta that he had succeeded Lord Mountbatten as head of the British Commandos and that he had been awarded Britain's highest decoration, the Victoria Cross, for an exploit early in World War II. As a young officer he led the raid on Rommel's headquarters in South Africa. He and his team were landed by night from a submarine and made their way to the headquarters where the great general was supposed to be dining with his officers that night. They burst into the dining room and killed all the diners, only to discover that the general was not among them. The article went on to say that Captain Laycock and a sergeant escaped, making their way through the desert to the British lines, hiding by day and traveling by night. And then – this is the part that makes me believe there will always be an England – the article said, "As they hid by night Captain Laycock sustained the spirits of his sergeant by reading to him from his pocket edition of *The Wind in the Willows*."

X

AMAZON

Above the broad entrance to the living room was a 12 foot-long object that looked like a curtain rod. On closer inspection one end had a mouthpiece. The other end was open, the end of a barrel. This was a real blowgun. It came from far up the Amazon, a thousand miles from the sea. The city of Manaus, just above the confluence of the Rio Negro and the Solimoes, the two rivers that flow into the Amazon, is the end of civilization. It is the last port accessible from the sea. I was there in 1965 with an expedition sponsored by the Niagara Falls Aquarium. I was commissioned to make a documentary film about the expedition, the purpose of which was to capture and bring back alive, for the first time, two species of freshwater dolphins, endemic to the Amazon and never seen in North America. Manaus was our staging area. The city was – and still is – a fascinating combination of Somerset Maugham jungle torpor amid the decaying splendor of a time long past. At the turn of the century, Manaus was the rubber capital of the world. Until some rubber plants were smuggled out of Brazil and replanted in what is today Malaysia, the Amazon basin was the world's only source of natural rubber. Consider any area having a monopoly on a substance as vital as rubber; and that the sale and shipping of that precious resource was entirely through a single city, Manaus. It was a boom town in the bush; a thriving, growing metropolis in the "heart of darkness;" a glittering, hedonistic capital of a commercial empire, carved out of the jungle and precariously perched on the mud/slime fetid banks of the great Amazon.

The echoes of that glorious opulence are still evident, muted by decay and disuse. The most prominent monument to the past glory of Manaus is the Opera House. Built at an expense of one million dollars during the rubber boom, it rivaled the great opera houses that ornamented the major cities and centers of world culture. In its pathetically brief flowering, hardly longer than a single season, it attracted Nellie Melba and other opera greats. The rubber barons built Renaissance townhouse palacios, many of which still turn up in the narrow, litter-strewn streets, occupied by several families, their stone facades pitted and crumbling. Their massive doors that were hewed from enormous primordial mahogany trees are still proof against the world of the street. The wood is dulled by time and neglect; but, on some, gorgeous, heavy bronze, dolphin-shaped doorknockers remain intact. Before we started up-river in quest of the living dolphins we had three days of stifling tropical torpor in this dead city during which I wandered the streets and, with a little imagination, relived its past.

I don't really wish to dwell on my recollection of that once-great city; but the vision of its decay contrasted markedly with the still vibrant, tenacious street life, which remains as colorful and pungent as any memory I have. There were no coffee-hued, magnificent Indian princesses, culled from some up-river tribe and mistress to a rubber baron, illiterate, arrogant, jeweled and ensconced in a box on the dress circle of the opera house. The "barons" are said to have drunk their champagne from the gilded slippers of their mistresses at the all-night orgies that followed the opera evenings. Why drinking bubbly out of any sort of shoe should be appealing puzzles me. However, my opinion is dated. It was apparently once considered the epitome of sybaritic excess and delicious wickedness.

The commercial streets were filled with shops, cement stalls hardly larger than a one-car garage, their wares spilling out onto the sidewalk. Live anacondas, tanned crocodile skins, poultry, garish fabrics, plastic baubles, dogs under foot, pungent smells of cooking meat, salt fish, urine and all-pervasive decay commingled into a sensual, powerful, chaotic, eclectic and living confusion. The riverbank could only be reached by balancing on narrow boardwalks laid down over 50 to 75 yards of muck and slime in which was imbedded the filth of the city.

This was dry season and the river was down. At the river's edge a flotilla of river boats, pulled up onto the muck gunnel-to-gunnel, were being off-loaded by brutish, powerful porters. Their primitive faces streamed sweat as they carried 120-pound loads of bananas on their backs from river's edge to the start of the city streets. Their only cover was a loincloth and a piece of burlap that started at their foreheads and covered their backs. At night they slept uncovered wherever they could find a dry place on the bank. Nearby turtle pens, containing hundreds of great animals weighing between 300 and 500 pounds, and all destined for slaughter, heightened the brutishness of the scene.

Sharply countering these dolorous sights were the acres of bright-hued produce set out in baskets or mats on the afterdecks of the boats or on the river bank: reds and yellows of peppers, rich greens and browns of beans, herbs, powders and grains, great bundles of sugar cane and baskets of silver fish from the river. And there were strange tiger catfish with monstrous barbel-ringed mouths, some weighing over 100 pounds.

At anchor in the river and beyond this border of boats was an antique riverboat, more like a tug. Its name: *Leida Mara*. It was right out of *African Queen*. One expected Humphrey Bogart to step out of the wheelhouse, clothed in filthy white ducks. It was one of the last wood-burning steam boats on the river, and it was ours. We had chartered it. I couldn't have been more delighted had a war canoe with 24 paddlers shown up to convey us up-river. The *Leida Mara* was almost a century past its time. Somerset Maugham would have had it crewed by raffish lascars; and – indeed – its crew, from captain down to third stoker, appeared to have escaped from a pirate time-warp.

The pure romance and sensual richness of our first night's passage up-river lingers in my memory more vividly than any part of that remarkable expedition. The *Leida Mara* was our power. Secured to its starboard side was the houseboat where we slung our hammocks and stowed our dunnage. It was nothing more than a wooden boat hull, about 50 feet long, open from stem to stern with a single deck and a roof which we could climb to using a ladder at the stern. On the port side of the antique tug was an entirely open wooden hull. If we succeeded in capturing the dolphins we sought, we would fill the hull with river water and take them back in a floating aquarium.

Our flotilla, bound together like a ménage à trois, got under way late in the day. The stench from that decaying city, golden and soft in the evening light, followed us until we were well beyond its suburbs.

Night enveloped us almost suddenly. While the river is a broad, brown highway one thousand miles from the sea and would continue to be for another 50 miles or so above Manaus, there are no horizons to hold the light from the parting sun. The jungle doesn't press in upon you but it is there, a dark barrier wall on either side, the darkness only occasionally relieved by the soft, orange point of a fire or an oil lamp in an Indian compound.

We had all moved to the roof of our boat where we spread our air mattresses and let the cool night air fan our bodies as we dozed or smoked or chatted quietly. The gentle rhythmic swish of a steam engine, powerful and quiet, is like no other motorized sound. The combustion engine emits an abrasive blatt, a whine or chatter as the strokes increase: the cacophony of traffic and generators and machinery that assails us during much of our lives. The steam engine hisses softly, the strokes slow and measured and beguilingly rhythmic. And from the smokestack a continuing shower of bright sparks soared 100 feet into the air. They became a glorious shower each time the furnace was stoked with fresh wood, an on-going Fourth of

July display that marked our passage up the middle of the great river. As the cloud of sparks fell astern the brilliance of the stars waxed and waned. The rhythmic swish of the engine was a hypnotic lullaby that eventually precluded any talk on our roof as we all succumbed to the enchantment of the time. Even the more garrulous among us lapsed into thought and eventual sleep.

The *Leida Mara* was lashed tight to the side of our boat. I could look down from the edge of the roof into the open sides of the stoke hole, a pit in which the engineer and the stoker worked. Their bodies, naked to the waist and bathed in sweat, reflected the hot red light from the furnace each time the door was opened. Sweat cloths were wrapped around their heads. Filthy shorts girded their loins. One of them, the chief engineer, was coal-black with a comically ugly face perched on a truncated, muscle-knotted body. He presided over a wonderful complex of copper tubes, bronze connector arms, hissing valves out of which thin jets of steam escaped, and massive steel cylinders. The conversion of power was from the corded wood to the furnace to the boiler to the cylinders and finally to the ponderous bronze camshaft that turned the three-bladed propeller that drove us with a rich, pulsing cadence up the Amazon. It was as simple as the miniature steam engines from Germany that I played with as a young boy.

A wood-burning steamboat consumes its own substance as it travels. It reminded me of the camel. That desert freighter can travel for days with the fuel stored in its body. A shark can actually live for months without eating, fueled by its own fatty tissue. The *Leida Mara's* decks were completely covered with stacked hardwood split and cut to two-foot lengths. At the start of our journey it looked like a floating, mobile woodpile. From stem to stern the decks were piled high, leaving just enough space for the captain to see out of his wheelhouse and for the crew to get about.

We steamed through the night. Dawn pushed through the mist that hung over the river and with it came a clear view of our escort. The woodpile was already down making the deck structures of the old tug visible. Wood must be the most ancient and inefficient fuel still used by man. It was obvious that a full-day's run and a furnace with an insatiable appetite would leave us in need of fresh fuel. Where would we get it? The riverbanks were now devoid of habitation save for the occasional native compound. The question of fuel supply was answered our second morning. We had spent the night with our flotilla nosed onto the riverbank. We refreshed ourselves with a swim only after we had taken the lead of our native guides. There was no way we would have submerged our bodies into that river without the assurance of what I call local knowledge. The specter of piranhas, snakes and other bad chaps we had heard about made us very apprehensive. We bathed without incident, ate what was prepared for us by our guides over an open fire on the shore and slept soundly in our hammocks. The symphony of sounds from the jungle was right out of a Frank Buck *Bring 'Em Back Alive* soundtrack. The next morning, as we breakfasted on the bank, one of our guides, intrigued by our fishing tackle, cast a spinner out into the river. The rod bent. The reel whined. We walked over to the angler carrying our coffee cups and looked on with keen interest and anticipation of what was giving him such a good fight at the end of the taut line. At length the biggest, meanest, most frightening piranha any of us had ever seen or imagined existed was beached. It was black and weighed probably close to four pounds. The Indian guide, handling it very carefully, squeezed open its mouth revealing a set of perfect triangular teeth, all razor-sharp. This, we learned, was the largest species of piranha, the great River Piranha. And this was where we had gamboled and splashed and refreshed ourselves the evening before.

The next morning the *Leida Mara* detached the flotilla from the boat and anchored it at the edge of the river before turning into a creek. There was no mark to identify the stream from many such feeder streams we had passed, but the captain obviously knew where he was going...or did he? The tributary quickly narrowed, the banks so close that the foliage brushed the sides of the boat. We were forced to crowd in the wheelhouse or on the roof forward of the stack. With the engine throttled down so that we barely moved, the eerie silence of the jungle sea was only broken by the hissing of the boiler valve and the occasional communication from the crewman stationed on the bow. About 20 minutes into our strange excursion we rounded a bend; there in a clearing rose a great stack of wood, split and measured to size for our furnace. The bow of the *Leida Mara* was driven into the high muddy bank. A gangplank was put over the side and we found out why we had been invited along on this excursion. We all formed part of a human chain, starting at the woodpile and ending amidships where the wood was carefully stacked. There was barely enough width in the creek for us to turn about and head out. These fuel dumps existed all along the river. No one appeared to collect payment. The system was as timeworn as the old steamboats that still existed on the river and it worked.

We had for some time seen the movements of dolphins, the little gray ones known as sacred dolphins, *Sotalia*. They rose often with rasping sighs alongside the bow wave of the *Leida Mara*. Two days up the river our net man, a veteran net fisherman from Delaware who had done much collecting for east coast aquaria, spotted a projection of the bank that created a small river pocket. There, on the morning of the third day, we set the net parallel to the bank then moved out into mid-stream with both of the big canoes. As the dolphins approached we beat on the sides of the canoes with our paddles, yelling like madmen, and had so positioned the canoes that the animals were diverted into the bay. One of the canoes quickly fastened its stern to the net's end and drew it across the opening of the pocket. The entire pod, perhaps 20 or more, were neatly trapped. As we drew the net up to the bank the pocket shrank, the animals sensing their danger communicated frantically. We could hear their shrill squeaks and staccato clicks as decreasing depth forced them to the surface. Finally they lay exposed in the shallow water, now docile and seemingly given up to their fates. They were such small dolphins that a single person could take one up in his arms. We had half filled one of the canoes with water. The animals were gently placed in the canoe and transferred to the barge that was also half filled with water. It now provided a floating aquarium in which the newly captured animals dashed about. In time, they quieted down, lying motionless underwater, surfacing only to refresh their lungs. The first capture had gone without a hitch, easier than we had possibly hoped. We were jubilant. A long journey still lay ahead before the dolphins would reach a new home. Keeping them healthy and alive was now the challenge. And their cousins, the pink dolphins known as *Inia* and almost three times the size of the little *Sotalia*, had still to be found and captured. We set off again upriver, spirits high, often looking down from our own barge into the dolphin barge to see how our new guests were doing.

The Niagara Falls Aquarium Amazon Expedition afforded enough adventure and unique experiences for an entire book. It is, of course, a popular statement by a lazy writer or raconteur: "I could write a book about that!" In fact, there were many facets of the experience, not only our final capture of the big pink dolphins and our struggles to keep them alive back in Manaus in a holding pond (we lost two of the *Sotalia*) as Brazilian bureaucracy held us up for the requisite greasing of the palm. Human relations on that long trip in close quarters became severely frayed.

When we had finally provided enough pounds of flesh to gain our release with the dolphins, we carried six of them back with us in that indestructible veteran of the air, the DC-3. Each dolphin had its own rubber-lined, water-filled box, and was carefully sedated and shot full of antibiotics and vitamins. We rode with them all the way, watching over them as lovingly as we were able. By that time we had all become emotionally attached to them. In hindsight I realize that we were escorting them to a life sentence. The jail would be benevolent, but hardly a fair trade for the freedom of that great river from which we had plucked them.

A good friend came out of the trip: Dr. Earl Herald. He was Director of the world-renowned Steinhart Aquarium in San Francisco. Two of the *Inia* were ultimately transported to the Steinhart and thrived. I visited with Earl a year later. We watched those curious animals with the long beaks and pink undersides. They were at home in their commodious tank at the aquarium and a prime attraction to legions of visitors, especially the children with their noses pressed to the glass windows. Not long afterwards Earl died of a heart attack while diving.

I am tempted to write that the 12-foot blowgun and the wooden quiver of poisonous, curare-tipped darts were acquired by bartering with an Amazonian tribesman. It was, in fact, purchased at the end of the trip in Manaus from an outlet for native crafts run by the missionaries. It was beautifully crafted, a bamboo tube inside another, both as straight as a gun barrel. It was accurate. I am told that the natives could pick a monkey out of a tree at 100 feet. We used to have target practice with it when there were guests. Even the biggest blow-hards could just barely push the dart through the barrel with their mightiest puffs. The darts were murderous-looking thorns about a foot-long. Raw wool was spun around one end to provide compression. Whether or not they were actually dipped in curare, which the natives are reported to do, my wife, Susy – always tuned to disaster – was sure the children would play with the darts, prick themselves and die. I was willing to gamble with their lives for the delight I experienced in having those bizarre missiles on display. Susy usually won out. I must admit that good sense was on her side; but what hairy-chested, hunter-descended, chauvinist male ever wanted to be told by a woman what to do with his weapons?

A three-foot-long and two-inch thick solid roll of cured black tobacco wrapped in palm leaves also came from that trip and stood on the other side of the living room arch. A bowl with a concave glass lining held an intricately arranged mosaic of gorgeous iridescent blue butterfly wings, another acquisition from the world of the Amazon. When, in my waking dreams, I think of the all-consuming fire, I envision each of those parts of the Punch Bowl collection adding their fuel in an explosive release of energy.

XI

POLYNESIAN ADVENTURE

The year I took my family to French Polynesia remains, to this day, the finest and the most meaningful year of my life. Let me say, "Our Lives." The year was 1965. My wife, Susy, and I lived with our three children in the affluent, stimulating university town of Princeton, New Jersey. The children were Gordy (14), Susy-dell (12) and at the bottom of the pecking order, Gar (10). Because there are two Susys in the family I will – in this account – refer to my wife as Susy. My daughter will be Susy-dell ("dell" is short for Liddell, her middle name). Gordy was short for George and Gar refused to be called Eddy or Edgar and so became Gar. Susy and I were very conscious of the social and economic environment in which our children were growing up. All three attended private schools. They were no more or less spoiled than a few million contemporary kids in North America whom fate had selected to be born into upper middle class families. The usual communication gap between children and parents existed, each busy with their own disparate social worlds. I was already embarked on a career of expeditions and filmmaking to the extent that Susy was virtually a single mother. Our family's decision to make such a bold move must have been motivated by years of reading about families sharing travel and adventure with their children. It might be described as a *Swiss Family Robinson* inspiration. We particularly wanted to share an adventure together while our family was still young. We hoped that a sustained daily life in a less privileged social and physical environment than American suburbia could inculcate in our children a sense of perspective, an awareness of the privileges they took for granted.

Where to go? We didn't really need to study a map of the world. I had traveled to Tahiti three times previously. The first time I shot underwater parts for a fellow film lecturer named Karl Robinson. The second time I documented a shark research expedition to Tikehau Atoll with the famous shark guru, Dr. Perry Gilbert. Our sponsors were Cornell University and the National Science Foundation. The third time I traveled with my Canadian broadcaster friend, Geoff Stirling. He paid our way and I introduced him to Tahiti life and diving. We made friends with both French residents and expats living there. On that third trip James Stuart and his wife, Janie, would become life-long friends. Their social popularity with the French Government paved the way for a government visa for a one-year visit in French Polynesia for the entire family. They also found a house for us and arranged the lease. Finally, I hoped that a year in the islands would provide the substance for a lecture film that would help to amortize the expenses for that entire year.

The time wasn't exactly right for us economically. An additional mortgage would be needed. But we realized that the time would never be perfect. "The days pass and never return." The time was NOW. We made our decision, both frightening and exhilarating, and Tahiti was it.

We started our preparations a good half-year in advance. U.S. Divers agreed to equip the entire family with essential scuba equipment and ship it to Papeete in advance. The German air compressor company, Bauer, arranged for a portable Bauer unit to be ready for us when we arrived. At that time the Bauer Compressor Company had the finest portable unit available. Jordan Klein subsequently secured the U.S. sales and distribution rights, renamed the product Mako and built a formidable market in the U.S. The Boston Whaler Company, Fisher Marine, quite new on the scene back then, provided a 16-foot boat. Johnson Outboards kicked in a 25hp motor. To say that help – and faith in our venture – was gratifying would be a prime understatement.

Susy had to start the long trip to Tahiti a month before me because of my lecture schedule, which ended three weeks after the lease for our Tahiti house started. Her resolution, enterprise and true grit were hard tested. She drove across the country with the children from New Jersey to Los Angeles. There she sold our car, embarked on Air France and was met by James at Papeete. The year in the strange, beautiful and totally different world had begun.

Our house was in the district of Paiea, 22 miles along the coast from Papeete, the capitol of French Polynesia, and the only town on the island of Tahiti. The habitations were strung out along the single coastal road that bordered the lagoon. Susy had already leased a vintage Ford station wagon from the only rental car agency on the island. A car for a family with children, equipment to transport and big food shopping needs was requisite when you lived in the boondocks as we did. Fortunately, Dave Cave, an American expat, owned the only car rental business in town. He and his vivacious half-Tahitian wife, Leone, had become good friends on one of my earlier trips. They inevitably were a big and vital part of our year.

When I arrived three weeks later Susy and the children had already put down roots. Using the Calvert home education system Susy had established a classroom regimen. Each morning after breakfast five days a week Susy labored to review and instill the essentials that would enable the kids to keep up with their peers at home. And it was a labor. Three different ages – 10, 12 and 14 – required three levels of texts, studies and homework. Outside the open veranda the lagoon lapped seductively at our very doorstep. The roar of the ocean surf on the outer reef was a constant, day and night, like so-called gray sound in the city. Neighborhood children had already bonded with ours and found common cause in the games that are much the same for children in both poor and rich countries. They required no toys, no bikes, scooters, roller skates and the like, just healthy bodies. It was not easy to hold our children to their classroom tasks with adventure and play in the sun and the lagoon awaiting just a few leaps and bounds out the door. Susy managed it.

The regimen became increasingly flexible after I arrived. I started planning excursions and activities for which I wanted the family – and especially the children – with me. My own serious mandate for that year in the islands was the shooting of a documentary about an American family experiencing the joys and hardships of an environment far removed from their home in the States. Susy and I were as one in recognizing that the experiences the children would have with their new friends, with me in the sea and all together with our daily lives would be the core of their education that year. They assimilated French from their playmates with the ease of water absorbed by a towel. Susy disciplined herself to learn the new language. They all became easy with French, enough to communicate for all our needs.

Our house was a step above the woven mat and straw thatch houses that, way back then 40 years ago, were pretty much standard out in the country. It had been provided for the director of the Fileriosis Research Clinic.

Fileriosis, commonly called elephantiasis, is a horrible disease that was at that time endemic in French Polynesia and still ravages remote parts of Papua New Guinea. It was eradicated locally by the Tahiti research. After the research project ended the clinic was not entirely a clinic any more, so the research director's house across the road was ours for the year. Our landlord was William Albert Robinson who became a good – albeit somewhat aloof – friend. There was, however, nothing aloof about his three vivacious, sinuous, beautiful daughters who were just the right ages for our nippers. "Robie" Robinson was almost paranoid about his daughters and suspicious of all young men. The girls, Nona, Tomata and Rompa were born of two native mistresses. He decided our boys, Gordy and Gar, were too young to be dangerous. So the Robinsons and Watermans became inseparable.

I took possession of the Boston Whaler and Johnson motor, ran it up the coast from Papeete and into the pass through to the lagoon just a quarter mile from our house. An unused cement pier by the shore most fortuitously had an inside sheltered berth that was perfect for the Whaler. Susy had already collected the portable compressor and crates of scuba gear from U.S. Divers. We could load the tanks into the station wagon along with all my camera gear, picnic baskets, towels and other equipment from the pier, park the car and head out for whatever the day's diving prescribed. We were in business.

The menu of opportunities for activity each day was endless. The sea at our doorstep, mountains behind us, a colorful, laughing and hospitable native population still tuned to the old ways in a changing world all combined to promise fine grist for a year of shooting. A Protestant work ethic pecked at my shell. I scheduled fresh activities for every day of our year.

I started scouting the island for scenic views including vignettes of island women (*wahines*) bathing and doing their wash in the rivers over which the road passed. When they noticed me with the camera they always laughed and shouted with unselfconscious humor. I would come upon 20 or 30 women in a long line on the beach pulling a net ashore. Just off the beach in outrigger canoes their men were guiding the net around a pocket of small, mackerel-like fish called *operu*. I would speed back to the house, burst into the morning schoolroom and shout, "Come with me! The whole village is pulling the net. You've got to see it. I want you all in it."

The kids would burst from the room like water breaching a dam. And Susy, no inflexible school marm, was of one mind with me. Calvert courses could wait whenever the priceless exposure to our new life called. The game was afoot. A half-hour from the time I had left the beach we were back there. Susy-dell and her mother now wore the loose native dress called the *pareu* daily. The boys wore surfer shorts with or without T-shirts. They had gone native. Their blond hair stood out as they pitched in with the ladies hauling on the line. When the silver harvest of ten thousand fish leaping and shimmering in the morning sun was beached, they helped gather it into big woven baskets. Their reward for the help: a kitchen pot full of fish, enough to feed us for a week. My reward: an achingly beautiful scene for the film, unrehearsed, unstaged.

One afternoon our new friend, Dave Cave, who was the President of the Gamefish Association, showed me pictures of a monster striped marlin that the bonito fishermen had brought to the central market at Papeete. By the time Dave arrived at the market the world record fish had already been cut up for steaks. Dave secured the bill and the tail. The tail was over six-feet high. Our house faced the mountainous island of Moorea, just 35 miles across the deep ocean trench that separated it from Tahiti. The marlin had surfaced from that trench among the bonito the fishermen were pulling in. They had hooked him with a lure on a heavy monofilament line, drowned him by dragging him behind the boat before he could fight for his life and pulled their prize to Papeete. So much for The King, perhaps the greatest game fish to have been plucked from the world's oceans. I have a picture of Dave standing next to it. He sent the measurement to the Smithsonian Institution in Washington for an estimate of the marlin's size. Their guess was around 3000 pounds. For the fishermen the great animal was only measured by the dollar-per-pound at the market.

The talk about the monster marlin led to an arrangement with one of the bonito fishing boats that worked the Moorea deep. The crewmembers were big, heavy built, solid muscled Tahitians. Fishermen all, they were proud of their skill. They made me easy aboard and shared their bread and coffee with me as we set out for Moorea at dawn.

The boat had a 40-foot hull and a cabin with four bunks forward, a flying bridge atop the cabin and a low, work deck aft. Bamboo poles were racked under the gunnels on either side. There were no rods with reels, just bare poles with monofilament attached and bare stainless steel hooks of two sizes.

We cruised the mid-channel for more than an hour before a big palm frond was spotted floating at the surface. They knew – and I learned – that a ball of small baitfish would be attracted to the flotsam. They tethered the frond to the stern. The boat drifted with it. Soon the bonito found the bait ball and the water became roiled with their attack, driving the school to the surface. Suddenly the air was filled with boobies and gulls. Pirate frigate birds appeared, harassing the boobies. Four of the pole men flicked their barbless hooks into this maelstrom and almost instantly the slender poles bent double. With a combination of body rhythm matching the springlike bend of the pole the 15- to 20-pound bonito were smoothly levered into a big open box in the middle of the work area. Most often the hook released and in less than a half-minute, the lure was back in action with another hit. I let the camera roll, shooting from the vantage of the flying bridge and well out of the range of flying hooks. I wound the old Bolex like mad, frantic to record every moment. Reloading the 100-foot spools was an exercise in frustration, my nervous fingers working too fast for efficiency.

Suddenly the action notched upward. I noticed no change in the seething mass – still a melee of screaming birds and panicked fish. But the pole men knew that a bigger, more powerful predator – oceanic yellowfin tuna – had arrived.

The pole men racked up their light poles and took up the heavier ones. Now there were two men to a team, two poles joined into one at the end with a heavier monofilament attached. There were now fins and the ominous dark forms of sharks cutting just under the surface. With bodies working in unison, the paired fishermen swung their hooks into the action. Almost immediately the twin poles bent; the men arched back against the great weight and heaved a big, shimmering tuna out of the sea and into the cockpit behind them. The backward spring of the bent pole perfectly coordinated with the anchored strength of the two backward leaning men was the most perfect marriage of natural and human force I had ever seen. I could only guess at the size of the tuna, very likely more than 200 pounds – every one the same as if they had been cast from a mold. The action was magnificent, powerful and exquisite. The way the great fish were literally plucked from the sea was magic. My grandsons would have called it "awesome."

As suddenly as it had started, the action stopped. The big poles were racked. The men, drenched with sweat, helped the deck men make some order of the bodies. The palm frond was cut loose and the boat headed home for Papeete and market. Hinano beers were liberated from an Igloo ice chest amid their laughter. Every one of the crew would have fine shares from the catch. As I downed my Hinano I felt a sense of pure euphoria. The action had exceeded my wildest hopes. I checked my meter readings and f-stops. The wide-angle lens on the turret was clean. All was in order, no horrible discovery after the action that I had blown it all with a careless move. It was a wrap. It was also one of the most dynamic scenes in the finished film.

Single fishermen in their small outrigger canoes at times caught great tuna on a hand line. One morning within sight of our house, I was lucky enough to be in the right place at the right time with such a lone fisherman. When the wind was offshore and the sea on the outside of the barrier reef gentle, I had noticed a cluster of small canoes concentrated in one small area. If the weather held they might be there all day long. I was told they were fishing in a "tuna hole." The barrier reef on the outside of the lagoon sloped down into deeper water gradually reaching the abyssal depths that always surround volcanic islands. The tuna hole existed in the slope of the reef. The opening was at a depth and location that I was never able to find on my own. The hole – as I understood it – extended into the coral like a great well and bottomed out at about 300 feet. Occasionally a big tuna could be caught in the hole.

The children were having their morning school time. I took the Whaler out through the pass and pulled up near a lone fisherman. He was sitting in his canoe, the only one over the hole that morning. I called out the morning greeting, "*iaorana*." He returned the greeting with a grin, accepted my presence no more than 15 feet from him as if there were nothing strange about a white *tane* watching and drifting with him. We rose and fell easily with the soft Pacific swells. The morning was glorious, the surf no more than a faint rumble. The mountains of Tahiti with their collar of palms along the shore rose up behind us. I settled in comfortably to wait, sensing that this pleasant vigil might very likely go on for hours. The monotony was interrupted when my companion commenced a small action. I rolled camera. He had set about freshening his bait. It was a learning experience for me that ultimately provided one of the luckiest sequences of my film.

Having retrieved his line hand-over-hand he secured a round stone about the size of a baseball to the line's end. He proceeded to cover the stone with slabs of fish, securing each layer by several winds of monofilament line around it. When the ball of fish was as big as a grapefruit he secured the windings with a slipknot. About a foot above the slipknot was an oval shaped spoon carved from the mother-of-pearl nacre that is the beautiful inner surface of the pearl oyster shell. A five-inch stainless steel hook was secured to the bottom of the lure. Over went the bait, with the line skillfully played out through his fingers. When the stone hit bottom far below he gave the line a jerk. Three hundred feet below in the dark the slipknot released the ball and the bait unraveled in a cloud of chum. He relaxed the line long enough to let the hook descend into the bait mass and settled back to wait.

The wait was surprisingly short. I saw him tense suddenly. His concentration focused on the line, hard-wired now to a whisper of vibrations at the far end. I started shooting. He braced his body, willing the hook to set and hold in the mouth of his prize. A series of quick, hard pulls and he settled into a steady, rhythmic retrieval of the line. Like the steady pressure exerted by the break on a big fishing reel, his body never relaxed.

My old Bolex camera had only three and a half minutes of 16mm film on a load. I knew the winning of the prize from that depth would be a long process and stopped shooting to keep enough ammunition for what I hoped would be a dramatic finale. It was. Peering over the side of the Whaler I was now close enough to the canoe to catch the first silver flashes of a big tuna powering from side to side, more visible every second as the hunter's inexorable pull never relaxed. The tuna was more than half the length of the canoe. The massive head broke surface; the fisherman snubbed the line tight on the side of the canoe with one hand. In the other appeared a combination gaff and billy. With the billy end he rained blows upon the tuna's head reducing what fight might be left in him. With the gaff secured to the tuna's head and his hand gripping the tail he tipped the canoe on its side, almost to the swamping point, and rolled the fat 200-pound still pulsing fallen warrior into the fragile shell. It was a fast, masterful performance. I cheered. He grinned. I tossed him a bottle of orange Fanta. He waved his thanks and with no pause for recuperation from the battle took up his paddle and started for home.

After all that I returned home in time for lunch. The children were outraged that they had not been with me. Increasingly through the year we subordinated the classroom to sharing such adventures.

One evening, Susy and I went to dinner with James and Janie Stuart. James, who was an encyclopedic source of information about native customs, filled me in on the whole story. That catch, he explained, could have been the only reward for many fruitless days of fishing over the hole without success. Its price in the market would support his family for a month. My prize was the unstaged recording of a native fishing technique unchanged by time.

As we were assimilated into the local life, we learned more each day about activities that would be fun for the family and, at the same time, grist for the camera. The Fataua Falls became a regular picnic place for us. We were often joined by the Robinson girls. One of the many rivers that flowed from the inland mountains to empty into the lagoon turned into a fast moving stream as we followed its course upward. A half-hour hike led to the first of a series of cascades. An hour of hard walking on a path that followed the stream brought us to a waterfall with a drop of about 200 feet. Above that was our favorite picnic place – a moss-covered clearing in a copse of giant ferns. As Susy unpacked the knapsack picnic, the children would line up for a ride down the cascade above the great falls. Smooth as a playground slide, their descent – always accompanied by screams and shouts – dumped them about 50 feet into a deep pool. They would scramble out, sprint up the path like monkeys and launch off again and again until Mum called them back for the picnic. They were brown, shimmering like wet otters and wonderfully healthy.

Over the weeks and months we often picnicked around the island. We discovered isolated black beaches – all the beaches were black volcanic sand – where Susy would lay the picnic on a big beach towel. I would join the children snorkeling out and over the fringing reef to explore the marine life. We all dove together when the sea was calm, exploring the pass near which the Whaler was docked, penetrating the tunnels that had been formed over eons of time by current, coral growth and stormy seas. We could only work the pass at slack tide. The children had become easy with scuba diving when we lived in the Bahamas. None of us had been certified. I was very aware of the unseasoned judgement in very young people; so I always watched my brood carefully and kept us together.

We ranged with the Whaler through the lagoon, threading our way around the shallow reefs and learning to navigate by water color all the way to the airport at Faaa (pronounced Fa ah ah). There a PBY, a twin-engined float plane from World War II, had sunk in shallow water at the end of the runway. Ever mindful of comic relief to season the film, I prepared a set scene. The side hatch of the plane opened. Susy and the children, carrying their handbags, exited in a line and swam away, their exhaust bubbles trailing behind them. It was the epitome of corn. It was also a huge success. The finished film with which I lectured for many years was punctuated with that scene. It always drew a good laugh and established a warm rapport with the audience.

In that same bay area off Faaa a two-masted schooner had foundered and sunk to the bottom. Its masts pierced the water's surface with the shrouds upon which the children could clamber. A line of running rigging, like vines in a forest, hung from the topmasts. The children, monkeys all, would swing out over the water, let go and fall ten or 12 feet with a great splash, screaming and laughing. They were tireless. The joy was so repetitive that I would finally have to round them up, haul them into the boat and head home for lunch.

Susy would always have lunch ready for us on the big table on the porch with Moorea, the lagoon and the sea our companions. If they had missed their lessons in the morning, Susy might ring the school bell after lunch. There were house chores, food management, laundry and other daily routines that kept our home life civilized and orderly. We had a native woman as housekeeper, but Susy was the boss, the mother hen. She adapted to the very modest goods and services that were available in the island world. She kept us nourished and healthy. She did wonders with the tinned corned beef, rice, breadfruit and yams that were the staple diet of the natives. Greens and root vegetables were mostly absent from the markets. Fresh fish could only be had at the big market in Papeete, and that, only if we got there early in the morning. Fruit was most happily abundant. Giant grapefruits called *pamplemousse*, juicy and delicious, were breakfast fare. Eggs were also readily available. But the diet was rather monotonous.

Later, when we moved our household to Bora Bora and the island of Tahaa, the children would beg me to tell them about "first class dining on the Queen Mary." I had never traveled first class across the Atlantic. That didn't matter. They would hang on every word as I conjured up visions of grand cuisine. Ultimately they would tire of waiting for the best part. They would shout, "Get to the desserts." Then literally slavering they would demand I tell them how many desserts one person could order. "Everything on the menu," I would tell them and they would groan with pleasure.

Generous friends opened doors for us around the island. They were all socially prominent in Tahiti's small society and accepted by the French as well as the old established native families. Nancy Rutgers was the daughter of James Norman Hall, co-author of *Mutiny On the Bounty* and *The Bounty Trilogy*. She was married to Nick Rutgers, a young heir to the Johnson & Johnson pharmaceutical fortune. Their gracious, sprawling home had the most beautiful location on the island. From a high knoll it overlooked Matavai Bay and Point Venus where, over 200 years previously, Captain Cook had recorded the transit of Venus. On a grassy slope descending from the house, a simple gravestone surrounded by flowers marked the resting place of the famous author. The house in which Nancy and her brother had been born and reared still stood at the bottom of the hill close by the main road. Her mother, Lala, as vivacious as her daughter, still lived there. Jamie, the youngest Rutgers, was Susy-dell's age. We along with the Stuarts and the Caves, celebrated Christmas and New Years and many dinner evenings with dancing and games at the Rutgers' home.

James Stuart, third son of the Earl of Moray, direct descendent of Mary, Queen of Scots, was the Director of the Pan Am office in Papeete. Urbane, charming, with a splendid sense of humor and a warm personality, he was enormously popular with the business community, the French colonial government officials and the island diving community. His wife, Janie, from Horse Cave, Kentucky, was equally vivacious and the most glamorous hostess on the island. Their friendship was of incalculable help to us and a source of delightful company.

We probably saw more of Dave and Leone Cave than anyone. Leone, one of the prestigious Bambridge family, had met Dave Cave when she was evacuated to California during World War II as a schoolgirl. She radiated energy, fun and high spirits and was the quintessential island lady with a handsome blend of local and western genes. She exuded animal female energy. When she danced the *tamure* with two or three men at a time the floor cleared to watch her. These ladies, Nancy, Janie and Leone were a formidable trio. We were the newcomers they accepted. All were instrumental in the connections and arrangements that initiated and facilitated almost all the varied moves and activities, the building blocks of our year.

Susy-dell caught the eyes of the neighborhood boys. It started each morning as she collected the fallen fruit from three mango trees in the front yard. The yard bordered the main road along which the boys rode their motorized bicycles. These low horsepowered machines were called mobylettes. Like high school kids tooling back and forth on Main Street, U.S.A., the Mobylette Gang – as we soon called them – appeared every morning at fruit harvesting time. They blatted past the yard, the high-pitched staccato tattoo of their little motors shattering the morning quiet. They showed off with suicidal abandon – steering with their feet, riding backwards and rearing back on their rear wheels. Susy-dell pretended boredom with it all, laughing despite her show of disdain. The amorous cowboys often crashed into the roadside ditch or tangled with one another. A yell of "Here comes the Mobylette Gang" would bring us all to the window to watch the show. Finally Susy-dell, her basket filled, would flounce back to the house without a backward glance at the mayhem left behind.

Through one of our friends, we were introduced to a native fisherman from the island of Tahaa. His name was Tavaa. He had command of serviceable English and communicated a cheerful, intelligent disposition. I was keen on extending our range of experiences to other islands less developed than Tahiti. Tahaa was part of the island group named *Isles Sous les Vents* (Islands Under the Wind). They included Bora Bora, Huahini and Raiatea. Tavaa had a family compound on the shore of Tahaa, the smallest and least developed of the islands. He had a house with a roof that he would be delighted to rent to us. His wife, Rena, and their little girl would cook and welcome the company. A deal was made, probably with the help of Leone Cave, and our sights were set on Tahaa.

Through the shipping agent in Papeete, we reserved cargo space on one of the Donald copra steamers that served the out islands. For a few francs more we might have space on the sheltered upper deck for ourselves and personal baggage. A week after the deal was struck our juggernaut clambered aboard a rusting freighter at the Papeete waterfront. Sailing time was indefinite. I was told that the ship would shove off when it was fully loaded. That turned out to be almost 24 hours later. When we boarded, the decks were already crowded with families going home. They sat and slept on their woven mats, their little traveling hordes of fruit, bread and soda pop carefully guarded. Children made common cause with families around them, creating a happy chaos and irrepressibly spilling out of their nests. We found space for our mats and dunnage and settled in for the voyage. We had been advised to bring our own pot and toilet paper. A big *pareau* draped over the head and down to the deck afforded working privacy. The contents of the pot were heaved over the side into the harbor. A shore breeze swept the deck reasonably clear of the omnipresent thick, sweet copra smell, robustly blended with sweat and human waste. It was quite an experience for us. Our neighbors on all sides welcomed us with smiles and nods that breached the communication barrier.

Last to be loaded aboard at the end of the day was our Boston Whaler. Our dive gear, compressor and fuel cans were packed in it. It was neatly plucked up from the pier and nested on top of a mass of soft cargo on the forward deck. We were on our way at nightfall.

I am unable to recall how we got from the ship to Tahaa. There were no roads on the island. We certainly arrived by Whaler with all the gear for our new home piled high. Tavaa's compound, nestled on an isolated stretch of shore, could only be reached by a footpath that ran along the edge of the lagoon and connected one household group with another, always at some distance. Contact with the main village on Tahaa was by boat. Outrigger canoes with outboard motors were the native vehicles.

The special recollections that each of us have of the three months we lived on Tahaa may provide a salient precis of that time with Tavaa and his family. The children loved the enormous sow that lived under our house. We named her Coney for reasons too obscure to recall. She had a litter of about 15 piglets, still nursing at her bank of dugs. The "oinks," squeals, snores and fights over the spigots went on all night long. During the day Coney rooted around the yard, followed by her family. The children delighted in the night sounds and the wallowings of the huge animal.

Holes dotted the yard like a giant cribbage board. In each hole lived a crafty land crab, a *tupapa*. Day and night they danced about their territories, always at a safe distance from the home hole. Tavaa showed the children a game with the crabs. A piece of bait on a string attached to a bamboo rod would be cast next to a crab hole. Very soon the crab would appear with beady black eyes focused on the bait and make a rush for it. The bait would be inched back drawing the crab further out. Then, at the critical moment the prey was allowed to seize the bait. The line would be whipped up, the crab deposited at the feet of the angler and captured. The sport was in the game and the prisoners were later released.

The island was one of the necklaces of small islands called *motus* that formed the outer boundary of the lagoon. Our *motu* was about a half-hour away from Tahaa as Tavaa could paddle his canoe. We became familiar with the reefs around the island and would speed ahead to start the day's diving. The children remember helping Tavaa collect the fish that he caught using a native root called *timba*. The technique was generations old. It was also shockingly destructive. In 1966 the environmental fervor had not yet seized our western world. I recorded the whole process because it was such a unique and interesting part of the native fishing culture.

The root of the timba bush grew wild and abundantly in the scrub woods behind Tavaa's house. I watched him pull up a bundle of the bushes, chop off the surface green and take the brown roots with him in his canoe. Over a section of reef he would crush the roots against a board with a stone until they were a semi-liquid pulp. With roots in hand he would drop over the side while breath-hold diving and with bare feet kicking for a full minute or more, he would shake the roots around the base of the corals. A milky cloud would appear and was carried by current in, under and around the coral. The effect was quick. In less than a minute the small, mobile life forms of the reef would begin to exit like a crowd from a burning building. From the smallest wrasse and butterflyfish to angelfish, surgeonfish, squirrelfish and small morays, the reef's population would pathetically lose balance, flutter in circles and sink to the bottom on their sides. The children watched the process as I filmed it. They helped Tavaa collect the catch, being well warned to let him handle the lion and surgeonfish.

The process was, of course, egregiously destructive to the reef. However – with few exceptions – everything went into the pot for human consumption. I learned months later that the poison element in the roots was rotenone, a toxin that apparently did not affect the human diner. I had previously worked with marine scientists who used rotonone for collection purposes, but never dreamed that it could be extracted from a root in the wild.

The people of French Polynesia love to party. No excuse is too small. A wedding is a very big excuse. It is apt to be a two or three day affair with marathon drinking, eating, dancing, music, fights and endless talking. We attended a wedding while living on Tahaa. The host was Tavaa's cousin, now my good friend from an earlier pig hunting venture. His niece was marrying a young man of the village. We loaded the Whaler with our sleeping bags, bottles of spring water, towels and a few necessities for camping out. At Raiatea, across the lagoon, Susy had purchased the requisite gifts for the bride and groom and family.

We arrived at the village and joined a dozen or more guests who had already spread their mats on the floor of the village schoolhouse. As the only foreign visitors the chief honored us with the most generous deference, introducing us all around and making us at home. A long copra shed with a thatch roof had been cleaned up for the banqueting and furnished with long tables and benches. The shed, open on the sides, had been decorated with palm fronds and flower couronnes (leis). The tables were already sagging under the weight of beer and wine bottles, baskets of boiled breadfruit and French bread. Pervading the whole scene with its happy, noisy guests was the mouth-watering aroma of roasting pig.

The bride and groom appeared, entering the village by a path along the lagoon. They walked together for about 100 yards before they reached the village minister who awaited them under a floral bower. The pair looked frightened, miserable and was apparently in physical stress. They both wore new shoes that were obviously killing them. The bride had a traditional white wedding dress. The lipstick on the dark glistening face was not flattering. She managed a wisp of strained smile and clung to the arm of the young groom. His black suit was too tight, his collar and tie an ordeal and his face, unbroken by the least hint of a smile, imparted pain stoically born. I was later told that he had all of his few remaining teeth extracted for the occasion. The good cheer and humor of the crowd that lined the path totally belied the funereal appearance of the wedding pair.

The minister intoned his ritual, the ceremony ran its course, and the newlyweds were escorted to the middle of the table. There they sat, grim and silent, looking straight ahead and stiff as cadavers. The guests stampeded toward the table and got on with the feasting. Two pigs had been roasted. The village women set great platters of meat along the table and kept it coming. We ate with our hands. There was orange Fanta for the kids. Hinano beer and Algerian wine flowed endlessly.

We stayed less than two days with just one overnight in the schoolhouse. The second day all formality and order were gone. Many guests had departed, but many stayed on to eat, drink and sleep, or nap, virtually where they were standing. There were fights. Horrendous blows were exchanged by those big men – blows that could fell an ox and would have crippled me for life. Within a minute after such a dust up, the combatants would embrace and weep and – apparently – vow eternal friendship. We quietly slipped away toward the end of the second day. That night we slept soundly with the reassuring snorts and grunts of Coney under the house.

A trip to the big city meant a half-hour run across the connecting lagoon to the neighboring island of Raiatea. A much larger island than Tahaa, Raiatea had a field hospital, a big fish and produce market, a general store to cover our needs from toothpaste to wine and, most welcome of all, the Bali Hi Raiatea. Three enterprising Americans had come to Tahiti years back and started chicken farming. When the chickens failed they landed on their feet with the construction of their first small island resort on the island of Moorea. They called it the Bali Hi Moorea. A main lodge and dining room on shore was connected to a number of full facility cabins built on supports over the shallow reef and joined by a network of raised boardwalks. Number one was an instant success. Number two followed, the Bali Hi Raiatea. There a Saturday dinner and overnight each week was our great joy. It meant dinner with real choices preceded by cock-tails. A hot shower and a bed with sheets were heaven. Between the twin beds in each cottage was a window set in the floor. A light switched on below illuminated the reef along with the small resident reef fish. It mattered not that the children had all been diving in that marine world and knew all the fish well. The novelty was so exciting that they usually fell asleep with their faces hanging over the sides of their beds.

A young American couple, Denny and Liz, managed the small inn (it hardly qualified as a resort). They enjoyed our weekly visits and usually joined us for dinner. You should know that back in the mid-1960s there were not many Americans in the out islands. That warm acquaintance with the two led to the most exciting diving adventure of our entire year.

The cottages were built so close to the edge of the shallow fringing reef that one could actually dive from the little balcony into the deep water of the lagoon. Denny told me that the lagoon in front of our cottage was about 100 feet deep. The reef's edge was a wall with a sheer drop to the bottom. He further told me that he thought there must be some sort of a wreck down there. Anchors had been fouled and pulled up with rigging debris caught in the flukes. No one wanted to try breath-hold diving to that depth nor had anyone come to Raiatea with scuba equipment before us. Following this rather intriguing information I loaded a brace of filled tanks into the Whaler for our next Saturday night special.

Gordy, our oldest, was elected to dive with me. As managers and staff watched from the dock I anchored the Whaler a stone's throw from our cabin. Susy and the two youngsters watched from the balcony. Gordy and I had no idea what we would find; and indeed, when we reached the bottom we found ourselves on a mud plain. We spread out within sight of one another and began a sweeping search. The first hit was an enor-mous spar as thick around as a small tree. We approached it from the deep side, away from the reef wall. It vanished in the gloom toward the reef. We followed it.

What emerged from that limited visibility mist was so shockingly dramatic and spinetingling that to this day the image remains clear in my mind. First came the shadow of a large hull. As we drew closer the shadow resolved itself into a ship so large that we were stunned. What we had discovered was an iron hulled sailing ship, a three-masted schooner on her side. I guessed she must have been over 200 feet from stern to the bowsprit that was still intact. All the wooden parts were, of course, gone. The steel deck supports formed a grid that we could enter. We both had hand lights. Directing them inside they flashed off the silver sides of a school of big jacks. We swam along the side of the ship to the bow and then angled up and away to bring us back to the Whaler. Our search had used up too much air for a further reconnaissance of the wreck.

You may imagine the excitement our shouts to shore generated among the small crowd that gathered at the pier. Our discovery was a complete surprise to Denny and Liz as well as the native staff. We stayed on for another night as guests of the hotel, made much of by all to whom we recounted our experience and puffed up like toads with all the hero worship.

On our return a week later I came with four tanks and a loaded camera. Gordy and I made two more dives reenacting the finding and following of the spar. We explored the inside of the ship, again encountering the resident school of jacks. In the hawse pipe forward a huge moray eel had made his home. He looked like a monster to us. His head filled the pipe. In hindsight I suppose he was no longer than about six-feet. He never came all the way out. We imagined he must be at least ten feet and so described him to our avid listeners.

News of our find had gone around the island by the time we returned. Denny had news for us. An old timer in his eighties recalled the trading schooner foundering. The ship had been docked by the reef, discharging cargo. A line squall caught it there, springing its seams as it pounded against the coral until it filled and sank.

Neither Gordy nor I will ever have another dive like that or experience the splendid epiphany of discovering a virgin wreck. A Hollywood fantasy adventure could not have been scripted more perfectly.

Thirty-two miles across open ocean the tallest mountain on the island of Bora Bora was visible on a clear day. Our friends in Tahiti had arranged for us to rent a cottage on Bora Bora and live there for as many weeks as we wished. Steve Ellicott, a French fisherman and landowner, was our landlord. An old friend from many years back was also a Bora Bora resident. Erwin von Christian had been manager of the Officers' Club in Bermuda when we first met and dived together in the 1950s. Our friendship had been renewed on my earlier trips to Tahiti where he had become the *maitre d'hotel* at the Hotel Tahiti. Now married to a beautiful native girl, Erwin had established a small diving business on Bora Bora. He was my guide to the reefs and a frequent diving partner during our weeks there.

The Whaler had a safe mooring with a dock about 50 yards from our small house. When the weather held fair we dove every day. If the sea was rough we dove around the reefs inside the shelter of the lagoon. The big adventures took us out through the pass to dive the outside of the barrier reef. There the endless flat expanses of low coral sloped gradually down into darker water and beyond sight into abyssal depths. Occasionally small schools of silvertip sharks, handsome animals six to seven feet long, would appear, always deeper. The children were thrilled but not frightened. They had long become accustomed to the blackfin reef sharks that were omnipresent in our lagoon dives. The larger open water sharks emerging from the deep held some menace in our minds even though they always showed little interest in us. The most enchanting encounters inside the lagoon were with the big Pacific mantas. Diving during late afternoon we learned that we could encounter them feeding along a sand ridge where an upwelling lifted plankton from the deeper lagoon water. The mantas, six to ten at a time in a column one behind another, would wing toward us and pass right over as we lay quietly on the bottom trying not to exhale. As they swooped over almost close enough to touch, their mouths were wide open like jet engines sucking in air. One of the finest takes in my finished film came from that experience.

The children rode on the outriggers of the sailing canoes. We climbed the hills of the small islands that bordered the outside of the lagoon, picnicking at the top and dreaming of "first class on the Queen Mary." Food was a problem. Amazingly, fresh fish were not readily available and I was reluctant to drop my camera for a speargun. At the Chinese general store green vegetables were almost nonexistent. Root vegetables, breadfruit, canned corn beef from New Zealand, eggs, powdered milk and an occasional chicken were to be had. Susy did wonders with our cuisine.

Twice a month the Chinese movie mogul would arrive on the copra boat. He would marshal local help to set up a sheet on a wooden frame for a screen and had a portable generator for his 16mm movie projector. The word would reach us that it was movie night. We would have an early dinner and drive in our rented 1938 Chevy to the open park by the lagoon. There, hours before dark, the locals had spread their mats on the ground. Whole families, perhaps 50 to 100, old and young would be there ahead of us, the children chasing about with a most festive air. The fare, as I recall, amounted to the equivalent of ten cents for children and a quarter for adults.

The program was apparently the same year after year. It consisted of 13 episodes of *Zorro* or 13 episodes of *The Green Hornet*. The audience was spellbound even though they must have memorized every line. The black and white film was so scratched that there was never a clear frame. We attended twice and loved it. After all, it was the only game in town.

The days passed happily and full. We made it so by programming activity. My remaining film stock was being used sparingly. We talked often of home and were, in fact, emotionally ready to go. Susy and I were determined to see the full year out; but we yearned for home.

The end came quite suddenly and disastrously, a happening that shortened our planned year by more than a month. I was bent, and badly bent. Following a dive, I had come up too fast, not allowing the nitrogen bubbles that accumulated in my body at depth to dissolve sufficiently. It is amazing that it didn't happen sooner. We had no dive computers, only depth and tank pressure gauges. The Navy dive tables were my general guide. Egregious liberties were taken and gotten away with UNTIL THAT LAST DIVE.

There was a sand slope on the outer reef densely populated by garden eels. At 132 feet they carpeted the bottom like grass. I discovered the location one day when Gordy and Susy-dell were with me. Erwin Christian and a native helper accompanied us with his boat. The water was so calm and clear that we could easily see to the bottom. I had been shooting garden eels inside the lagoon in shallower water and was fascinated by the animals. So down I went to the bottom, settled on the sand and filmed away. Erwin accompanied me and shortly left for the surface. I was too busy to notice. I did not notice that my air was running out, until I began to pull a little harder for each breath. I stayed on, crowding in the last good take and started for the surface as fast as I could ascend, exhaling, pausing a second for a short breath and continuing to exhale as I shot up like a Polaris missile. I climbed into the Whaler and was immediately hit by a severe cramp across my middle. I was doubled over with pain. In the other boat Erwin called across, "What is the matter?" "I'm bent." I shouted, realizing full well and too late what was happening. "Nonsense!" he called back. "It cannot be. You'll be okay. I'm going back for lunch." With that he pulled up his anchor and headed home.

I was too preoccupied with my pain to notice. Gordy helped me off with my tank and on to a spare. I told him I was going back down to decompress and dropped over the side again. At 25 feet the cramps disappeared. I started my decompression on the anchor line. Time passed; I didn't know how long. Chill invaded my body. My teeth began to chatter. Picnic debris drifted past me. The children were having their picnic while I was shaking like a rattle down there. I decided I had had enough and surfaced. To my profound relief the cramps were gone. I had beaten the rap. The children shared my relief. In their ignorance about decompression sickness they had nonetheless sensed the seriousness of the emergency. I thought, and so did they, that I was in the clear. On the way home I was aware of heaviness in my legs. I was willing to believe that it was just lassitude and fatigue brought on by the trauma of the experience.

Late that afternoon, a little before dinner, I knew I had not gotten away with my careless abuse of the rules. I needed to urinate and I could not. I was also losing feeling in my left leg and motor control in my right. Too late I picked up the *Navy Diving Manual* and read it thoroughly. I confirmed what I already knew; I was in serious trouble. I had sustained a central nervous system hit. From the waist down I was becoming paralyzed on the left side. The immediate crisis was the need to pee before my bladder ruptured.

The nearest hospital was in Raitea, 32 miles over open water. By the time we started taking action the radio contact with Tahiti was closed down for the night. Thus began a series of moves, an odyssey that would four days later find me in a recompression chamber on a French warship 900 miles east in the Tuamotu Islands. The island was Mururoa. The chamber was the only one in all of French Polynesia.

But first I had to relieve myself or burst like a swollen tick. With Steve Ellicott to guide our Whaler through the pass and a neighbor along to help we ran for the open sea. Grateful for a calm sea and clear night we made the passage to Raitea. I was helped to the field hospital where a catheter was finally inserted. That wave of relief will never be forgotten.

The following days merged into a misery of suspense and hope and obligation to many people who pitched in to help. The Flying Club of Tahiti was contacted. A small plane and pilot arrived mid-day to fly me to Papeete at low altitude, to avoid aggravating my condition. I was met by James and friends who took me to the hospital in Papeete. The hospital had been built for Napoleon's occupation force. Its facilities were just as ancient. The staff knew nothing about the bends. There was no chamber on the island. Friends went to work. Susy and the children were contacted. They would wrap up our small affairs on Bora Bora and return to Tahiti. The boat would be sold to the Bali Hi Company along with the diving equipment. It was determined that there was a chamber aboard a French warship at the islands farthest east in the Tuamotu Group. There the French were preparing to test their first atomic bomb. Meanwhile, I languished in the hospital, not at all in pain, just in limbo, much visited by friends and finally by my weeping and alarmed family. I did make headlines in the local news. That was small consolation since I knew that my stupidity had gotten me there.

James Stuart went to work. He and Janie were popular in the social circle of the French top brass. He asked them to help and they did most generously for which I will always think well of them and be in their debt. It was arranged that I should be flown to Mururoa in one of their regular cargo military runs – a twin-engined, pressurized transport.

At the airport the family saw me off – Susy tearful and not knowing if she would ever see me again. The children were hushed. Gordy, in the best tradition of the adventure movies he had seen, blurted out, "Gee Dad, I hope you pull through. These long years since we still joke about that.

The chamber on the French cruiser had had no previous customers. A junior officer had been put in charge. I was not reassured as I watched him studying the manual. The chamber had an air lock and a single pipe berth inside. The officer and a corpsman entered with me and joined me down to a pressure equivalent to 160 feet. With that they exited through the lock. I learned that I would undergo a treatment for table four bends. That called for three days and nights in the chamber. A classic French treatment followed. About an hour later the corpsman joined me again, bringing with him blankets, pillows, a *National Geographic*, a plate of baloney sandwiches AND – this is the winner – a carafe of red wine. He also had a bucket should my urinary system open up. He departed. I was left with my thoughts – rather bleak – and a sterilized catheter with which I could skewer myself when I became desperate. There was cold comfort from the friendly faces looking into the porthole and making "V" symbols. There was also a determination not to take any liquid including the red wine. The long isolation in stir had begun.

I recall that I sat on the bucket frequently straining for relief as my bladder became stressed. I believe it was about a day into the term that I tried again. A trickle became a stream. I must have shouted "Eureka" and let go. Talk about "epiphanies" – I shall never again discuss or write about my urinary tract or anything that personal; but that time I shouted it to the world. From then on it was downhill.

Halfway through the long decompression the airlock clanged shut, presently opened on the inside and through the opening a tall gentleman appeared, smiling and bearing gifts. He was a friend of the Stuarts and Rutgers whom I had met. He was also a French pilot just arrived from Tahiti. He brought letters from the family, greetings and gossip plus a care basket of goodies for munching and drinking. After the first success on the bucket my appetite had revived. The visit was pure gold. The next day-and-a-half passed easily. I exited on the final morning to a greeting by the officers of the ship, an invitation to luncheon in my honor with a hot shower and some clean clothes with which to enjoy the honor.

What a year it had been. Living together for many months, sharing the adventures and adapting to new friends in a very different social world: it came at the right time for all of us. The children were old enough to absorb and recall their new experiences. They were a part of their dad's work. They were also a part of their mother's work and enterprise in making a home for us as we moved about the islands. An *esprit* within this family emerged from that year and has not diminished. The timing for that adventure together was perfect. We seized it and that has made all the difference.

We departed for home soon after I returned from Mururoa, pausing for a week in Honolulu to stay with old friends, the Zadoc Browns. We also visited the Institute for Tropical Medicine for a check up even though we felt fine. Blood tests revealed that a half dozen types of parasites had set up housekeeping inside us. We had never been aware of them any more than the islanders who carry that parasitic baggage with impunity all their lives. I went to the Tripler Army Medical Center for a post-bends check up. It was decided that I would live to play the violin again.

It was midsummer and the siren song of Maine and the Punch Bowl sang within us all. I had taken the current when it served. My family, all of a mind, had pitched in with enthusiasm and so shared the adventure. Ultimately *National Geographic* purchased the rights to the film, entitled *Polynesian Adventure*, after I had presented it in their Constitution Hall Travel Series. Fortunately, the purchase price met the year's expenses. We came home with a "goodly store of memories for company." Most valuably, we had gained an expanded perception of life far removed from home, and a discerning appreciation for what we have.

XII

BLUE WATER, WHITE DEATH

The half-year odyssey that took me away from home for the production of *Blue Water, White Death* was one of the finest adventures in my life. Peter Gimbel was the moving force behind the major film production: it would be the great white sharks' public debut. He had recently carried out some seminal cage diving with blue sharks off the Jersey coast and had even exited his cage to film them in the open. Peter had in mind the harrowing idea of doing much the same with Great Whites. At that time, 1963, so little was known about shark behavior that primitive fear of "man-eaters" reigned. Peter did not lack for courage and enterprise. He had already achieved celebrity status as the first diver to reach the *Andrea Doria* and bring back pictures of that colossal wreck. They were published in *Life* magazine.

During the summer of 1964 Peter visited us at the Punch Bowl to put forth his idea for producing a major studio release, with a search for the great white shark as the plot. The first larger than life-size moving images of that most feared of all predators would be the capstone of the production. Without enough imagination to even wonder how it would all be accomplished, I enthusiastically applauded the idea and agreed to join Peter in the film's development. As usual, I was in over my head with ongoing projects, and preoccupied with my lecture circuit. It produced the majority of our limited income. Much later I came to understand the advantages Peter had to offer with such a bold venture. An heir to a great department store fortune and with many business connections as well as his celebrity status, he was well endowed to proceed with the scheme.

Except for occasional letters from Peter I lost all connection with the enterprise while I carted my young family off to French Polynesia to experience island life for a year. While we were away Peter had been busy and most productive negotiating backing from Cinema Center Films, the new filmmaking division of CBS, and dabbling in more shark diving escapades. At a machine shop in New York City he designed and fabricated two shark cages with adjustable buoyancy controls. Cameras, housings and supplies were stored and ready for shipment when our itinerary was finalized. Personnel to make up our production team had been contracted. I was surprised, amazed and excited with the reality that the improbable production was going to fly.

Shortly after my return from Tahiti, Peter flew to Durban, South Africa, to scout the hunting grounds of a shore-based whaling station as a possible production site. The Union Whaling Company hunted sperm whales as they ranged between the Indian Ocean and the Atlantic past the tip of Africa. The whalers assured him that when they harpooned a whale and buoyed it to be picked up later by one of the homeward-bound whale catchers, they often found their waiting whales shredded to the bone. White sharks by the hundreds, they said, feasted on the carcasses before they could be collected. It sounded like a perfect location with plenty of great white action guaranteed. We would nail down the climactic target footage at the very beginning of shooting and then fill in with a string of underwater sequences shot in a range of other locations.

It did not turn out that way. Peter had no way of knowing that the whalers' "whites" were oceanic whitetip sharks, *Carcharhinus longimanus*, not the great white shark, *Carcharodon carcharias*. Only with the Latin name can one be sure. As fate would have it, that communication error provided the most exciting experience during our entire half-year travels. Even our eventual encounter with the great whites toward the end of the lengthy adventure did not compare to our introduction to raw fear in the open ocean off Durban when we ventured outside the shark cages with dozens of oceanic whitetips rabidly plying bloodstained water.

The underwater camera team included Peter, Ron Taylor and me, always supported underwater by Ron's wife, Valerie. With her long blond hair, fine figure and vivacious personality Val was frequently on-camera during our travels. She and Ron were Australia's most famous diving couple. They had worked with the "White Pointer" as the great white was called in Australia. Both were, of course, superb divers and Ron was an experienced underwater cameraman. Peter Lake, a young friend of Gimbel's, joined the expedition as the underwater still photographer. Peter Mathiessen, a much-celebrated novelist and wildlife author, would join us periodically to gather material for a book documenting the production, entitled *Blue Meridian*. Mathiessen and Gimbel were both Yale men and old friends. Mathiessen had been with the Rockefeller expedition in New Guinea, when young Michael Rockefeller mysteriously disappeared.

Once our boat, equipment and team finally arrived in Durban, and things were put in order, the offshore weather made a turn for the worse forcing the whaling boats to remain in port. After several anxious weeks ashore, waiting for the weather to break, the wind and seas laid down enough for us to make it out of the harbor, although the seas were still roiled by the hard blow. Additional days passed before the weather, whales and sharks decided to cooperate. Our boat was tethered to the giant whale left buoyed in the gentle rolls by the whalers. We descended into the two cages that had been attached to the whale carcass. Gimbel and Valerie were in one cage, Ron and I were in the other. In the deep-blue, crystal clear water we viewed a scene that was stunning, overwhelming to our senses. The predators – oceanic whitetips – circled the prey at a leisurely pace, so many that it was impossible to determine their numbers. I can tell you that Ron and I had no intention of exiting the safety of our cage. We were shocked to see the door of the other cage open and Peter issue forth into the mainstream of the circling sharks. I like to think of myself as more prudent than brave, but the situation called loud and clear for someone to back Peter up. I went out. It was like stepping off the edge of a precipice. I have never been so scared in my life. Peter and I took up a station back-to-back and started to shoot.

We were jostled and bumped by the oceanic whitetips and so busy pushing them off that we soon drifted apart and found ourselves shooting toward one another to catch the action of cameramen being besieged by sharks even as the sharks were besieging us. Had even one attacked there was nothing we could have done. But they didn't. The first contacts – perhaps a nose in the back delivered with jarring impact or a side swipe on one side when we were shooting the other diver – were heart-stoppers. In hindsight we guessed they were sensing us. Our neoprene wet suits were certainly not as appealing as the whale banquet awaiting them.

On successive dives our entire team worked in the open water. Valerie Taylor rode shotgun while we concentrated on the shooting. When she saw a shark approaching one of us from behind she would rush over and rap it on the snout with her shark billy. She rapped so many that she developed an ache in her elbow and so was the first lady to develop "shark elbow."

Ultimately we pushed the intimacy of our contact with these animals by joining them at the side of the whale carcass on which they were feeding. We filmed at point-blank range as their mouths scooped out gobbets of blubber and they thrust their reeking noses into the carcass. Apparently we were accepted as fellow banqueters, sharing the feast. We suspected that once these animals committed themselves to the bait they paid no further attention to the human presence. Our footage proved exceptionally vivid and powerful, but alas great whites never appeared.

During the years since those first nerve-bending trial runs, Ron Taylor and I have directed much of our filmmaking to sharks. We put to use the lessons learned off South Africa, the most useful enabling us to take advantage of the sharks once they were committed to the baits. Thus the astonishing and impressive close ups of gnashing teeth and bloody snouts.

Many adventures occurred during the long months it required to track down our elusive prey. Even a trip across the Indian Ocean proved futile to our search, but that voyage did provide a most memorable encounter in Ceylon (Sri Lanka). When we were there in 1968 the large island at the tip of India was famous for its tea and its gentle, beautiful, smiling people. Now it is known as Sri Lanka and is synonymous with violence, ethnic pogroms, and implacable hatreds spurred on by vengeance.

The ancient city of Kandy is situated in the middle of Ceylon. The princes of Kandy once ruled all Ceylon. Now the city stews in the inland tropical heat, marinating in the backwash of history. There is, however, a shrine that is sacred to the Buddhists. There the tooth of Buddha himself is displayed in an ornate glass reliquary. The tooth is large enough to fit the chops of a hippo. Its extraction must have required a forklift. However, belief is in the mind of the beholder. The tooth is, no doubt, as potent in its spiritual force as fragments of the True Cross. Enough True Cross fragments showed up during the Middle Ages, hawked by friars and mendicant monks, to provide framing for an entire fleet of Spanish galleons.

The production team was crossing Ceylon by road from Columbo on the west coast to Batticaloa on the east. Our expedition ship, the retired whale catcher *Terrier VIII*, would meet us there. Our intention was to find and film the wreck of the *Hermes*, a British aircraft carrier, the first ever built. It was sunk early in World War II. We did find the wreckage, resting in 175 feet of water, but the currents and visibility were horrid and no sharks or large animals appeared. On the way there we took a break from the road trip for two days in Kandy. Having exhausted the novelty of Buddha's Tooth and blown our allowances on what turned out to be fake moonstones, we sought diversion and any subject that might be filmed that added to our adventure story. True, the great white shark had not penetrated inland that far, but we were encouraged by the size of the venerable tooth. Then we heard about the fruit bats.

They are the biggest bats in the world. They can weigh up to four pounds and have wingspans up to four feet. By night fruit bats swarm over the countryside in dense clouds like locusts and decimate the fruit orchards. The farmers might wish that the fires of St. Anthony would dart up the fundament of every one of them, but bound by religious strictures, they will not lift a hand against them and so the bats thrive and multiply. We heard about a rainforest on the outskirts of Kandy where the bats literally hang out. We further learned that a spectacular scene could be witnessed when the bats were made to fly en masse by frightening them. Since one could go for days – or even weeks – in Kandy with no more excitement than being cheated by a gem merchant, we decided to film this bat-o-rama. To this end we acquired a pair of enterprising urchins. For a trifling sum plus free cigarettes as required, they would take us to the hangout of the bats.

The edge of the rainforest was a short way out of town. Bat City turned out to be an immense dead tree, well over 100 feet high. Its great branches, barkless and bleached white by time and weather, stretched skyward like ghostly arms. And festooning these limbs, hanging upside down like evil fruit, were the bats – tens of thousands of them. They appeared so loathsome and menacing that we almost recoiled from our purpose. Of course, there's nothing wrong with bats, but our mindset places them in league with snakes, spiders, toads, and other unpleasant creatures. So we gaped at this world-class horror. At this point the urchins revealed the contents of the newspaper bundle they had with them. In it were rockets, regular old-fashioned Fourth of July rockets. They let us know that for a rupee a rocket they would waken the bats from their pastoral torpor, causing them to fly. And that was the very end we sought. The 35mm Arriflex was set on top of the tripod, manned by cameraman Jim Lipscomb and his assistant Tom Chapin (brother of the late Harry Chapin). Stu Cody, our soundman, set up his Nagra, hoping to catch a few frantic bat squeaks. Peter Gimbel, the producer/director, stood by ready to give the time-worn signal that would start the action. Ron and Val Taylor and I stood by, trying to look busy out of water. The urchins conned one more cigarette each, essential to light the rocket fuses. The scene was set; all eyes shifted between the urchins with their rockets and the somnolent bats.

"Roll sound," said Jim, with calm professional assurance. "Sound rolling," intoned Stu. "Camera rolling," bounced back from Jim. "Action!" called Peter with an authoritative gesture to the urchins. The fuses sputtered and hissed. Two rockets simultaneously shot upwards with a whoosh and, to our immediate satisfaction, exploded in the upper branches in the very thick of the napping bats.

Several things happened. First, the urchins ran like hell as soon as the rockets fired. We were too keenly intent on watching the bats to wonder why the boys had lit out so suddenly.

Then the bats all awakened unpleasantly and decided – as one – to leave. The sound of their mass departure was like summer thunder. The sky darkened as their sheer mass blotted out the sun. At the same instant several thousand sphincters lost control, opened, and let go. A cloudburst of excrement rained down upon us, a flood of bat shit, a deluge, a tidal wave, a disgusting force field, a Mt. Pinatubo of feces, unimpeded by any umbrella or protection for our group. We were directly in the line of fire. We panicked. Production equipment was abandoned in our mad flight for the shelter of the van. The rocketeers were already there. No one noticed in the stampede for the doors that they were grinning broadly. The fecal torrent continued to splatter the roof of the van as we cringed in the stifling heat with the windows tightly shut. A growing sense that we had been had added to our outrage.

Then the final blow, the aftershock, occurred. One of us – I can't remember who – gargled incoherently, a horrified strangled "Arrrrgh," and pointed to his ankle. On it, well seated and prospering, were five slimy brown leeches. An immediate inspection of our own ankles confirmed the success of the leech assault. The urchins had the last kick from the disaster. Bumming two more cigarettes they showed us how to remove the loathsome parasites by touching them with the lighted end.

And then there was the clean up of the equipment, abandoned on the battlefield, and perhaps a germ of thought that some day, ages hence, I might be telling about this with a laugh. Encounters with bats, the biggest in the world and legion in number, are not apt to occur often in the career of an underwater cameraman. But who knows. For a rupee a rocket and a pair of good running shoes I would be delighted to set the scene up for some people I know.

Since we had run our budget to the end and were delivering a film that never achieved its goal, one might suppose that the hard-nosed producers would have bagged the whole thing. Instead they came through. They were so impressed with what we had put in the can that they took a chance and put another quarter million into the project. That was enough for us to take our production team to South Australia, cages and all. There we hit the jackpot.

We worked out of Port Lincoln, a summer resort and grain shipment port on the coast of South Australia. An overnight run south into Spencers Gulf took us to Dangerous Reef. There Ron and Val had regularly encountered the "white pointers" and filmed them at the surface. A world record catch with heavy rod and reel fishing tackle had been made there. The isolated rock island, less than 300 yards across, was inhabited by hundreds of fur seals and thousands of sea birds. In a dense fog one could have navigated to it by the smell on the wind.

We started a chum slick of fish guts and blood that was carried by the wind and current 15 miles and more across open water from the island. A shark crossing that slick would home in on the source. We were ready for action. Watches lay aloft all day. Expectations ran high. We waited and waited as the meter ran. The days passed. The budget dissolved. A full week passed with zero appearance by Mr. Big. The usual high spirits and laughter in our crew gave way to pervading gloom. Peter called the shots. He decided to give it one more day beyond the week. With desperate hope he gave the situation still one more day. Nothing.

On the tenth day we began preparations to wrap up the failed attempt. That morning the fickle finger of fate, having toyed with us most cruelly for half a year, relented. An impossibly high gray fin appeared off the stern. A shout – several shouts – brought us all tumbling to the stern to watch the biggest shark we had ever seen in our lives cruise about at the surface in the chum slick. It looked like a minisub. We were all thrilled, excited to the core and perhaps a little stunned now that our quarry had appeared.

The action was galvanic. The shark cages, already hoisted aboard for the retreat, were prepared and lowered. Wet suits, not really adequate for that 60-degree water, were stretched on. The big 35mm Arriflex cameras were loaded. Before our first team could get into the cages a second monster equally huge appeared. Ron, with his seasoned eye, estimated they were both about 16 feet.

The sharks were hungry and aggressive. One mouthed the outboard on the skiff, shaking the small boat like a toy. Another seized the rudder of the *Saori* with such force that the wheel in the wheelhouse spun right and left. We paired off in the cages as we had off South Africa. Ron and I shared one, Peter and Valerie in the other. Peter Lake substituted in one or another during the course of the day.

That single day provided the entire action. Both sharks were male, their claspers as large as Louisville Slugger baseball bats. They appeared even more massive underwater as they pushed at the cages, mouthed the bars and cruised by over and over again, their bodies brushing the bars. We ran through our 400-foot film magazines almost without stop as the action continued. Out of the cages for a fresh magazine and in again, as fast as fresh magazines could loaded. The deck was a barrage of shouting, cheering and backslapping as we climbed out of the cages with our exuberant accounts of the performance below.

It continued all day. Everyone had stories to tell. On one dive Peter Lake, alone in a cage, was turned almost upside-down as one of the sharks tangled in the cage line, panicked and dragged the cage about, turning it on its side. Lake, impressively cool, cut the line and released the shark. Its thrashing had bent the bars. I was able to catch the incident from the other cage.

My own little drama was not recorded. As one of the great animals brushed by the cage I reached out and grabbed the nearest clasper. The shark twitched, slapped the cage with his caudal fin and accelerated past. There was no glory in the move, but for one second I held a one-ton shark "by the balls." That has to have been an all-time first and last.

As that wild, wonderful, lucky day ended we had it in the can. It was a wrap. The cages were secured, left over chum went over the side along with several small crates of far-gone vegetables from the galley. In the dusk the sharks surfaced again. As we weighed anchor and departed Dangerous Reef our sharks were savaging the debris with wild eruptions at the surface. They were still at it as night closed.

We were so energized by the day's spectacular success that sleep was out of the question. The champagne, saved for that occasion, flowed freely. The best dinner of the entire ten days went on 'til midnight: the talk and laughter never abating. With no element of bragging those of us who had been in the cages agreed that any sense of fear had been obviated by the action we were catching on film. We had waited a very long time for that action. The only fear was that a camera would jam.

Blue Water, White Death did well in theaters across the country. It almost won the Academy Award for Documentary of the Year in 1968. As I recall, it was nosed out by The *Helstrom Chronicle*, an excellent documentary on insects. Looking back I could not put a price on that experience. It had been a real odyssey of epic stature for all of us. Not long after our production Rodney Fox started dive tours for cage diving with the great whites. I went into the tour business and subscribed annually to so many of Rodney's tours that I have lost count. They were hugely successful. Over the years the size and numbers of great white sharks diminished. A 16-footer became a rarity. They were not hunted but were inadvertently killed in commercial nets. Toward the last years of my trips to Spencers Gulf I had three no-shows. That was a hard roll for guests who had paid to travel so far. Thanks in large part to Valerie's vigorous lobbying the White Pointer was declared an endangered species in Australia and put under protection.

XIII

EXPLOSIVE DIVING

J ust to the side of the living room arch in the hall was a 90mm shell case, gleaming like gold, its brass polished at least once a summer. It was raised from 110 feet deep at one of the biggest underwater ammunition dumps in the world, located in the Solomon Islands just off the Russell Islands, north of Guadalcanal. The battle for Guadalcanal opened our Pacific war with the Japanese during World War II. It was also the first setback for the Japanese war machine, which until then, had rolled uncontested southward through the islands of the western Pacific, with sights set on Australia. We checked the Japanese at Guadalcanal and from there started the long, costly drive northward, through the Solomon Islands. When that campaign was concluded and we moved north into the islands of Micronesia we found it less costly to dump the hundreds of millions of dollars of equipment and ammunition than to load and transport it onward to the next battle area. Thus the "Million Dollar Points" were created, high shores off of which millions of dollars worth of construction equipment was run into the sea. And off one of the Russell Islands we had dumped hundreds of thousands of live rounds of ammunition.

In 1968, I had chartered the *Waioona*. Today there are two fine live-aboard dive boats that operate in the Solomons, but when I first went the only boat available for diving around the islands was the *Waioona*, captained by an ex-salvor named Bryan Bailey. Rick and Jane Belmare, a Canadian couple, had created an excellent shore-based dive activity out of Honiara on the island of Guadalcanal. They put their roots down there and eventually instituted the first live-aboards.

As it turned out, Bryan was a perfect guide for us. From his salvage days he knew the locations of most of the World War II wrecks that were within diving depth. My youngest son Gar was with me and that year's Our World Underwater scholarship winner, Rocky Strong, who would in time become one of the foremost shark researchers in the marine science field. Bryan's wife Marie Clair cooked. His eight-year-old daughter, Rowena, amphibious from life aboard the small sloop, joyously renewed friendships with her peers when we touched at the island villages each evening. She was as easy in the fragile outrigger canoes as a suburban American child is on a bicycle. Two native islanders, Brian and Lowell, completed the ship's complement. I remember cheerful betel-nut-stained smiles and their capacity for tearing a coconut apart with their blood-red teeth. We were happily assimilated into the family and easily adjusted to the close quarters. Eight people on a 54-foot sloop is pretty snug; but Gar and I remember that cruise as one of the happiest of our adventures.

Bryan and the legendary Australian diver, Wally Gibbons, had salvaged tons of brass from the Russell Island dump. By his admission, they had hardly put a dent in the great mass. The dump started at 90 feet on a sand slope that dropped at a 35-degree angle into the depths. The ammunition, still in its boxes, had been disposed of in deeper water. The boxes disintegrated, leaving mounds of shells scattered about the bottom and continuing down the slope beyond sight.

There is a special intensity to the excitement and the suspense that attends diving on a wreck when the wreck is so deep that it is out-of-sight from the surface. Any diver will tell you that. You know it is there, but the first sight of it, the vague shape emerging out of the gloom as you reach hand-over-hand down the anchor line, awakens all your senses and is deliciously exciting. The first sight of those mounds of 50 caliber and 90mm shells had a particular fascination. Each one, especially in the case of the 90mm shells, comprised a rare and beautiful artifact; and there were hundreds of thousands of them. I experienced the euphoria of a kid loose in a candy factory. That the artifacts were live and deadly hardly impressed itself on me. Each 90mm shell was a magnificent three-foot cylinder of brass. I ranged further down the slope, the piles of ammunition even more concentrated as I went deeper, and finally fetched up at 170 feet by an urgent flashing warning on my Edge decompression computer: ASCEND IMMEDIATELY. And I did, gathering Gar and Rocky with me as I ascended. We found Bryan at the ten-foot decompression stop, shaking his head and rolling his eyeballs at us. He still used the standard Navy decompression tables. We relied on the recently developed decompression meters, especially The Edge, which at the time was the most reliable. Bryan would have none of it. He was still on the line when we surfaced. Our meters were more user-friendly and, as it turned out, served us well.

On a second dive – with plenty of surface interval credit time – I filmed Bryan using an airlift bag to raise one of the 90mm shells and then shot him coming out of the water and onto the shore with the live shell in his arms. The beach was virtually covered with 90mm projectiles, detritus from the disarming of thousands of shells by Bryan and Wally Gibbons during their years of salvage. I wanted to do a sequence of Bryan going through the disarming process, so I set my Eclair 16mm camera on the tripod and started shooting. In the film that came out of that trip, "The War Reefs," this sequence evoked the greatest audience response. First Bryan dropped the shell on a piece of coral rubble (the audience gasped and so did Gar and I). The projectile detached itself from the brass shell case. Bryan picked up the steel head and tossed it into the sea, at the same time declaring, "There! Now it's safe." He further explained that it was an explosive head and so safer in the water. Gar and I wondered at this point if we should ditch the camera and just run like hell. Bryan topped up the shell case and poured out the black cordite, which was still dry. That, he explained, meant that the shell was still very much alive.

"Now, this stuff is very volatile," he explained. This was not entirely news to us and not at all reassuring.

Bryan took a handful of the cordite and ran a thin trail of it about five yards away from the pile.

"I'm going to set this off," he said. "You may want to move your camera away a little farther." We hardly needed the prompting. He then touched a match to the end of the trail. The fire raced along it with alarming speed and the pile erupted in a sheet of flame (this always had a gratifying effect on the audience). Bryan had not yet finished his remarkable performance. He put his foot on the shell case, suggesting again that we move farther away from it, and struck the primer with a hammer and center punch. The shell emitted a great spurt of flame and the report sounded like a French 75.

"There," he said. "Now it is entirely safe" (relieved laughter from the audience).

I lusted after the shell to take home as a souvenir for the Punch Bowl. Getting it out of the Solomons was not simple. Some while earlier an outgoing baggage inspection at the airport had turned up a live 30-caliber round in the dive bag of a departing tourist diver. The round was confiscated, the diver fined and narrowly missed going to jail. Since then it was forbidden to take any artifacts out of the islands. All bags were to be rigidly inspected before being loaded on the departing planes. How to get through the rigorous inspection with a large brass shell was a challenge I did not relish. In fact, the only baggage it would fit into was my dive bag and it stretched along its entire length. At the airport I watched the guard unzip my bag and fumble about the dive equipment. Fortunately every one in that equatorial climate and non-air conditioned airport was sweating as much as I was. The bag was zipped up and passed along. The purloined shell stood handsome sentinel at the hall entrance to the living room for many years.

Except for those ships that beached themselves before they sank, the wrecks in the Solomon Islands are deep. Those that are accessible to scuba divers often start at 140 feet or more with the rest of their hulls extending down along the steep slope, well beyond safe diving limits. The temptation to explore deeper was always there and always dangerous.

There was something else in the hall that Susy would have been delighted to make firewood of. I was delighted with it and went to considerable trouble to acquire it. Its genesis was in the small museum in Honiara. Honiara, incidentally, is the only town of any size in the islands. It is on Guadalcanal, as is the airport. At the end of World War II it was a motley collection of Quonset huts. Now, a half century later, it is a town of about 20,000. In the museum were several very antique examples of shark worship which was once much practiced in the islands. One that fascinated and delighted me was a three- and a half-foot long carving of a shark with a little man riding on his back. Like a jockey he was bent forward over the shark's neck. On his head was a derby and hanging out from between his legs toward the sharks tail was a considerable part of his penis. I was so taken with it that I asked the Belmares to arrange an interview with the island's finest wood carver at my hotel. For $300 (a princely sum for him) I commissioned him to duplicate the carving with wood as dark as the antique one in the museum. Rick undertook the finances and agreed to bring it with him when he and Jane attended the annual Diving Equipment & Manufacturer Association (D.E.M.A.) conference in Las Vegas some months later. They did just that – an act above and beyond the call of friendship in my books. I took possession and was only partially pleased. The carver had accentuated the schlong and left out the derby. While I had to agree that the rider's one-eyed snake was more important to his anatomy than the hat, it was the derby that really gave the carving the raffish look I found so appealing. All was made right when Gar, my youngest son and a professional wood and marble carver, fashioned a proper black derby for the jockey. I tried for years, without success, to impress Susy with the appeal of this artwork as a centerpiece on the dining room table.

XIV

CLUNIES-ROSS

Now the view passes the French doors on the left side of the fireplace to the table in the corner. In a glass case was the model of a jukong. The memory evoked by that model takes me back to an atoll in the Indian Ocean, a man who would be king and an expedition by the Philadelphia Academy of Natural Sciences. The atoll is named Cocos Keeling. It lies 1,200 miles west of Perth, Australia, alone and far out in the Indian Ocean.

Late in the 19th century the atoll, which was an uninhabited British territory, was given by Queen Victoria to a Scottish sea captain named Clunies-Ross. He successfully colonized it with a community of Malaysian workers, developed a copra plantation on three of the islands that ringed the lagoon and built his own home and the workers' village on a fourth island, which he called Home Island.

By the time I reached Cocos Keeling in 1974 with my expedition group, a fourth generation Clunies-Ross, a great grandson, was the king of Cocos Keeling. The original Scotsman had a sense of noblesse oblige along with a Protestant work ethic. He looked after his workers and their families, provided a healthy, contented social environment and was, in fact, a benevolent dictator. He isolated his happy kingdom from disruptive influences in this way: there were two boats a year from Singapore that brought needed supplies and materials to the atoll. Any of the workers and their families who wanted to leave the island might do so when the boats returned to the mainland. However – and this was the big control factor – they were not allowed to return to Cocos Keeling. Once out of Paradise, there was no way back. In that way over the years labor agitators, drugs, and many of the ills that plague urban society today were kept out. Few chose to leave. They had a good life on Cocos Keeling, a wise and fair master, and no illusions about the outside world. All successive Clunies-Rosses had successfully retained that pattern of isolation.

In 1955 the atoll was ceded by Britain to Australia. However, the property was owned by the Clunies-Ross family. It was virtually autonomous.

At the start of World War II the Australian government pressed Clunies-Ross to sell one of the islands to them. It was to be used by Qantas as a fueling stop on westward flights over the Indian Ocean and also as an advance weather station. This was West Island. When we arrived on the bi-monthly flight from Perth to Cocos Keeling, we found a colony of approximately 280 souls, well established with a small field hospital, a communications and weather station complex, a six-hole golf course that paralleled the landing strip and had packed sand greens, and three drinking clubs. The Australian government personnel had two-year tours of duty there. If you were abstemious when you arrived you were very apt to be alcoholic when you departed.

We were billeted in guest quarters on West Island and messed with the personnel in their main dining room. We quickly learned that there was no social intercourse between West Island and Home Island. In fact, no one was allowed to visit Home Island without express permission from Clunies-Ross. The doctor visited the island daily to attend his clinic there and a teacher commuted to run the small school. Otherwise, the isolation was still very much intact, even though you could pop over to Home Island from West Island in 15 minutes by fast outboard.

The purpose of our expedition was to sample the marine life of the atoll. Two prominent ichthyologists, William Smith-Vaniz and Patrick Colin, directed the collecting. The backers of the expedition along with their wives, a retired Air Force general, who at 81 had more pizzazz than the rest of us together, and I made up our group. I was the expedition cameraman.

We rented a wretched cement hull boat that we named *Concreetee*. We took picnic lunches with us and stayed out all day collecting either in the lagoon or outside where the coral shelved off into deep water. Rotenone poison was released in a small area and the fish collected in nets as they drifted out from their hiding places in the coral or under the sand. We also used dynamite two or three times. I expect that today both ichthyologists would blush to admit it. The damage from dynamite was not extensive, being confined to a limited area. But within that area practically the entire marine ecosystem was destroyed. In two weeks of collecting, 12 new species of tropical reef fish were found. Evaluation of the collection at the Academy would continue for almost half a year.

The jukongs were the open sailing dinghies used by the natives on Home Island to commute round trip each day to the copra groves on the uninhabited small islands that ringed the lagoon. Each family built its own jukong. Depending on the care, time, materials and skill they put into the building, these lovely little craft were either the Ford or the Cadillac in the garage. They were 12-feet long with lapstrake hulls, tapered fore and aft. Each carried a single sprit sail and was steered with an outboard rudder yoked to lanyards. All affected wonderfully bright colors for their sails. The finest ones had brass fittings with natural-grain varnished wood – the kind of finish that is only kept up with much love and elbow grease. Each morning about seven a.m. the flotilla set sail across the lagoon; the early morning sun catching their sail colors with all the joy of bright facets from a crystal. They raced one another. Their laughter and shouts carried across the lagoon by the brisk trade wind that took them over on one tack in the morning and, holding steady, returned them on the other tack at the end of the day. It was a joyous sight and it never failed to make me pause and take in the scene on my way to *Concreetee* for our own work.

The jukongs were just about the prettiest small sailing craft I have ever seen and later I had the good fortune to acquire a splendidly crafted model for the Punch Bowl. In time the opportunity came – I received an invitation to visit Home Island. Dr. Virginia Orr-Maes, a malacologist (a specialist dealing with mollusks) at the Philadelphia Academy of Natural Sciences, had researched some years back at Cocos Keeling. As an eminent scientist she was graciously received by the Clunies-Rosses. She was kind enough to write a letter of introduction for me. The first day of our arrival I learned that a schoolteacher, employed by the Clunies-Ross, crossed the lagoon each weekday morning to teach at the small school there. He, too, however, was forced to return each evening to West Island. I entrusted the letter to him to deliver to the great man, but the more I heard from our fellow residents on West Island about the aloof Clunies-Ross family and the curtain of isolation they enforced between West Island and Home Island, the more dismal I considered my chances of being invited over.

At the end of our first week there, royalty smiled upon this lowly visitor. A message was delivered to me; my companions were envious. I pretended modesty while soaking in the warmth of this special attention. The message read: "You are invited for an overnight visit with the Clunies-Ross family. A launch will pick you up at the utility pier tomorrow morning at eight a.m. Dinner dress is informal." The last sentence was a great relief to me. I had not packed my black tie along with my dive gear.

The next morning, having indulged in cruel jibes at my expedition fellows as they went off in the cumbersome *Concreetee*, I awaited the express to Home Island with as much pleasure and sense of adventure as I had enjoyed in a long while. The swift launch was not an admiral's barge. It was an outboard motor skiff. A cheerful young man, who turned out to be the manager of the Clunies-Ross estate, had come to fetch me. He introduced himself as John McKay and, as we made the short 20-minute run across the lagoon, he set forth the day's activities. I would be staying with him and his wife at their cottage, but joining the Clunies-Ross family for dinner that evening.

We drove directly to Oceana House, the Clunies-Ross home, a white, clapboard two-story Victorian with verandas on two sides, both facing the lagoon. A screened porch, heavily shaded by a dark-green, big-leafed ivy also faced the lagoon. It promised cool comfort. The house had been built early in the last century by the grandfather of the present Clunies-Ross. It was beautifully maintained as were the gardens that surrounded it. These latter, I noticed, were being tended by teenage Malaysian girls. They giggled and waved as we drove by.

As we pulled up to the front door the king of Cocos Keeling himself, John Clunies-Ross, stepped out of the house and awaited my own descent from the Jeep. He extended his hand and welcomed me to the island with a gracious but diffident greeting. To my eye Clunies-Ross was the reincarnation of Rudolph Valentino. From the black hair, brushed straight back, to the olive skin, theatrically handsome features and slender body, the great Latin Lover of silent films lived again. He wore dark canvas slacks, sandals, a white shirt open at the throat and with sleeves rolled up. A large knife, perhaps half the length of a machete, hung in a tooled scabbard from his belt. His straight, graceful carriage was borne with informality yet everything about him was regal. He advised me that I was expected at dinner, cocktails at seven, and that the manager would take me on a tour of the island after lunch.

We might have toured in the Jeep, but instead we walked along the trim, navigable streets and alleys of the tidy, appealing village of 411 Malaysians. The single-family thatched-roof houses with cooking areas in the rear were generously spaced and well kept. There was no litter, half-starved dogs, children with bloated bellies, or other evidence of poverty.

The manager was greeted from the doorways and yards with amiable deference. It was evident that he was liked and respected. I was eyed with a curiosity devoid of any hostility. Visitors here were infrequent, to say the least. Other than old men and small boys I had seen no males. I commented on this to my new friend. He replied matter-of-factly that this was a workday in the week and the men were at work.

Around a bend in the lagoon shore a group of large sheds, one housing the island's diesel generator, heralded the working part of the island. In one I was shown through a tool room that would have drawn the envy of a German engineer. All the requisite machinery for carpentry work was here: table saws, planers and routers. And all the hand tools were mounted on the walls over red-painted outlines. Another room contained a machine shop with drill presses, lathes and milling machines as well as a fully equipped electrician's work area. Adjoining the shed was the boat shop. This was where the jukongs were built. I learned that the workmen could buy the lumber, fittings, sailcloth and other necessary materials with their wages and would have use of the communal tools to construct their personal boats.

At the end of this line of buildings was a large thatched frame structure with an open veranda that bordered the entire length on one side. This was shaded by two ancient banyan trees that provided a wonderfully cool environment for about 15 young women. They were seated on cushions and working on a variety of woven articles: mats, baskets, hampers and generally useful household objects. They chattered and laughed and made eyes at John and me. Several were knockouts, with full figures and long, thick, shiny black hair. None were shy. They bantered with John, who spoke Malaysian fluently, and were obviously having a ribald series of exchanges.

If all this sounds idyllic, the dream republic, I found it so. The first Clunies-Ross had, in fact, established what can only be called a benevolent dictatorship. From the very beginning, when he took possession of the atoll and established a colony of Malaysian families to develop and work the copra resources, he inculcated into the native force what may be called a Protestant work ethic. Weekdays were workdays; weekends were free. A decent quality of life was uniformly established with a minimal housing standard. Newly married couples were subsidized in the building of a house. Patterns of hygiene and order in the village were enforced until they, in turn, became a natural way of daily life for successive generations. A clinic was established and also a school. Education was provided for girls up to the age of 12 and for boys to the age of 14. For the girls the focus was on domestic skills. The boys learned trades. The brighter ones were given advanced training in the skills needed to run the machinery. In other words, aside from literacy and basic arithmetic, the schooling was practical. Education at a higher level was not considered realistic. I suppose that some undeveloped genius might never have achieved his or her potential; I must also admit that I thought the policy very practical.

I attended dinner at Oceana House that evening. Mrs. Clunies-Ross proved to be an ample-bosomed, homey matron with a warm smile, as comfortable as a "Mum" in a Brighton cottage. I was made at home and spent the evening pleasantly enough chatting with her. The Great Man was reserved, taciturn and not given to initiating conversation. Two children in their teens were at school in England, I learned. I also learned how Mrs. Clunies-Ross, whose first name was Hermione, came to the island. The manager told me the story; and it was right out of a Victorian romance.

The father of the present Clunies-Ross had married a beautiful Malaysian girl from the village; thus the handsome dark looks of my host who had grown to manhood without getting married. Now a curious and whimsical tradition had become part of the passing of the P&O passenger liner by Cocos Keeling several times a year in her passage from Bombay to Perth. A lonely Australian telegrapher, stationed by the government on Home Island, but isolated from the community there, always made wireless contact with the ship. On Christmas day some years past, the ship's captain had invited the lonely operator to meet the boat offshore where it would heave to and toss over a barrel with books, food and Christmas cheer. As the passengers crowded to the rail the barrel was dropped and picked up by the telegrapher in a bobbing jukong. The passengers cheered and shouted Christmas greetings. The isolated telegrapher felt less lonely and no doubt made good use of the spirits that had been included in the barrel.

The P&O Line was so pleased with the entertainment afforded by the dropping of the barrel that it became a tradition. On or near any major Christian holiday, the barrel was dropped. And so it fell out that when the present Clunies-Ross was 22 years old and still a bachelor, the telegrapher (now a radio operator) was indisposed. The prince volunteered to sail out for the barrel himself, he being a fine sailor and expert jukong-handler. The great ocean liner usually hove to about three miles offshore, an easy-weather sail for a jukong. But the weather worsened before Clunies-Ross reached the ship. As the passengers watched in alarm and before the barrel could be dropped, a line squall capsized the jukong. It foundered with its royal occupant. A lifeboat was immediately launched, Clunies-Ross was taken aboard and then, because the liner was on a scheduled run, there was no time to return him to the island. He became a mid-ocean entry on the passenger list and the guest of the P&O Line for the remainder of the voyage to Perth, 1200 miles on eastward.

Needless to say, his dramatic arrival and his identity caused quite a stir among the passengers, which included a young schoolteacher emigrating from England to Australia. Her name was Hermione and she had a well-turned ankle (as the expression went in those days). She caught the young prince's eye and romance blossomed. When he finally returned to his island kingdom his new princess Hermione accompanied him.

To me this is one of the most delightful stories I have encountered, made all the more poignant for having spent the evening with that lovely, serene lady.

XV

NEEDLE IN A HAYSTACK

Nestled on the floor in the curve of the stairs was a cannon, a handsome iron piece from the late 18th century. And there's another story. Gar had made a beautiful carriage for it. Covered and preserved with paraffin, its dull black body was one of the dominant artifacts in the big hall. I must admit that it is not easy for a cannon to "nestle"; but it suited that alcove perfectly and its bold size was right for the big hall.

In 1977 I joined Teddy Tucker and Peter Benchley for a wreck-hunting expedition to the Turks & Caicos Islands. Peter and Teddy were good friends of long standing. With the success of *Jaws*, Peter had moved from a modest house in Flemington, New Jersey to a large, attractive house in Princeton. Our houses were within easy walking. Our friendship led to 11 ABC *American Sportsman* shows that we did together and some productions for ESPN. When the Discovery Channel decided to produce a two-hour special on my family and me, Peter narrated the production. Our friendship survived my move with the family to Lawrenceville, ten minutes down the road.

Teddy Tucker was also an old friend. He was – and still is – Bermuda's most successful salvor. He has few rivals for his knowledge of maritime history. The gold and emerald bishop's cross that he recovered from an early 18th century ship is one of the most valuable antique artifacts ever recovered from the sea. He was forced to sell it to the island government since, by law, treasure recovered from the sea in the territorial waters of the island could not be sold outside of the island. The government placed the cross with other artifacts in a poorly arranged museum that was part of the pitiful aquarium. Teddy was asked to take the cross from its case and clean it in preparation for a visit by the Queen; in doing so he discovered that it had been replaced by a cunningly crafted plastic model. The scandal and the mystery is still the substance of island gossip today. The real cross was never recovered.

Teddy had a fine 40-foot workboat, equipped with an air lift system, scuba tanks and everything needed for light salvage work. And most vital to the success of the expedition was an advanced model magnetometer, an electronic device that detects metal anomalies on and under the sea bottom. The magnetometer is towed behind the boat while the operator watches a console of instruments in the cabin and sings out when there is a hit. The technician and veteran wreck diver who would operate it was Denny Breeze, one of the finest in the business and also an old friend. Denny had been divemaster, director of all diving activity and support systems in the film production of Peter's story, *The Deep*. The problem posed by this splendid tool was somewhat unique to the Turks & Caicos. There were so many wrecks and the device was so sensitive that we had a hit almost every five minutes as we towed along the northwestern shore of Providenciales (Provo for short), the largest of the Turks & Caicos Island group. That northwestern shore borders the southeastern side of the Caicos Passage, a thoroughfare for ships' traffic for three centuries. The treasure galleons, having loaded in Cuba, often headed back for Spain through the Caicos Passage. Northwesters would force them onto a lee shore, and the lee shore was the shallow coral shelf that extended out from the island.

We spent almost a week towing the magnetometer along the edge of the dropoff that marked the deep ocean. At first, when there was a hit that registered on the instruments, a buoy and weight would be thrown over to mark the spot. Teddy would locate any wreckage that was visible and, if possible, determine from it the period of the wreck. A single pottery shard, an anchor fluke, some elements of ballast, almost anything visible from the wreck was enough for Teddy to postulate period and nationality. The wreckage was prolific, everything from late 19th century paddle wheelers to privateers from two centuries past and merchant ships that spanned three centuries. On some wrecks that seemed promising we paused and dug for a half-day or more before moving on. It wasn't until the second week that we hit a wreck that Teddy deemed worth spending time on.

It turned out to be the wreck of a late 18th century privateer. A disparate assortment of cannons in a disorderly mound was visible above the sand. We soon discovered that the cannons were not loose. They were imbedded in a concrete mass of coralline lime that had settled around them and around most of the wreckage. Loosening the cannons required sledge and crowbar application; this was accompanied by heavy breathing and the expenditure of massive amounts of calories. It was hard work, but fortunately in only 25 feet of water.

As the cannons were worked loose and raised an increasing variety of debris was revealed, mostly weapons and projectiles, all still imbedded in the coralline mass. There were four different kinds of bar shot as well as grape shot in cemented masses and cannonballs. The handsomely carved hilt of a dress sword broke loose, encrusting coral clinging to it. Only the outline of the steel blade remained, as the coral split away from it like the shell of a mold. A residue of rusty pigment remained from the actual blade. Similar molds broken apart revealed cutlasses and pistols, a wide variety of weapons typically found on privateers. These predators of the sea armed themselves with the best from the ships they plundered and sank.

The cannons we raised varied in size. The choice ones that we decided to take back with us were small guns once positioned on wishbone swivels, which were typically mounted on the rails of the ships. They were, of course, most easily handled. Two persons could lift one of these small cannons. One of them made the long journey from the Caribbean to my front hall with a one year stopover at the Philadelphia Maritime Museum for preservation.

Perhaps the most valuable artifact raised from the wreck was a physician's clyster with a set of attachments. Medicine in the 18th century was a rather hit or miss science. A ship's surgeon's tools probably consisted of little more than a lancet, a set of knives, a saw, cups for cupping and a clyster. This last item was a large syringe with attachments for introduction into any orifice in the human body. Among its uses, oil could be shot up the rectum for constipation, vaginal flushing could be done, and ears could be washed out.

There was no bullion in the wreck and it's likely that there were no survivors. If any managed to reach shore over the storm-lashed shallows studded with reefs, the mosquitoes would have drained their blood as surely as Dracula.

And speaking of mosquitoes, we ran the gauntlet each day from our screened-in quarters to and from the boat. There were golf carts to make the quarter mile trip. We would run for the carts, fire them up and try to outrun the mosquitoes, great angry clouds of which followed the carts. I recall the battery failing on one I was on with Peter. We abandoned the cart and ran like hell for the house, breaking all Olympic records.

The cook on Teddy's boat was a derelict redneck Bermudian named Billy Penniston. Teddy collected derelicts, down-on-their-luck fishermen and boatmen no one else would hire. Teddy would pick one up, give him a job on the boat and win his undying loyalty. Billy was not only a stubborn redneck. He was also the most bigoted, ignorant, surly boatman any of us had ever met. He was hardly prime company, but he loved Teddy and did his job. One of his jobs was cooking on the Turks & Caicos trip. And one of his favorite, regular dishes was pig snout. If you dared ask him what was for lunch he would bark "SNOUT."

For all of his bum-like demeanor and appearance, Billy was very proud of his way around a boat and knew how to handle himself at sea. One day he tossed a bucket into the water through an opening in the transom while the boat was under way. The bucket had a line on the handle so it could be retrieved, a common way of scooping up seawater with a bucket. There is always a jerk when the bucket catches the water. This time it jerked Billy out through the open transom. He disappeared in the wake, his straw hat marking the place of his submersion. The alarm was sounded. Teddy circled to pick him up and he was hauled aboard, still clinging to the bucket. There were no thanks. There was outrage, sheer violent outrage on his face. He certainly believed that we had somehow been responsible for this ridiculous performance. He spoke to no one and disappeared below. For several days the snout as well as all the other messes were so hot with pepper as to be even more inedible than usual.

During the two weeks that we worked on the wreck we raised a formidable collection of guns, weapons and artifacts that were enough to start a creditable museum on the island. In our agreement with the new Turks & Caicos government (their independence from Britain was less than a year old) we had agreed to leave with them the largest part of the recovered materials, taking with us only a representative sample of what was recovered from the wreck. The materials we left were arranged in a display on the dock. While we were there no representative of the government showed up to see what we had found. We later learned that the collection on the dock remained there, disintegrating in the sun, until it was accorded the status of junk and pushed off the dock back into the sea from which it came.

We flew home in a World War II B-25 bomber, and with us were five of the small cannon, one of the clysters, the dress sword hilt and several of the expanding bar shots. A flight of the famed bombers, led by Jimmy Doolittle, took off from a carrier and successfully bombed Tokyo. A 1944 movie, *Thirty Seconds over Tokyo* documented the heroic action. The preserved and fully operational relic in which we returned home was owned by Richard duPont. If I may reach for a little serendipity in the connection: our cannon were being carried north by the descendent of a family whose fortune was made in the production of gunpowder for General Washington's Army in the Revolutionary War.

Without extensive preservation treatment the cannon would have literally disintegrated before our eyes. Like Robert Frost's "Slow smokeless burning of decay," oxidation will accelerate immediately when any iron object that has been in the sea returns to the air. The process is almost as fast as the growth of bamboo and kelp, which may be measured day to day. At the Philadelphia Maritime Museum our cannon were immediately submerged for a year in freshwater to leech out the salt. They then spent another year in a solution of sodium hydroxide and what Teddy called "mossy zinc." This bath removed all remaining moisture from the iron mass and arrested the oxidation. For the two that Peter and I kept, the finishing touch was applied in his Princeton basement. Melted paraffin was brushed over every exposed surface and quickly hardened to provide an airtight envelope.

The cannon alone survived the fire that destroyed the Punch Bowl in 1994. There are so many other inside parts of the house that await finishing by ourselves that the cannon is still well down the list. For lack of money we are doing our own work. Both boys are remarkably fine carpenters. Last summer Gordy and one of Susy-dell's boys laid the hardwood floors for the entire downstairs. Gar and a carpenter friend finished the stairs and railing using the oak salvaged from our own trees. Ah, progress.

XVI

SEA ROVERS

The memories are golden but also green. I will continue with the living room, as I close my eyes and let them range around the space, pausing every few seconds at an object with a rich store of memories behind it. The survey might start with my desk in the corner with its angled view of the great fireplace and the French doors on either side of it. The desk chair swiveled and was shaped like a giant hand. The palm was the seat and the fingers were the back. They were fashioned of leather. Two of the fingers, the ones flanking the index finger, could be bent down, thus effecting the rude "up yours" sign. The chair was designed by that prince of all diving humorists, Dick Anderson, and presented to me at one of the Boston Sea Rovers film festivals at Hancock Hall in Boston.

The Sea Rovers were my chosen dive club. I still attend their annual "Clinic" each year if I possibly can. They are no ordinary dive club. Their membership included many prominent divers and marine scientists. To name a few: Dr. Eugenie Clark, Dr. Harold Edgerton, Dr. Robert Ballard, Dr. Melville Bell Grosvenor, Dr. Joseph MacInnis, Peter Gimbel and many others. I have never been more honored than I was to be counted in this company. Their riotous parties that followed the film festivals reached legendary proportions and approached the recklessness of Shriners conventions. One such party was held on a barge in Boston Harbor. Dr. Grosvenor, publisher of the *National Geographic* magazine and the grandson of Alexander Graham Bell, was the honored guest along with his wife. They were isolated in a small anteroom and protected from the bacchanalian orgy that was reaching ten on the Richter scale in the main room with the open bar. They held court in the small room, meeting and chatting with the sober club members who stopped by to pay their respects.

Now it happened that the distinguished pair sat on a sofa with their backs to a window. I had not yet abandoned myself to the orgy and so was at the time it happened visiting with them. As we chatted I was stunned – horrified – to see two of the most prominent and incorrigible Sea Rovers appear at the window behind the Grosvenors, drop their pants and press a moon on the window. The distance from the elderly couple's heads to the two bare butts was no more than six inches. Those of us facing the unspeakable irreverence struggled to mask our panic and give the honored guests no intimation of what was going on behind them. In the next room the party had reached that orgy level at which beakers of vodka were being poured on the heads of unwary victims. In fact, it was a bit of inebriate horseplay that gave rise to the annual tradition of dunking that year's recipient of the "Diver of the Year" award headfirst into a bowl filled with vodka and orange juice. The tradition survives to this day. The bowl is always a beautiful silver bowl in a pattern originally designed by Paul Revere and so known as a Revere bowl. Mine, presented in 1987, sits on the top shelf of my office in Lawrenceville. It was well worth the dunking; however, it was the Anderson finger chair that reminded me of the Sea Rovers.

XVII

THE PUNCH BOWL REMEMBERED

We have made a compass of the living room, recalling only those special artifacts that related to my expeditions and experiences. The furnishings and *objets d'arts* were acquired over a period of years by Susy and me, mostly by Susy. Without having been raised in a house of such grand dimension, she nonetheless had intuitive good taste and a sense of dimension and style for that wonderful old house.

My brother and his wife Ali took much of the practical furniture from the Punch Bowl and much of the beautiful furnishings that were in storage from the old Montclair house. I had returned to college and had no responsibilities or real home at the time; so when we split the chattels my instinct, as we divvied up the loot, was to trade for the esoteric things and heavy furniture that had actually been created for the house. Thus, the tiger skins that dominated the front hall and the bearskins on either side of the living room and the heavy, dark-stained, "antiqued" Grand Rapids oak dining room set were my lot.

My stepmother, Herta, who had risen from second maid in the household to my governess, then housekeeper then second and last wife to my father, had taken what she wanted from the Punch Bowl after my father's death in 1943 and furnished her own home in North Carolina. She well deserved whatever she took with her. She had given my father a 14-carat loyalty, managed his home exactly as he wanted it run and saw him through with unflagging care and singleness of devotion to the time of his death. She was a good woman and the nearest thing I had to a parent when I was mustered out of the Navy.

All this background is pertinent. It explains why it was really up to Susy to furnish the nest. The sort of big sofas that could seat five people abreast and elegant, real antique side furniture that complimented the spacious grandeur of the house was well beyond our means. If anything good could have come out of the great fire that devastated Bar Harbor in 1947 it took the form of elegant furnishings for us. After the war and after the fire the big houses went up for sale and their furnishings were auctioned off. Susy attended many of these sales. Few homemakers wanted the big stuff. The desperate auctioneers knocked down great tables and sofas and charming bedroom furniture to the little blonde lady with the determined blue eyes for a song. The Punch Bowl came alive. It began to recover the air of graciousness.

Two enormous sofas flanked the great fireplace in the living room. One of them, bought up at auction, had eiderdown upholstery so that when you sat into it you were virtually enveloped. The children and then their children used to leap upon it with great glee, almost disappearing in its softness and the dozen or more cushions at its ends. Always draped along the top of its back was a huge, stuffed cloth carrot that young Susy had made. Between the two sofas and filling the space in front of the fireplace was a handsome, low round table of polished dark wood, five feet in diameter. It was always piled with books, the sumptuous coffee table type, by the finest boat photographers in the world: Rosenfeld and Beakin. A magnificent leather-bound portfolio of drawings of the great Americas Cup defenders and challengers was a gift from our son Gordy. He had filmed the Australian defense in Perth for CBS and returned with that collector's prize as a gift for the Punch Bowl. That had been on the table along with many wonderful old books on maritime history and Maine islands.

There was more. My memory will not release them from my early morning waking dreams. It is then that so many of the small parts, the stuff of the collector, the fabric of an interesting, well-aged and well-used home scroll across my inner eye.

The living room opened onto the screened-in porch through French doors on either side of the fireplace. The outside of the chimney was centered on the house wall of the porch and supported on either side by great wooden caryatids with bare bosoms as opulent as Dolly Parton's. Susy had rescued them from the wrecking crew when one of the grand old buildings in the center of Princeton was torn down to make room for a modern building. That porch was my domain, my serene joy at the end of the day. On golden evenings, when the wind slowed to a soft whisper or died completely, I could hear the occasional sound of laughter and voices all the way across the reach from Little Deer Isle, a quarter mile away. Sitting quietly in my favorite rattan chair at the northwest corner of the porch I could hear the murmur of voices from the kitchen and the sounds of pots and pans as the ladies prepared dinner. That last summer the loons were in great voice. Their demoniacal laughter carried from as far away as Dead Man's Cove, up the shore a half mile. I sipped my vodka. *The New York Times*, which arrived a day late in the mail, nevertheless provided just enough contact with the chaos, chicanery, tragedy and horror of the outside world to put the supreme grace of the scene around me in sharp relief. As will happen when you are sipping a goodly measure of strong drink, I would absent myself from the paper and its stark reality and let my eye feed on the world immediately around me. The western sky would so often start the progression of red hues that might develop into an *Arabian Nights* phantasm from a beginning of light pink against eggshell blue. With such sunsets I would call loudly to the rest of the house to come and see; and we would all sit on the curve of the lawn – two generations of parents with grandchildren and dogs. Even the youngest of the grandchildren would be drawn into the hush of the moment as we bent our eyes to the blood-red tapestry that set off the dark lines of the Camden Hills on the western rim of Penobscot Bay.

Nature is never entirely a free gift. On those still evenings dense populations of mosquitoes were abroad, all hungry and persistent. I could take cover in the bug-free haven of the porch. My daughter's three boys, Durry, Jesse and Lonson chased around the house endlessly, each time attempting to set a new circumnavigation record. They outstripped the mosquitoes. The joy of their shouts and rapid pounding of their feet as they thundered past the porch, just a few feet from where I sat, never seemed to interfere with the enchantment of the evening. It was, in fact, part of it.

The nickname "Boonie" for my daughter started when her irreverent brothers called her "baboon." It later evolved to the affectionate "Boonie." Lonson derived from husband Steve Becker's family. I was in California at the time of Lonson's birth and called his mother at the hospital in Connecticut. When I asked what she had named him I thought she said Manson. That was the name of the cult murderer then serving life in prison. I was horrified. I yelled "Did you say Manson?" With her reassuring laugh she pronounced "Lonson" very carefully.

Steve Becker was the captain of the Middlebury Ski Team, one of the finest in the country. Boonie was a sophomore in the same New England college when Steve and his best friend, Bill Packer, graduated. They planned to sail around the world in a 46-foot ocean-racing sloop and wanted Boonie to join them. She was taking a year off from college and waiting on tables in Hanover, New Hampshire. Steve located her there, put the proposition to her, and – being a Waterman – she jumped at the chance for the great adventure. In the course of two years of sailing off and on, returning for the big holidays and rejoining the boat where they had left it, the sea-worn and now very salty sailors got no farther than Tahiti. There they were so hospitably received by the party-loving Tahitians that they lingered for months. Bill Packer's father finally cabled, "Am sending professional crew to bring boat home. Return immediately and go to work."

Steve and Boonie had paired up while Steve attended Harvard Business School, Boonie waited tables in Boston and silversmithed. After graduation Beck (as we called him) took a job in Chicago and helped to put Boonie through the prestigious Art Institute of Chicago. They finally married, moved back east and ultimately raised their three boys in Westport, Connecticut.

The boys were all dedicated to sports and bodybuilding like their father, starting to pump iron in their early teens. All three became captains of the high school football teams and superb athletes. Durry, the oldest, joined the Marine Corps for the experience before returning to college and was by hard circumstance sucked into the war in Iraq in 2004. He was, of course, a natural for advanced training with the Marine's elite RECON Division and was sent into the thick of battle at Fallujah.

Let me return to Maine and again pull back those happy memories. Another sound that blended into the harmony of those evenings was the medley of boat engines idling and revving up, the occasional laughter and voices of the lobstermen as they pulled their traps, and the clear splash of the trap as it went over the side. I looked down upon this scene from the house and its west porch, perched on elevated ground which fell away steeply through 50 yards over bayberry and tall grass with a scattering of spruce, then plunged over the granite collar to the weed-wigged rocks and finally to the sea.

In the quiet of the evenings, when the Becker boys were not stampeding around the house and when it was well into July, I would become aware of a muted chattering, something like a dimly overheard argument between a company of fairies, only with intonations of satisfaction. I knew what it was and never failed to crane my neck to look down into the water's edge. There a male and female eider duck, followed by their miniature brood, could be seen doing a progress over the seaweed beds. They would disappear under water, diving for crabs and shrimp, the mom and pop no doubt teaching their young survival techniques.

If there is a Heaven – which I doubt – and if I go to it – which is not likely – I hope it may be an eternity of evenings in summertime on that west porch. And if required, I would even be happy to substitute ambrosia for vodka.

The living room opened into the entry hall through an arch, over which hung the Amazonian blowgun. This was perhaps the most beautiful part of the house. As you entered through the double doors from the south porch, you faced the graceful curve of the double stairs, dark mahogany railings bordering the polished hardwood treads. And at the landing, from which the stairs diverged right and left, was a handsome stained glass window. The leaded panes in rich reds, greens, purples and yellows depicted a jolly gnome ladling wine from a punch bowl into a goblet. The wine was royal purple. The nose of the imbiber had just a tinge of salubrious red. Both the goblet and the punch bowl were transparent so that the wonderful purple stood out. Under this scene was the legend, "Ye Ol' Punch Bowl." In the center of the hall were two splendidly shocking Bengal tiger skins. No one ever expected to find tiger skins in a Maine coast summer home. We loved them and used them long after they had become somewhat tatty from the depredations of grandchildren and dogs. One tooth was missing in the head of the smaller female. At various places the felt base under the skin had detached and was lovingly pushed back together every time I passed through the hall, only to be put all askew by the children as they charged from the kitchen area to the south porch. When visitors asked me how we had come by these skins I was fond of telling them that my father had bagged them at the corner of 45th Street and Madison Avenue in New York, at Abercrombie & Fitch.

XVIII

BITS AND PIECES

Letting my mind's eye swing clockwise around the hall, I can recall with pleasure almost always noticing as I walked by the framed glass box of mounted spiders – horrible great things – the largest being a tarantula that was fixed into the middle of the display. I purchased it in a hotel gift shop in Saudi Arabia, when I was doing a pair of dive shows in the city of Jedda. Another similar glass box with bizarre insects had been acquired in Port Moresby, Papua New Guinea and, knowing that my children loved these weird displays, prizing them as home decor, I had given similar displays to them at Christmas times. All these mounted boxes indicated that they came from Kuala Lumpur, Malaysia. Ultimately I found myself in that exotic city with my daughter, Susy, on our way to produce a film for Malaysia Airlines about diving at Sipadan Island. The driver/guide, to whom we had been assigned for a day of touring about the city, was rather taken aback when I requested that we visit the place where these displays were manufactured. This was not at all what he had in mind for a scenic tour for visitors. We did locate the factory on the outskirts of the city. It was just a deep dark hole-in-the-wall, cottage-size industry with chattering women sitting at benches while pinning and mounting the insects. However, outside and at the entrance to the workshop, was a concrete pit about five feet deep with a dirt floor. And on that floor swarmed hundreds of giant scorpions, alive and mean and lashing about at one another. By giant I mean eight-inches long from claw to the venomous tail barb. I can imagine arch villain, Stavros Blofeld, suspending James Bond over that pit with diabolical glee. We were invited to reach into the pit with a pair of tongs and select one of the dreadful animals for closer inspection. I might have known that my daughter would jump at this chance. She did and then pursued us around the pit with the beast lashing about.

A bench seat with storage space inside sat on either side of the center stairs. They were piled so high with glorious cushions that no one ever sat there. It was in the left-hand one that we stored the semi-automatic assault weapons, so loathed by my wife and loved by my two boys. Peter Benchley, the author of *Jaws* and my best friend, had given them to me when New Jersey made them illegal. I should add that Peter is not homicidal nor does he aspire to terrorism. He just loves collecting guns. We lived near each other in Princeton and shared the friendship of one of the great military ballistics experts in America, Jac Weller, who also had an enormous gun collection and was Peter's mentor and conduit for his own collection. One of the weapons was a Valmete, a Swedish gun, which Peter purchased as part of a protection arsenal when we went on an expedition with Teddy Tucker to the Turks & Caicos Islands for wreck hunting. Hijacking of boats by drug runners was epidemic then, making an onboard arsenal and great vigilance requisite in that part of the world. The other two guns were Rugers, all with great banana clips and all more powerful than any peaceful, domestic household should have. The boys fired them once or twice each summer while our dogs hid under the house.

Above each bench and mounted to border the angle of the stairs were a pair of great two-handed broad swords. I commissioned them from an Edinborough swordsmith when Susy and I were in Scotland visiting our friends, Jane and James Stuart. James, incidentally, had been my best friend when we lived in Tahiti. He is the third son of the Earl of Moray and the direct, linear descendent of Mary, Queen of Scots. When we met in Tahiti he headed the small Pan Am office. He was a superb diver, an expert spearfisherman and a warm, self-effacing gentleman. He and his charming wife, Janie, live in Scotland now. Their crofter's cottage is on the fringe of the enormous estate his brother inherited by the law of primogeniture. One day we drove into the country to visit his older brother, Douglas, who was then Lord Dune and had inherited a handsome manor house and property. We were shown to an upstairs drawing room and introduced to Douglas's father-in-law, one Lord Mansfield. This rubicund, porcine and haughty gentleman merely grunted at the introduction to James's friends from the States and looked away as he warmed himself by the fire with the back of his kilt elevated. It happened that the previous evening we had dined with Douglas's wife, Malvina, and this truly lovely lady had told me in conversation that her father had once visited the States and returned with a taste for Jack Daniels sour mash bourbon. It also happened that I had in my baggage in the trunk of the car two bottles of this fine elixir, the black label best. I fetched one of them and approached the aloof old warrior at the fireplace and addressed him thus: "Sir, your daughter, Malvina, has told me that you are partial to Jack Daniels whisky, which is not easily come by here in Scotland. It happens that I have with me for our travels more than I need. I would be pleased if you would accept this with my compliments." Now, as I was making this spiel my target slowly turned to face me. His eye fixed on the package, which – as it happened – was in a black Christmas box with a plastic statue of Jack Daniels himself, in a niche. A smile spread over his face and as he extended his hand he said with great warmth, "What did you say your name was?" Before the day was out we were invited to visit with Lord and Lady Mansfield should we pass through their territory.

Back to the swords. They had great burnished steel blades and leather-bound hilts and were replicas of the terrible weapons wielded by the ancient Scots. The alcove by the benches had other swords mounted at the sides, perhaps the most valuable of which were a pair of regulation U.S. Navy cutlasses, the kind that were issued to boarding parties as late as the Civil War period. They were the real thing, and I am shamed to admit that I smuggled them out of the Naval Air Station at Jacksonville, Florida. I was stationed there during World War II and discovered them in a crate, packed in Cosmoline and stuck far back in an area that stored naval aviation supplies. How they got there is a mystery. How I discovered them and smuggled three of them out of the base will remain a mystery. One I gave to my Uncle George Waterman for his gunroom. The others graced the hall. They were beautifully balanced and real weapons from a time gone by.

Bagpipes are not appreciated by everyone. Some, who find their skirling abrasive, refer to them as the ill wind that blows no good. My own hung on one of the floor to ceiling posts that bordered the beginning of the stairs. I had acquired it through a bagpiping friend on Prince Edward Island where I had spent some time developing blueberry land. There is a large Caledonia society there. I had always associated the pipes with romantic images of Scots clans and recall weeping copiously in the Claridge Theatre in Montclair, New Jersey at the end of a movie about Mary, Queen of Scots. It was in the thirties. Katherine Hepburn played Mary. When she walked to her death on the headsman's block, the camera panned upward to the heavens and the sound track was filled with the skirling of the pipes. Mine were not the only wet eyes in the theatre. We took our movies seriously back then.

The romantic madness had been indulged when Susy and I were in London on our honeymoon. At Scott Adie, known as The Scottish Warehouse, I ordered a kilt made for myself, the tartan being that of Clan Forbes. Susy's ancestors on her mother's side were Forbes, a thin connection, but better than none. I went almost the whole nine yards and also ordered a highland tweed jacket with bone buttons, a fine leather sporran with tassels, a tam with the Forbes pattern ribbons on it, ribboned garters for the knee-length stockings and a silver-mounted dagger, called a *skean dhu* with a fake amethyst in the hilt. This last bit of frumperie is worn in the stocking with the jeweled hilt sticking out, ready for a quick draw should the stag charge or an insult require a strong answer. So it followed that I should learn to play the pipes and acquire a set, myself. Those long winter evenings in Maine during my blueberry farming time were perfect for learning the fingering on a practice chanter. And when the pipes were in hand, the Punch Bowl was the perfect place to practice. The nearest neighbor was a half mile away and the lobstermen, pulling their traps a stone's throw from the house, couldn't have cared less. So I played the pipes to the vast amusement of Susy and the delight of my children. I used to take them with me when I worked with my men on the blueberry land I owned in Penobscot. At noon, as they relaxed over their donuts and whoopee pies, I had an audience that was captive since I was their employer. So I would fire off a round of "All the Blue Bonnets" or "The 79th Farewell to Gibraltar" while they lay back in the herbage and snoozed, happy for my eccentricity, which gave them a little more nooning.

In time, when we moved from Maine to Princeton, I let the pipes go. If you don't keep them in condition with use it is a real grunt to fire them up again. So they fell into disuse and hung decoratively by the stairs.

1. The peninsula that forms the Punch Bowl. The house,
hidden by the trees, was lost in the 1994 fire.

2. The young snark, age 12, 1934.

3. Dartmouth, 1950.

4. Susy and Stan starting out on their honeymoon, 1950.
"Young America."

5. Father, William.

6. Mother, Ethel.

7. Stan sailing with brother Bill (L), 1947.

8. Joyce Stirling and Stan, on his charter boat, the *Zingaro,* in the Bahamas.

9. With the Jordan Klein 35mm housing, filming *Blue Water, White Death,* 1969.

10. With Geoff and Scott Stirling on the *Rotterdam*. Stan was a guest speaker.

11. Shooting with Ron Taylor.

12. The Waterman children riding the sailing canoe on Bora Bora lagoon.

13. Family quarters at Tikehau Atoll, with the Explorers Club flag.

14. Gar down the slide at Fatua Falls.

15. The Robinson girls teaching the kids the *tamure*.

16. Susy with the
Bora Bora mountain
in the background.

17. Stan with all three
children, heading down
the reef.

18. Susy-dell with
butterflyfish.

19. The family's 1965
Christmas card.

*Merry
Christmas*
and a happy new year!

The Stan Waterman Family

20. Filming the hermit who lived at the southern end of Tahiti.

21. Dave Cave with the tail of the estimated 3000 pound marlin.

22. Big news in Tahiti when Stan was bent, July 1966.

23. The *Leida Mara* heading up the Amazon with barges.

24. *Sotalia*, known as The Sacred Dolphin, 1965.

25. *Blue Water, White Death* movie poster.

26. The *Terrier VIII* on her way to sea.

27. Peter Gimbel preparing to dive.

28. Jim Lipscomb shooting Tom Chapin playing the guitar, 1969.

29. First sight of "Mr. Big" at Dangerous Reef.

30. Council of war in Stu Cody's workroom, aboard the *Terrier VIII*.

31. A page
from the
*Blue Water,
White Death*
pressbook.

32. Stan in his
cabin aboard
the *Terrier VIII*.

33 - 35. Montage of the old Punch Bowl house interior.
It all went with the fire in 1994.

36. Maine days picnic-bound on the *Rabecca H.*
(L-R), Susy-dell (Boonie), Fang (the poodle) Gar, Susy, Gordy and Stan.

37. Young Watermans: The core family on the steps
of the old Punch Bowl house. (L-R) Gar, Gordy, Susy, Stan and Susy-dell.

38. Gar (L) as assistant cameraman working with Gordy (R) during the shooting of "The Man Who Loves Sharks".

39. Susy-dell, finishing her giant squid for a show at the Norwalk Maritime Museum, 2004.

40. The Waterman clan, 1996.
(top row L-R) Gordy, his wife Mary Sue, Gar's wife Thea, Gar, Susy-dell, her former husband Steve Becker. (middle row L-R) Susy with Gordy's two boys, Torry and Gar, and Stan. (bottom row L-R) Susy-dell's three boys: Jesse, Lonson and Durry.

41. Gar at the dedication of his sculpture
for the Cornell Medical Center in New York City, 1987.

42. With Susy-dell on her wedding day, 1977.

43. With Sony's first underwater housing
for the new Hi-8 video, 1991.

44. With Al Giddings and Chuck Nicklin on the set of *The Deep*, 1976.

45. Filming *The Deep*, 1976.

46. Ron and Valerie Taylor, 1978.

47. With Michele and Howard Hall aboard the *Tahiti Aggressor.* A Royal Birthday Party, 2003.

48. Peter Benchley, during the filming of "The Man Who Loves Sharks", 1991.

49. With his pipe and a good book – both old friends –
waiting for shark action in South Australia, on the *Ninad*, a shrimp trawler.
Sleeping accommodations were in the shrimp hold which had been
scoured and provided with mattresses.

50. With Peter Benchley during the filming of "The Man Who Loves Sharks".

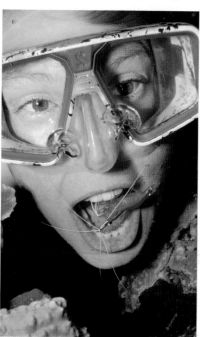

52. Rob Barrel, Master of the *Nai'a*, and crew, Tomasi Tokea and Rigamotu Fullman with Stan at Yasawa Island.

51. Cat Holloway and tiny friend on a Fijian reef.

53. Diver of the Year initiation by the Boston Sea Rovers. The dunk was in a bowl of vodka and orange juice. The Paul Revere Silver bowl was the award, 1968.

54. With Jack McKenney, editor of *Skin Diver*, film producer and lecturer.

55. With Jim Church.

56. Presenting
the Reaching
Out Award
to Sylvia Earle, 1999.

57. With Nancy McGee, Stan's business manager, 2004.

58. The publishers of *Ocean Realm*, Charlene deJori and Cheryl Schorp.

59. The many faces of Stan, 2000.

60. Never the technician.

61. Portrait by Howard Hall, 1991.

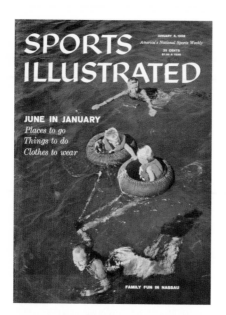

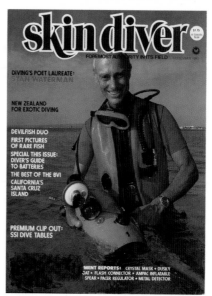

62 - 65. Some of the magazine covers on which Stan was featured.

Sports Illustrated, January, 1958. Taken during his first season charter boating in the Bahamas. He is towing Gordy and Susy-dell, with wife Susy following.

Skin Diver, September 1982.

Sub Aqua, January 1994.

Sort of Diver, 1988. With a skeleton acquired from a medical supply house and used for boffo humor.

66. The famous Howard Hall photograph
of Gordy riding the big manta in the Sea of Cortez.

67. The new house rises at the Punch Bowl, Maine.

IXX

LIGNUM VITAE

On the long table in the hall were some "collectibles" that I cherished. One was a lignum vitae dead eye that I found on a ledge in Eggemoggin Reach, actually within sight of the house. I was scalloping, an illegal activity with an aqualung and out-of-season in the summertime on top of that. At the same time, the activity was wonderfully rewarding. There's nothing like a succulent, illegal scallop in the middle of summer, right out of the sea just hours before dinner. Dead eyes were wooden discs with four or six holes through which cordage was threaded to create and hold the tension of the stays that supported the masts of sailing ships. A great three-masted square-rigger with top masts and top gallant masts would have used hundreds of them. A two or three-masted schooner, from which the one I found probably dropped, would have a hundred or more. They were made from the hardest wood in the world, lignum vitae. Before the era of plastic, bowling balls were turned with that wood. It was as hard as iron. As iron replaced wood in the construction of sailing ships, iron turnbuckles replaced the wooden dead eyes. They are collectors' items today; so I was delighted when I spotted it on the bottom, encrusted with pink coralline algae and barnacles. I did not clean it. I left it as a gift from the sea and a physical remembrance of things past. Those things were the schooners that passed our house early summer mornings before the war. I remember while lying in bed and snugged in under two blankets and comforter on a foggy, windless morning, listening to the mournful cry of the fog horns and the staccato, rhythmic blatt of the one-lunger, make and break engines on the yawl boats that pushed the schooner from astern. The antique dead eye, raised from the sea, shared the table with my son Gordy's "death mask." He had created this macabre but rather handsome bronze in an art class at Bucknell University. It was the product of his one-shot, entirely brief excursion into art, inspired by the reputation of that class as a "gut course." The object was heavy bronze and a perfect likeness. To make it he allowed his face to be covered with liquid plaster, breathing through a straw as the plaster set. Thus a mold was created and a bronze alloy poured into a mold shaped from the plaster. As it turned out Gordy, in a way, would earn his living in part as a creative artist. He became a professional cameraman, a very successful one and far more creative than his dad.

There was another bizarre object on the table, a gift from Peter Benchley. Over the years of our friendship we vied with one another at Christmas time in the presentation of weird and sometimes gross gifts. The one on the table was a brass mold, in two parts. The thicker part had eight perfect tube-like intrusions, very like a bullet mold. The top secured to the bottom with wing nuts. It was heavy and handsome and a complete enigma if you were not told what it was for. No one guessed. The molds were too shallow for candles. It was, in fact, a mold for suppositories. It was also a conversation piece that even drew a laugh from Susy. She rather frowned on gross objects in the house and would never let me use as a centerpiece for the dining room table the Solomon Island shark sculpture of the naked boy riding on the shark.

And just behind that copy of the ancient shark god image and well hidden under the long table were two richly-oiled leather gun cases. Now there were quite a few guns in the house, and Susy hated them all. They ranged from muzzle-loader long rifles and pistols, an antique eight-gauge double-barrel cap and ball shotgun, three semi-automatic assault weapons – dreadful things that the boys dearly loved to shoot across the cove and into the uninhabited woods on the other side, an assortment of contemporary sporting rifles and finally the two splendid shot guns in the leather cases. They had been given to us by a dear old friend, Charles C.G. Chaplin, not the actor but a quintessential English gentleman. He was an accomplished, self-taught ichthyologist, married to one of the wealthy Catherwood family of Philadelphia. Our friendship dated back to my charter boating in the Bahamas. Charlie had a private aquarium on Hog Island (today called Paradise Island) across the harbor from Nassau Town. He endowed the Chaplin Chair of Ichthyology at the Philadelphia Academy of Natural Sciences, co-authored the definitive book on reef fishes of the Bahamas and introduced me to the Academy. The association led to three expeditions on which I was the expedition cameraman and to a life-long friendship with Charlie and his wife, Louise. They had a summer home in Bar Harbor and often visited overnight with us at the Punch Bowl and had us to dinner with them in Haverford, Pennsylvania. They were, of course, very wealthy and moved with an intellectual, wealthy set. We were their somewhat pedestrian friends. One time we were part of a large dinner group and seated at individual tables for four. Susy and I were separated. At her table the conversation touched on nylon, the magic synthetic that had revolutionized fabric. It had such an enormous impact on western civilization that Susy was momentarily overwhelmed by the thought of its discovery. She blurted out, "I wonder who actually invented nylon? Where did it start?" In the pregnant silence that followed her question the gentleman sitting opposite her said, with a self-deprecating smile, "I guess I did." The table exploded with laughter and Susy was dumb-founded. The gentleman was Crawford Greenwalt, then the president of DuPont. At the time that nylon made its debut he had been the head of their experimental laboratories; so – indeed – he might lay claim, with some reason and also some levity, that HE invented nylon. At that time Greenwalt had also finished a book on hummingbirds, which was soon to be published. Interesting, isn't it, that a productive person can be the president of a giant corporation and still have time to turn a hobby into a definitive book on an esoteric totally unrelated subject like hummingbirds? Churchill wrote a history of the English speaking people plus a history of World War II while he guided Britain through its time of peril as head of state. Most people, including me, find they are too busy with their small affairs to find time for such additional productivity.

I was writing about the guns. One thinks of all British gentlemen of means as having fine guns – if not matched Purdies – and growing up with them. Young gentlemen are given their first shotgun when they are about 14, usually a .410. A 12 or 16 gauge follows when they are about 18. And if they are the progeny of very wealthy aristocracy, the guns may well be Purdies. They will certainly be hand-made, custom guns crafted by one of the fine London gunsmiths to the physical dimensions of the client. They are always cased, which means that they are carried in a wood, velour-lined case, compartmented to hold the stock, the barrel, cleaning tools and usually two empty brass shells with which to test the ejection action.

Such guns are often handed down from father to son. Charlie's son, Gordon, was uninterested in guns and shooting; so two of his beautiful guns were given to us. The light, elegant .410 double-barrel shotgun was specially presented to Susy. I received the 16 gauge gun that had been custom designed for a left-shoulder man. Both cases had Cunard Line First Class stickers on them. And stamped on the fabric that lined the inside of the hinged case lids were the declarations of patronage. The .410 proclaimed, "By Appointment to the Maharajah of Jaipur." The 16 gauge: "By Appointment to Her Royal Highness Queen Victoria." It was all very impressive and pretty meaningless, since such "appointments" are actually purchased by the manufacturers. However, the guns and the cases and the echo of pomp from the days of the great empire were fun to show off, when we occasionally had guests who knew something about guns.

We shot them from time to time. I had a clay pigeon thrower that hurled the discs out over the Punch Bowl as we fired from a stand on the shore. None of us were very good but the sport was a small but elegant part of the Punch Bowl activities. We cherished the privacy of the cove, but legally could prevent no one from entering the cove and anchoring their boat. When occasionally the company on a strange boat was noisy and obnoxious we used to fire up the skeet shoot and send the clay pigeons near enough to the boat to precipitate a hasty up anchor and away.

Long after Charlie went to that great trap shoot in the sky we remembered him kindly, cherished the guns and recalled his splendid, dry wit. When he was outraged by the failure of his Nikonos camera at a critical encounter with some marine animal he would level a curse on the inspector who had passed the camera before it was sold. Charlie C.G. Chaplin embodied all the best qualities that characterize English gentlemen: wit, classic education, urbane intelligence and ineffable grace. He was the best of company. Susy and I both loved him dearly and miss him.

The livingroom and the main hall contained so many of the things that I had collected over the years that it was my intention to confine my remembrance of things past to my remembered visual image of those rooms. I shall keep to that original design, although there were many other cherished objects scattered around the other rooms in the house. From Susy's great adventure in Nepal – when she hiked through the high country with David Brown – a three-foot-high elephant, carved from solid wood, reposed in the kitchen. The grandchildren loved to climb on it and ride it until they were big enough for their feet to reach the floor. On the back stairs that led to the servants' wing I had mounted the 25 pound lobster that was given to me by the Philadelphia Sea Horses, a club for which I used to do film festivals. And on another part of the stair walls, mounted in a glass case, was an enormous crab. Its mandible claw, grotesquely large in proportion to its body, was about two and a half feet in length, folded against the entire front of its body like an impregnable defense engine. I had seen it landed from a fishing boat at Port Lincoln, South Australia, when we were there for our first great white shark encounters in 1968. I was told it was the biggest ever seen there and had come up from deep water in a giant trap. I offered to buy it and struck a deal. It was mine for two bottles of Johnny Walker Black Label and it was to be cured, mounted and shipped to me in the States at some later date. Almost a year later it arrived by ocean freight.

That splendid big house was perfect for housing all those things that I brought back with me from my travels. Had we lived in an apartment I would have been far less acquisitive. When I took possession of the Punch

Bowl much of the furniture had been removed. My stepmother and my brother both had the right to take what they wished and did so when they filled their own homes. As both Susy and I gradually filled the house with our own collectibles and furnishings it truly became ours.

Our children so loved the house, having grown up surrounded by all those things and having reached an adult sense of pleasure in having them around, that they would all their lives love keeping it as it was, perhaps adding some keepsakes from their own travels.

We knew what we had. We never took it for granted. While we could hardly know that it would be totally destroyed, we were acutely aware of its vulnerability to fire. I am grateful that it was a part of our lives and that we loved it and appreciated it while we had it.

We are building again, something very modest by comparison. At least in the generation to which my children belong there will be no affluence approaching my father's. The future for the grandchildren is still over the horizon. Maybe one will strike it rich and a big house will rise again on the point. It won't have tiger skins; but there will be at least one adventurer among those five boys. In time strange and wonderful things will fill the house and it will be a full-bodied Waterman home again.

Epilogue

The beat goes on but the rhythm I march to has very much slowed down. The cars we have inevitably develop troubles. The machinery begins to wear out. So, too, my own body shows big signs of wear and the scars from patchwork and repairs are plenty evident. There are no complaints, just intimations of mortality as I do look forward to new experiences and adventures within less demanding schedules. It's the long air travel I find onerous, the long security lines at airports, the immobility of 18 hours in the air. The aging body, I find, does not take easily to sitting still, and it is the far away western Pacific that still has the siren song. I will continue to write for two fine dive journals, *Fathoms* and *Scuba Diver*. As I write we are turning the corner into 2005. My schedule includes a return to Northern Sulawesi and the Lembeh Straits, Tonga with the humpback whales on my favorite live-aboard, the *Nai'a,* and a return to Guadalupe Island with "Whitey" and good friends on the *Horizon*. There will be a return date with the *Sea Hunter* to Malpelo and Cocos Islands plus tours with the Aggressor Fleet, my long-standing and welcome regulars. From those experiences there will be grist for the essay mill and my video-editing bench.

And that brings up the time for writing and editing. How do I find it? An angel with prodigious energy, enterprise and expertise became my business manager. There has been no mention of her in the book although her good and generous offices to me are virtually essential to my travels and adventures in the marine world. Her name is Nancy McGee. She is a Canadian who moved with her family to Dallas, Texas. She has her own successful dive tour business. Years back she chartered the *Red Sea Aggressor* for a tour that Jim Church and I co-hosted. She offered to take over my annual bookings as well as travel ticketing, public relations and – ultimately – the sale of my video productions. Those were office work activities with which I had little patience and even less ability. She and her staff were so efficient that they enabled me to attend to my writing and editing as well as long daily walks with Susy and long evenings of reading by the fire at home. I credit her with saving me from early retirement and retreat to Sun City with Bingo and shuffleboard as my lot. At a modified pace the game is still afoot.

When I ship out on a live-aboard dive boat I generally leave the world behind. Communication with the outside world is always available. You can send and receive your e-mail. You can ask the captain for news coming through the radio at the bridge. I do neither. For the days' lengths of your tours you can retreat to the peace and quiet of the marine world. The sea air is clean. The horizons are so sharp and straight that you can almost feel the earth turning on its axis. The regimen is eat, sleep, dive. Inevitably there is a warm camaraderie with your fellow divers. More friendships than I can recall have hatched over the years under those aegis. Some have been life-long and close: Peter and Wendy Benchley.

Howard and Michele Hall, Rod and Jacqui Stanley, Malika and Jean Claude, Geoff and Joyce Stirling, Gregg Aslinger, Jim Perminter, Martha Gilkes, the lady publishers of *Ocean Realm* and many more who I see too seldom but "...grapple to my heart with hoops of steel." We have shared splendid adventures. I am grateful to them all for coming into my life. They are the stuff that makes living in a depressingly troubled world still the most rewarding course I know.

Martha Gilkes was listed above and deserves more than a name on a list. A superb professional diver, author of two books on Caribbean Diving and, herself, a prominent figure in Caribbean diving, she was as close to a regular dive buddy as I have ever had. She lives in Antigua with her husband, Tony, and always brought with her on our tours a half dozen or more guests from her coterie of island friends whom she had certified. That I was not long ago either dead or crippled by bends I owe to her vigilance. Too often, when I was fecklessly eager to get the last take of some special marine life action in deep water I would finally check my computer, find that I had about 200 p.s.i. left with a first decompression stop of five minutes at 25 feet, I would rightfully panic. Then I would look up to see Martha far above, waiting for me with about 1,500 p.s.i. in reserve and an octopus. Saved thanks to Martha. But nothing stays the same. Her regulars dispersed or dropped out of diving. The ranks of delightful Antigua friends thinned. But she still joins me from time to time as she is able in her busy world. She was recently elected President of the Women Divers Hall of Fame.

The special guests I invited to my 80th birthday party on the *Tahiti Aggressor* were all companions in diving and friends with whom I had shared some of my most memorable experiences over the years. They were Ron and Val Taylor who had been with me during the *Blue Water, White Death* production; Howard and Michele Hall, friends from the many network shoots; Rob Barrell and Cat Holoway, my Fiji connection with the beautiful live-aboard, *Nai'a*, and Doug Seifert, a first class underwater photographer and author. You will have read my essay, "A Royal Birthday" and know that Peter and Wendy Benchley were my hosts. That generous act by Peter was characteristic of his warm friendship and generosity over the years. The friendship grew as we did many *American Sportsman* and ESPN productions together. The Benchley family also live just ten minutes away in Princeton. To this day the friendship is nourished by almost daily communication when we are both home.

Our children and six grandchildren all live in Connecticut just two hours away. That year together in French Polynesia developed a bond that has strengthened through the years and is a great source of happiness for Susy and me. Gordy married a lady doctor and is a highly successful independent cameraman, shooting all over the world and experiencing adventures that easily match his father's.

Susy-dell lives just 15 minutes away from Gordy. She is a professional artist and muralist. She works with the Norwalk Maritime Museum. Her three boys all in turn captained the high school football team and are superb athletes. Her oldest boy, Durry, took a leave from college to enlist in the Marines and graduated from their advance training for the RECON Division. At this writing he is in the thick of it in Iraq. Gar, our youngest, became an artist. Having graduated from my college, Dartmouth, he went to Italy to learn marble sculpture and returned to develop a studio in New Haven. He is prospering with commissions, projects and grants and happily married to a lady with business smarts. They are all my best and most enjoyable friends. As the expression goes, they are a comfort to Susy and me in our autumn years.

And what of my very good wife, Susy? She and two friends started the first organic food store in Princeton, The Whole Earth Center. It prospered and is today a multi-million dollar success. She visits the store almost daily, impacts on their functioning and is on the board of directors. She also grandmothers our third generation brood and keeps a snug and trim house for me to come home to. We quietly read by the fire for a thousand and one nights and are happy as clams at high tide. Surely I am blessed and well know it

I will wrap up with a thought full of hope by the Seafaring Rat in *The Wind In the Willows*: "When the play has been played and the cup has been drained come home to your river with a goodly store of memories for company. I shall linger and look back. At last I will surely see you coming, light footed and strong, with all the South in your face."

Sea Salt
&
other writings

We need a newer and a wiser and perhaps a more mystical sense of the animal. Remote from universal Nature and living by complicated artifice, man - in civilization - regards the animals through the glass of his knowledge and sees thereby a feather, greatly magnified, and the whole image in distortion. We patronize them for their incompleteness, for their tragic fate in having been formed so far below ourselves. And thereby we err, and greatly err. For the animal shall not be measured by man. In a world older and more complete than ours, they live finished and complete, gifted with extensions of the senses we have lost or never attained, living by voices we shall never hear. They are not brethren. They are not underlings. They are other nations, caught with ourselves in the net of life and time, fellow prisoners of the splendor and the travail of the earth.
— *Henrey Beston* THE YEAR OF THE WHALE

The Rambo Out-Of-the-Cage Club

Some years ago, 1967 to be exact, Ron and Val Taylor, Peter Gimbel and I exited our cages in open water 100 miles to sea off Durban, South Africa. We were trying our luck in the open with 20 or more oceanic whitetip sharks. The attraction was a sperm whale that had been killed by the Union Whaling Company. It had been floated and buoyed with a radio beacon for later recovery and transport by one of their catcher boats to their whaling station in Durban.

We were all scared. The adrenaline was pumping full time. The risk was calculated, founded on our hope that the oceanic predators would not attack the strange animals venting bubbles and swimming among them. It was a benchmark experience, a theory that had not been tested. I do thank Neptune, Poseidon, Proteus or whatever gods may be that our guess was right. I have often recounted that experience when asked about my most frightening dive. Ron and Val and I harkened back to that "moment of truth" and agreed that we shared the same feelings.

In the years that have passed we have all worked safely with sharks, observed patterns of their behavior that allowed us to film the great predators and to earn our bread doing so. A mindset of abject fear by divers has gradually changed to a desire by most to see sharks. Hundreds of thousands of divers have watched the hand feeding of sharks with impunity, excitement and ultimate delight as the sharks circulated among them. The stars of the one-ring circus have been the feeders – divemasters outdoing one another with ever more daring feats of intimacy. Off Grand Cayman I watched a feeder tempt a full-size reef shark with the bait until his lips touched the shark's nose. In the Maldives a celebrated shark feeder had his daughter feed the gray reef sharks with a fish held in her teeth. I heard that she did this topless and never experienced an un-programmed mastectomy. All this stretching of the limits was bound to happen as individual divers and dive operators sought to entertain customers with derring-do and individual courage. That brings me to the Rambo Out-of-the-Cage Club.

For years I have annually taken dive groups to South Australia to realize the ultimate fulfillment of their macho imaginings. An encounter with the great white shark was the right attraction. Peter Benchley's *Jaws*, even more the movie so brilliantly directed by Steven Spielberg, provided the siren song. Rodney Fox, using first the shrimp trawler, *Ninad* and later the splendid old topsail ketch, *Falie*, had the cages and all the logistics to make the expeditions viable.

Spencer's Gulf, the Neptune Islands and Dangerous Reef were the arenas. Legions of divers, thrilled deliciously and safely frightened, photographed the huge animals from a distance of one foot with only the steel mesh of the cage between the gaping jaws, gnashing teeth and the camera lens. That sufficed for a long time. But there was always the protection of the cage. Even the most craven wimp could enjoy that exercise. The next step was pushing the envelope of safety by leaving the cage and facing "Whitey" in the open.

Years back Ron Taylor and I speculated on the possibility of abandoning our usual shark cage and meeting the great white in the open. We both had extensive experience filming other shark species in open water. We actually thought our chances were favorable for an open encounter with the white. However, the difference between speculation and execution was too great. Prudence checked us both.

As far as I know Al Giddings was the first to give it a try. In the making of his series, *Ocean Quest*, a cage was lowered to the bottom. Al exited the cage, leaving the door open for retreat. Three whites appeared and curiously circled the strange animal. Al got his shots. When the predators closed the diameter of their circles, Al found it prudent to return to the cage and close the door. If you are doing that sort of thing to prove you can, it's always satisfying to be shown doing it. Chuck Nicklin nicely documented the scene.

I heard about the next open encounter from San Diego diver and cameraman Howard Hall. Howard was filming for *Wild Kingdom* near Guadalupe Island off the Pacific coast of Baja. The star of the show was tagging blue sharks when two whites suddenly arrived on the scene. As Howard described it, the divers retreated to the safety of the cage and observed the whites cruising about. Instinctively they felt the whites were in a non-aggressive mood, so they left the cage. Howard filmed as the star tagged one of the whites.

Later, Howard was again filming for *Wild Kingdom*, this time off South Australia with Rodney Fox, who arranges all the great white shark encounters there for filmmakers. At the end of the shoot, Howard and still photographer Marty Snyderman took one of the cages to the bottom and got out, as Al Giddings had done, to try their luck with the big animals.

This time the sharks approached the divers so closely that they had to be fended off with a short billy. One opened his mouth in a bite attitude that Howard described as being "rather scary." When it became impossible to anticipate the movements of several sharks at the same time, the two men wisely retreated to the cage.

Courage loses much if not all of its value after the ice has already been broken. Now that the "four-minute mile" of shark encounters had been accomplished, I was determined to break through the reserve barrier and try an open-water meeting myself. I joined four other men and two women who had all converged on South Australia for encounters with the great white shark. Upon hearing that I planned to leave the cage at the bottom and meet my destiny with the great white in the open, all six became determined to try it themselves.

In the gloom 40 feet down, four men climbed out of the cage. Some sat on the top and others clung to the outside like kids on a jungle gym. Minutes went by with much apprehensive swiveling of heads to peer into the murky perimeter.

When a not-so-great white did finally appear (a relatively small ten-footer), there was a rush to re-enter the cage. The open hatch would only accept one diver at a time. Adrenaline flowed; masks were knocked off; friendships were strained. Rodney claimed he saw the shark smile as it cruised by the cage.

On a second bottom dive, the two women and one of the men went to the bottom with Rodney. One of the female divers was so determined to be the first woman to have an open-water encounter with a great white that she started to climb out before the cage settled. In the process, she stepped on Rodney's head. For the titillation of this second team, the shark flexed its jaws a bit.

Everyone was pleased except Rodney. He saw a precedent that he did not want to encourage and closed the option of divers consorting with the sharks out of the cage at the bottom. With liability suits gone out of the ball park these days, one cannot blame him. And, indeed, there is no commendable reason for leaving the security of the cage to encounter the great predator in the open.

The line between foolish risk and macho courage is very thin. Al Giddings claimed scientific investigation, which lends an aura of responsibility to such an exercise. Actually, it introduces a new thrill level to a film and that in turn can be serious box office. Dave Barry, a columnist, points out that it is getting harder to find a great white shark these days. "Most of your top sharks probably have commitments to do documentaries," he writes.

Not long after Howard Hall filmed his dive companion, Jeremiah Sullivan, actually grabbing the tail of a 14-foot white as it swam by. I have a hard-worn still picture of the mad event. Howard recounted the moment of contact: "The shark panicked, shook Jeremiah off and vanished into the distance. The ride lasted two or three seconds."

The end was not yet in sight. Like the ancient Minoan bull leapers, who somersaulted over the horns of charging bulls, further exploits to entertain and astound the public as well as prove the superiority of the diver have been generated in South Africa. There, in the waters off Capetown, divers have attracted great white sharks to the sides of their small boats. As the sharks follow a bait out of water with their heads the local divers have learned that they may cup the very snout of the shark with a hand, causing the animal to become transfixed, almost anesthetized, as long as the hand is held in place. The sensation achieved is called tonic immobility.

To top it all a world-famous diver was filmed free diving onto the back of a great white shark and briefly catching a ride. The length of the ride beat Sullivan's record by several seconds. Who knows? Perhaps we will achieve sustained shark flight one day even as the Wright Brothers' brief flight at Kitty Hawk evolved through the years.

So what are my thoughts about all this? I, of course (now that I've had my go in the arena), hope there will be a lid on such activity. We don't want the "Rambo-out-of-the-Cage Club" to become any less exclusive. But in all seriousness, I begin to think that such stunts demean the magnificent predators. We prove for the consumption of our own human egos and the titillation of the public that we don't know the meaning of fear. The sharks themselves are not impressed. They have no sense of machismo; they just survive. I have filmed these antics over the years. They are great for "show biz" box office. The great animals don't even get Actor's Equity. They are the foils of our superiority displays. Rambo could be your next-door neighbor when he returns from his dive trip, as a certified member of the Rambo-Out-of-the-Cage Club. After many years of diving with sharks, I believe I would rather see and film them in the wild, unmolested by man and be happy that they do not eat me. I like to think that intelligent fear may be synonymous with healthy respect.

Henry Beston wrote in his book, *The Outermost House*: "For the animal shall not be measured by man. In a world older and more complete than ours, they live finished and complete, gifted with extensions of the senses we have lost or never attained, living by voices we shall never hear. They are not brethren. They are not underlings. They are other nations, caught with ourselves in the net of life and time, fellow prisoners of the splendor and the travail of the earth."

The Confessions of a Retired Spearfisherman

During the spring of 1950, I spent my days traveling by foot along the western coast of Corsica. I carried fins, mask, snorkel and an Arbalet speargun in addition to the few traveling essentials in my knapsack. The romance of the lone hunter was upon me. I fancied myself an aquatic Daniel Boone.

The coastal road was only a dirt track and distances between villages were long. One day I encountered no other human or human habitation during the entire day. Where there was access to the sea from the high road, I frequently made my way to the water's edge and entered the sea to hunt. Fortunately, I was incredibly inept with my speargun. Also, there was little to shoot at. More practical hunters than I had already created something of a wasteland by using dynamite. The entire marine ecosystem had been flattened.

Had I actually speared a fish, I could have done nothing with it. I had no adulating female companion to gasp with wonder at my courage as I came out of the sea with a limp octopus. I also had no means for cooking my catch before the sun's heat ripened it to a stinking mess. Yet I fired at anything that moved.

Years later, when I was a charter-boatman in the Bahamas, I did something so reprehensible and bizarre that I'm amazed by it in hindsight. In order to extricate a large jewfish from a deep coral recess so that I could produce a movie sequence for a client, I blew it out of its hiding place with dynamite.

How did I happen to have dynamite aboard my boat? Because my client was also interested in treasure hunting. I thought we would blow up a few wrecks here and there to get at the gold that we knew was always under the wreck.

Never having used dynamite, I thought three sticks would be an adequate charge for chivvying the jewfish into the open. We realized that it might even leave him with an Excedrin headache.

Of course, the explosion completely demolished the reef, vaporized the great fish and would have sunk my boat had not some shred of common sense prompted me to withdraw to a considerable distance before touching the wires to the battery.

In the Bahamas I took diving clients to a selection of favorite reefs with abundant marine life. One reef was always loaded with lobsters and groupers; another had a favorite moray eel.

Few divers had cameras back in the early 1950s, but they were enthralled by simple observation of an active reef community. I allowed no spearguns. It had become patently evident to me that the dynamics of each area depended on the preservation of the living community. One hunting party could wipe out an otherwise renewable resource.

I suspect that at the time economics had much to do with my philosophy. Letting divers off at dead reefs did not produce satisfied customers. I had also started filming in those days. Increasingly, I resented the destruction of an animal that I could have captured on film – or, at least, with whom I could have begun to establish the kind of rapport necessary for better, more intimate filming.

Today underwater photography is the dominant interest for divers. The latent hunter in us finds that to bring 'em back alive on film is far more satisfying than to impale them on spears. I like to think this evolution from destructive fun to constructive and satisfying hobby is a natural process in the maturation of a sport.

Mind you, I have seen spearfishing done under circumstances that made it a magnificent, primordial and entirely admirable activity. When I lived in French Polynesia, I watched local men who speared for the table. They matched wits and endurance with their prey on a level with a Masai warrior stalking a lion with a hand spear.

Like silent spiders, the men descended the steep walls of a pass, pulling themselves down hand-over-hand without fins. At 80-100 feet they would reach a ledge and freeze, motionless. Using a glossary of guttural grunts and clicks passed down to them by their fathers, they would pique the curiosity of a passing jack or grouper.

As the fish swam close, they would track it with a smooth arc of their home-made thumblatch speargun and fire. Most of the time the shot was instantly fatal, hitting high and into the vertebrae just behind the head. Even so the click of the speargun was enough to attract gray reef sharks. The men made their long trip to the surface with the game held close to their bodies in defiant protection, running a gauntlet of marauding predators. Elapsed time: often two and a half minutes or more. Now that is what I call spearfishing.

Legions of divers have watched and filmed the famous potato cod of Dynamite Pass on the Great Barrier Reef where four or five of the mottled white, 100-pound groupers were regularly hand fed. Since any diver could approach them virtually nose-to-nose, shooting one would be like firing a spear into the side of a barn. A few years ago a party of spearfishermen wiped them out. Fortunately, other potato cod replaced them in time and are now protected by law as a natural and valued resource.

The quarter-ton jewfish of the Florida Keys and the Bahamas are long since gone, as are the magnificent giant sea bass of the West Coast. Today most divers would give their left strobe to catch one of these behemoths in their viewfinders. I am ashamed that in my own time I helped to speed their virtual extinction.

There is nothing new in the depletion of our resources. The tragedy of the buffalo and the carrier pigeon is paralleled in the sea. We entered the reef world just 30 years ago with all the predatory exuberance of the westward trekking pioneers. We seem to have grown up in our approach to the marine world and the sport of diving in a wonderfully short time. Perhaps the camera has been the main catalyst for that maturity, and surely the era of environmental awareness has accelerated the process.

I say "Bravo!" With care, patience and the benevolent click of the camera's shutter, the kelp forest, old rigs and tropical reefs may again become the forest primeval we knew when we first began exploring them three decades past.

Descent into the Maelstrom

Some years ago I attended a ship's christening and launching at the Brooklin Boat Yard just down the coast from where we live in Maine during the summer. It is situated at Center Harbor at the eastern end of Eggemoggin Reach, which in turn connects Penobscot Bay with Frenchman's Bay. Any more detail than that would involve you in a geography lesson burdened with so many quaint, incomprehensible names for Maine islands and notorious ledges that you'd think yourself on another planet. Let's just shorten it to "way down east" on the Maine Coast.

The manager of the yard is a young man named Steven White. He is the grandson of the late E.B. White, beloved author of *Charlotte's Web*, *Stuart Little* and one of the great humorists and essayists of our time. Steve White's father, Joel, started the yard and designs the fine wooden sailing boats that come off its ways. He designed a beautiful, sleek, fast ocean racer for his son, a sloop that subsequently stood tall in competition.

At the christening Steven would announce the name for the new boat, a name so curious that it demanded an explanation after which his wife, Laurie, would smash the long, graceful bow with the champagne bottle and cry for all to hear, "I christen you *Vortex*."

But first, the explanation. The name *Vortex* astonished and mystified us all. Steve recounted a true experience had by the radio operator at a charter boat office on the east coast of Florida with a customer on one of their boats. A distress call had reached them from the weekend mariner. His voice, transmitted from a small harbor across the Gulf Stream near one of the small northern islands in the Berry Islands, part of the Bahamas, was shrill and frantic. He announced that his small motor vessel was caught in a vortex. Almost incoherent with fear he screamed that at full throttle he was unable to break away from the fatal suction of the terrible whirlpool. At increased speed he was circling the dread force and would soon be sucked into the vortex.

Steve went on to recall the amazement of the radio operator. It is unlikely that he had read Edgar Allan Poe's *A Descent into the Maelstrom*, but whatever the force and malignancy of a vortex might be, the hapless mariner appeared caught in it. Over the radio he could hear the plaintive shriek of the engines as the owner frantically revved them. There seemed no doubt that the hapless man, his girlfriend and his plastic jazz boat were going down the tube. All the questions by the operator shed no light on the enigma until a way-out consideration entered the back of his mind, a last ridiculous possibility. He shouted through the babble of the panicked man: "Have you pulled your anchor?" Sudden silence at the Bahamian end of the line. The engine noise diminished. Then an astonished "Oh Jesus," and the doomed mariner went off the air with a tremulous "Thanks."

Our laughter and delight, as we raised our glasses, sent the *Vortex* down the ways.

And then there was my experience with a real vortex. You may find the real thing at the ocean entrances to some of the great underground water systems in the Bahamas. The island nation is undermined by one of the most extensive systems of subterranean caverns and tunnels in the world. Once above ocean level and carved out by great rivers and millennia of rainwater coursing through the porous limestone, they were flooded by the rising of the sea level after the last Ice Age about 12,000 years ago and now respond to the rise and fall of the tides.

Blue holes are entrances and exits to the miles of labyrinthine passages. When they occur underwater on the shallow reef that borders Grand Bahama on the east, millions of gallons of ocean water exit through the hole as the tide drops and are sucked back into the hole with the flooding tide. Where the tidal movement of the water has eroded the surface of the reef around the actual entry hole there may be a blue collar of deeper water, easily distinguished from the transparent shallow water over the reef. Such blue holes are easily spotted from the air.

A popular children's program, *3-2-1 Contact*, produced by ABC, had contacted me to do the underwater shooting for one of their productions. Their format: a pair of young teenagers has encounters with scientists and naturalists around the world and have a learning adventure on location. The production for which I would shoot took the young pair to Grand Bahama to dive on the reefs with Dr. Jill Yager. The previous year Dr. Yager, while exploring deep into the underground system, discovered an entirely new class of fish living in the stygian darkness. The discovery had vaulted her into some prominence in the marine science community. Part of the story would acquaint the two youngsters with the blue hole described above.

A delightful part of the shoot was provided by the local children playing in the pillow of outgoing water from the blue hole at ebb tide. The force of the water exiting actually pushed the water level over the hole above the ocean level around it, providing a pillow into which children jumped, shrieking with laughter as they were hurled aside. It was an aquatic trampoline. At slack tide the flow stopped, the water calmed and the children went home. From infancy they had been warned about the vortex, the terrible suction that would pull them down into the bowels of the earth should they continue their play after the slack tide.

I asked one of the little kids what would happen if he got sucked down. With eyes white and round he said, "You don't never get seen no more." He hurried after his friends, away from the place of frolic and joy, now an evil force until the next tide.

The actual entry hole in the center of the wider indented circle was about ten feet down. It was approximately five feet in diameter. As the flood tide picked up force, a real, very visual and very ominous-looking vortex appeared. The whirlpool above the hole became more strident...more powerful and rather frightening as a thin, transparent column appeared from the center of the hole, dancing higher and higher, swaying slightly like a cobra poised for the strike. It reminded me of action pictures I have seen of tornadoes, weaving their way along their paths of destruction; only here the entire force of an ocean-size bathtub was being sucked down into that small drain.

Small reef fish, butterflyfish, wrasse and little cardinalfish darted into the perimeter of the whirlpool and with imperceptible movements of their fins, harnessed the force to bounce up and down as they whirled about. It was an engaging sight. Lying on the bottom with scuba support I filmed the scene from just inches outside of the whirlpool's reach. Mindful of the terrible force within close proximity, I had a safety man holding my legs. We had been repeatedly warned by Dr. Yager not to take chances that might deliver us up to the grip of the vortex. Her words: "Once caught in that suction and drawn into the hole there is no way a person could survive." I believed her and assumed a posture of macho courage by having worked so close to the terrible force. And that sets the stage for what happened on the last day of our shoot.

The rest of the production team were involved with indoor shots. I wanted one more round of filming the vortex. A divemaster was assigned to me and drove me to the location. From the shore we swam out to the blue hole, both of us snorkeling at the surface of the shallow water. I was equipped with scuba so that, when we reached the broad blue hole declivity, I could lie on the bottom alongside the vortex without holding my breath.

I got my shot. For my part of the production it was a "wrap." Prepared to start back, I was surprised when the dive guide asked if he could borrow my scuba equipment. I was happy to lend it to him, though I hadn't the least idea of what he might do with it in that shallow water. I soon learned. As I watched in utter amazement he descended into the pit and swam directly into the whirlpool. He was carried round and round, at first slowly near the top of the action, then more and more rapidly as the vortex drew him down toward the dreaded opening. With one kick of his fins he could propel himself out of the circular grip. It was a bold stunt. I watched, fascinated, and having anticipated the conclusion to his stunt I had started to shoot, documenting the maneuver.

Faster and faster he whirled about. I remember thinking that he was rather pushing the whole thing and had better make his break…and then he was gone. Down the hole! Swallowed up! Disappeared into that untraveled nether world of darkness and violent forces from which no traveler could return.

It had happened while I was shooting, viewing the action through the viewfinder of my camera. For a shocked moment I couldn't believe what I had seen. I stopped shooting, looked closely at the hole and the evil spiral of water snaking up from it. He was gone…GONE! VANISHED!

I circled the perimeter of the great sump, fixing the hole in my view from every angle, knowing at the same time that it was futile. I had never presided over the death of a fellow human and vaguely thought I had better swim ashore and notify the police. Still, I lingered on, without any logical hope but so overwhelmed by the horror of what I had witnessed that I was compelled, body and soul, to hold my focus on the hole that had swallowed a full-grown, six-foot, 200 pound man.

Beyond any reason the play had not been fully played. Did my eyes deceive me? Had there been some slight alteration in my vision of the hole that mesmerized me with its black, empty interior? Was that a hand emerging on a part of its rim? I did have the wit to start shooting. Very slowly a head appeared. The mask was gone. In increments both arms and the shoulders appeared and then, a body grossly bloated like some Michelin Tire ad, rose from the grave and shot to the surface. Lazarus – and so I will think of him all my days – kicked out of the whirlpool and faced me, his head thrown back, his whoops and shouts explosive. I, too, was caught in a hysteria of laughter and shouting.

We swam toward shore until we could stand and face one another. "What, in the name of Jesus, were you doing?" I shouted, even though I could have reached out and touched him.

"I planned it," he said.

"You what!?" I shouted again, my voice more an accusation than a question.

"I've planned to do that for a long time; I suppose I really should have let you know what I had in mind." Any intonation of apology was masked by his obvious pleasure in having pulled it off. Then, as we continued standing in the waist-deep water, he told me how he had planned the spectacular exploit and carried it off.

Some while back, during a half hour of slack tide, he had entered the hole by himself, penetrated just a little way in but far enough to see with his light that there were eroded niches in the sides of the passage, large enough to shelter a man. At this time he knew that the tide was within a half hour – more or less – of reaching slack. My tank had over 2,000 p.s.i. of air still in it. Inside the hole at the start of the long passage the water was still only 15 or 20 feet deep. His plan was to take refuge in one of the interstices out of the torrential incoming current, bide his time there, with plenty of air, and when the tide turned slack and the current stopped, he would return the way he had come. He had not counted on his facemask being ripped off and decided on an immediate ascent by inflating my buoyancy compensator vest. He was not sure the lifting force of the inflated vest could counteract the current. With the help of his arms, and the rapidly swelling vest, he was able to counter the force and gain on the entrance. When he popped out he looked like a swollen tick.

Cost: one mask, a near heart attack by me and a story – on film – so bizarre and imprudent that ABC did not dare include the footage in their finished production.

The Middle of Nowhere

"Filial ingratitude, thou marble-hearted fiend!" Shakespeare couldn't have put it better. The lady's face was a mask of outrage as she heaped scorn on the cowering occupants of the departing Zodiac. Her invective, enough to make a lumberjack blush, reached out across the widening gap of water, wishing us ill luck and shrilling: "I hope a shark eats you, Gar."

Alas, the vituperative harridan was my lovely daughter, Susy. The cause for the maledictions? We had decided to reduce the number of divers attending a shark-baiting exercise. The more divers there are in the water, the less likely it is that any self-respecting shark will approach a bait. I had elected to take her brother, Gar, with me and Howard Hall and leave Susy behind on that dive. Of course, it could be argued that one might go for days and even weeks before discovering, in a completely random selection of human beings, one who would consider not being allowed to bait sharks being discriminated against.

As it turned out, three divers were too many. In a wild area not yet frequented by divers and well populated by tiger, Galapagos, and silvertip sharks, we had set out our juicy, gourmet baits, withdrawn a respectable distance, and waited motionless and inconspicuous (we thought) while we breathed away our air supplies. For now, we would have to be content with mantas. On our return I found a contrite, apologetic daughter, tactful enough not to gloat over our dry run.

We were at San Benedicto Island, part of the small, isolated group that includes Socorro Island. They are 260 miles due south of Cabo San Lucas in the middle of nowhere. Have a look in your atlas. If they are there, they will be pinpoints at best. Few dive boats care to travel that distance from the mainland. But Howard had been there four times before, always on the *Ambar III*. So the combination of Howard and the *Ambar III* was, for me, my children, and a Discovery Channel film crew, a passport to this pristine, virgin diving area.

Did I say mantas? Oh my! I still wake up sobbing when I think of the manta madness that we encountered there. We first dived around a boiler that Howard had located on previous trips. Don't mistake this for a rusting ship's boiler on the ocean floor. A rock that is just under the surface and reveals itself by cresting waves as the ocean swells pass over it is called a boiler. This one was a real pinnacle, with sides that reached down in steep steps to an ocean bottom 130 feet below. It was honeycombed with moray and lobster habitats and attracted a wonderful variety of reef fishes, schools of moorish idols and angelfish along with visiting schools of pelagics. There are currents, not as swift as those at Cocos Island, but enough to keep the nutrients in suspension. And that rings the dinner bell for mantas.

Mantas were there every day that we dived, on both sides of the island. On the first day, the first dive, they arrived as we waited for sharks. It required more singleness of purpose than we possessed to remain motionless on a ledge watching the morays and jacks eating the shark bait we had put out when a gaggle of mantas arrived. There were three to start with, as big as spaceships and doing wing-overs in the open water just to the side of us. Sharks are exciting, but mantas are inviting. We joined them and, in short order, they offered their bellies for scratching. They hovered over us, their undersides like vast, white-washed barn doors, the tips of their wings quivering as we scratched their rough skin. The experience was so enchanting and the pleasure of the rapport with these great animals so appealing that we didn't realize we were scratching away the skin on our hands and fingers. In the spirit of these wonderful encounters one was not apt to think: "Now this is an elasmobranch. Like the shark, its skin is composed of microscopic teeth, and what I am doing with such joy is massaging a sheet of #40 sandpaper." Later, out of the water, we would find our hands raw and bleeding.

To comprehend the serendipity of this moment you should know the reason for our being there with a film team. The Discovery Channel production was titled, *The Man Who Loves Sharks*. It focuses on a superannuated underwater cameraman whose filming of sharks over the years had helped feed and educate his children. Thus the fondness for sharks (an unrequited love at best). The children, growing up, had worked in the sea with their father, and the family had had many adventures together. That cohesion, plus the shark element, appealed to Discovery. The long-of-tooth diver, hanging out with his children, was me. The children were no longer short-of-tooth themselves. At 39 Susy was the mother of three and a proper suburban matron living in Connecticut: car pools, PTA meetings, little leagues, and all. Gar, a struggling artist, was a superb marble sculptor making his own way in a difficult trade. Both were renewing the fun of working with Dad. And so, as we swept through the open sea space with these magnificent animals, we rolled our eyes at one another and laughed and shouted to the extent that one can with a mouthpiece gripped firmly between the teeth. Adding to the joy of the moment was the realization that the finest underwater cameraman in the western world was documenting the experience on 16mm film. Howard was there, shooting head on and swimming furiously backward in front of us like a crazed sea otter.

The mantas apparently loved the attention as much as we did. They followed us to the surface at the end of the dive and hung around as the Zodiac picked us up. Mantas are not always that accommodating. The ones at San Benedicto were more accommodating than most I have encountered, but we didn't have such an extraordinary experience again.

For the last two days we shifted location to the other side of the great, black, volcanic cinder cone that dominates San Benedicto. On the eastern side of the island, the lava had burst through the base of the cone and flowed into the sea. It formed a massive black shelf as it cooled and broke off at the water's edge. An extensive jumble of lava rubble spread another 50 yards out into deeper water and terminated in a featureless sand slope that disappeared into ever-deeper water. At the edge of the slope, in 60 feet of water, Howard set the baits. Twice a ten- to 12-foot tiger shark nosed around. Galapagos sharks came and went. All were wary, even though we had retreated to the edge of visibility. Mantas appeared, swooping and banking around the big boulders and hovering over us. They virtually begged for attention. The temptation to play was excruciating, but our minds were on sharks. Little good it did us. Even as we ascended the surface, with our gauges at zero, we could watch one or more sharks move in and make off with the baits. That is, until the last day.

To understand what happened that last day it is necessary to understand the causes. We, ourselves, didn't until we later analyzed the danger-fraught experience we emerged from.

That morning, while we waited for the sun to be high enough for good light, we fished. I have small patience for the usual fishing characterized by hours of trolling without a strike. Fishing at San Benedicto was constant action. I have never encountered anything like it. With two lines out we had strikes about every three minutes, often on both lines at once. Yellowfin tuna, wahoo, barracuda, and sailfish came in with wild regularity. We ate the best of them, noon and night, and used their carcasses for bait. They were cleaned promptly on the transom so that a rain of blood, guts, and scraps went over the side. That morning, although we didn't know it, that delicious chum was carried by a strong current some distance astern of us. Now it is said that a shark's olfactory system can pick up one part in a million of diluted scent, and tuna caused sharks to sob aloud with anticipation. When Howard and I dropped over the side of the Zodiac a good 150 yards astern of the boat, the action had already started.

As usual, Howard had the stringer of bait plus his camera. The drill was for Howard to attach the baits securely to a rock while I established an observation post at some prudent distance. But this time within seconds of hitting the water, a seven-to eight-foot Galapagos shark, fast and aggressive, came charging in. Howard dropped the baits and fended the premature guest off with his camera. With tight turns the shark continued to make passes at Howard. I started shooting right away, delighted with this fast action. Thirty-five years of shooting underwater coarsens one's instincts. My reaction to all this was, "If Howard gets eaten by the shark, I sure as hell want to catch it on camera." Then again, if it wasn't someone as shark-savvy as Howard or Ron Taylor or Bob Cranston, I would have been somewhat more solicitous. Howard's defense was effective. The shark departed, ignoring the bait – at least for the moment.

Howard wasted no time in securing the bait, while I did the decent thing and watched his back. Then we took positions opposing one another at a little distance from the bait. There would be no tedious waiting this morning. We were sure of that. Within a minute our friend was back, and with him two of his buddies. The word was out. The action accelerated.

They didn't take the baits at first. They glided in from all directions, their handsome, torpedo-sleek bodies filling the viewfinder as they almost snubbed their noses on the dome port. At the last split second they would swing aside with one powerful thrust of the caudal fin. We could feel the soundwave from that movement, like a sheet snapping in a high wind. While we could see them approach, this was great filming. With just a moment's preparation we could fend the animals off with our cameras. As long as we could see from what direction they were coming and, more importantly, as long as they could see us clearly, we were reasonably secure.

Then an already lively and somewhat dangerous exercise was exacerbated by diminishing visibility. There is an overlay of volcanic ash that permeates the bottom sand all around San Benedicto. The movements of the sharks – and now there were five – stirred up the bottom, especially as they began to make passes at the bait, lashing about to tear it loose. Visibility deteriorated to about ten feet. I could barely see Howard. There was less than one second of lead time to swing the camera into position as they suddenly appeared from the gray curtain just ten feet on every side. There was no feeding frenzy yet. We both knew instinctively that we were better off hunkered down on the bottom with lowest possible profile than fleeing from the scene.

As the scenario worsened, two large tiger sharks, probably ten-to 12-foot bruisers, cruised by above us. We could make out their silhouettes against the light. At that point I think we both had the same thought: Let's get out of here! I practically crawled along the bottom to Howard's position. Together we started moving laterally away from the bait action center. As we did so, two of the Galapagos sharks moved in on the bait. With twisting, convulsive gyrations they finally tore the bait loose and vanished. And with that, it was over.

There were no curtain calls. The tiger sharks did not appear again. We moved even farther away before we surfaced, turning as we ascended to watch every sector. But we both knew the sharks would not return. That's the way it is. The bait's the thing, not the humans. However, in that mad scene, the usual rules didn't apply. That was the time for even the most veteran shark filmakers to be scared, and we were.

Our director, and our editor and the executives at the Discovery Channel were ecstatic. They thought we should have shot more of that fine action. At this writing the film is being edited in the Times Square area of New York City. Compared to the action in that part of the world around midnight, our encounter might easily have taken place in the Christian Science Reading Room. Everything is relative.

An Embarrassment of Whale Sharks

I have just returned from one of the most extraordinary, unlikely, and thoroughly wonderful experiences in 45 years of diving. Now before I relate to you what happened off the Ningaloo Reef on the northwestern coast of Australia, let me give you some perspective about the animals we encountered there. Until four years ago I had never seen a whale shark. I had traveled all the way to South Africa, trying to encounter these largest of all fish in the oceans of the world, drawn by the report that they abounded in the Mozambique Channel. They were conspicuous by their absence on my visit.

Having reached the age where Sun City and the shuffleboard court are the lifestyle for many of my contemporaries, I began to suspect that I never would have the privilege of diving with a whale shark. Then, four years ago, encouraged by Howard Hall, the ABC *American Sportsman* show launched an expedition to find the whale sharks in the Sea of Cortez. Howard had encountered whale sharks in those waters before. We assured the ABC producers that a whale shark on-camera was a virtual certainty. It transpired that we lucked out way beyond our just deserts. With the help of aerial reconnaissance, we located one whale shark. Howard and I filmed Genie Clark riding its huge dorsal fin all the way down to 190 feet. We later learned that that was the only whale shark spotted in the Sea of Cortez that summer. But I had my whale shark, and if I never encountered another, my giant was as magnificent as I had expected. I was in free. Just set me up with a rocking chair and bocci and a goodly store of memories for company. Then along came Exmouth.

It was only by chance that I organized a tour to Exmouth. It was a substitute, tossed to me by Rodney Fox, when my 1992 great white shark tour to South Australia canceled. Memories of the Mozambique Channel dry run provoked a healthy skepticism in me about the big animals being there when "Lucky" Waterman showed up. Rodney's boat could only take six guests. That many signed on before I even advertised the tour, such is the magic appeal of the leviathan. We had a "go."

When we reached Sydney on the eastern coast of Australia, we still had a continent as wide as the United States to cross. Westward for five more hours. I looked down upon the Great Australian Bight and Port Lincoln. Twenty-four years ago I had sailed out of that port with Peter Gimbel and Ron and Val Taylor for our film-history-making first encounters with the great white shark. I slept with those memories as we continued west across the trackless wastes of the Nullarbor Desert and on into Perth, fresh and green in the Australian autumn. We did the jet lag stagger into a Perth hotel for an overnight and continued three hours north along the coast to Learmonth, the airport for Exmouth. We exited the plane with a gaggle of school kids home for the Easter holidays. Their parents, sunburned and lean, were the owners and managers of the great sheep stations. Their dust-powdered four-wheel-drive vehicles all had roobars over the radiator grills, to protect them from kangaroos and wallabies.

On the half-hour trip by van to the little coastal town of Exmouth, Rodney Fox dispelled much of my skepticism with his account of a successful tour that had just preceded ours. The group had "wallowed" in whale sharks. That sounded a little like hyperbole to me, but nonetheless it was encouraging.

The next morning we started an action routine that would continue for the entire week. The 58-foot *Nordon* was loaded from the beach via Zodiac. We had paid for aerial reconnaissance for four hours each day. Our captain, George King, salty and seasoned, wanted to be there when the band started playing. Less than 30 minutes from the beach, we were on the shark grounds. Here, off the Ningaloo Reef, the continental shelf for western Australia is at its narrowest point. The Leeuwin Current swings down from the north further encouraging the phenomenon we were about to experience in Exmouth Gulf by stirring up the coral spawn and algae blooms on which the whale sharks feed and then circulating outside the Northwest Cape and mixing with the blue water along Ningaloo Reef.

The spotter plane was in the air. Within five minutes, the radio crackled. The captain on the flying bridge relayed the message to Rodney. Action central was the cockpit and the diving platform. Rodney called out the first contact of the day, an announcement that would become familiar during the week: "All right, folks. We have a whale shark about a quarter mile to the south. It's a big one. Get ready."

In fact, we were too ready. We were so ready and excited that at least one diver tried to put both feet into the same leg of his Lycra suit, and I strapped on my tank before I thought of my weight belt. We had been briefed by Rodney. "When Gary [the crewman] yells 'Go,' if you aren't over and in within five seconds, all you may be lucky enough to see will be the tail of Mr. Big disappearing into the murk. You can have breakfast again from the egg on your face." So we were ready and quivering with much needless fiddling with camera adjustments and checking of straps. This would be no leisurely exercise. We wore Lycra skin suits only, with perhaps an eighth-inch shorty over it. To cut down on drag, we had eliminated our buoyancy compensator vests and strapped on 40-cubic-foot mini-tanks. There would be plenty of hard swimming. The leisurely cruising speed of the leviathan would be matched by a lot of flat-out finning on the part of his human pursuers.

"Three hundred meters and closing." Rodney handed the walkie-talkie to Gary and took his place on the gunnel next to me. Six guests and two crewmen were in position, ready to go.

Gary had the walkie-talkie pressed to his ear. All eyes were on him. "Get ready. He'll be on the starboard side; he's amid-ships now, 20 meters out and heading right for us. Go! Go! Go! Go!"

Before his last "Go!" eight bodies had hit the water. Eight pairs of eyes were trying to penetrate the chrysalis of bubbles, then a desperate sweep of the perimeter ahead. Nothing. Where the hell was he? An animal the size of a submarine just 20 meters away must be visible. But these were plankton-rich waters. That's why the beast was there. And then, he was there. The first thing I saw emerging from the gloom was a straight horizontal line. Holy Neptune! It was a mouth, six feet wide, slightly open, dark between the lips. Then the full head appeared. We converged quickly as the huge animal turned away from the appalling cavalcade that he must have seen bearing down upon him. Now he was broadside, banking as he turned. He was about 35 feet long, not as big as they can get, but he looked like a nuclear sub to me. He had more passengers than a cruise ship. Two big cobia swam under him, shar-ing his bottom side with a plethora of remoras. I swam parallel to his head and saw three small, striped pilot fish swimming just an inch in front of his mouth. They obviously didn't know the meaning of fear. His eye was amaz-ingly small. It obscured any clue to an intelligence or response that might be behind it. His skin – more like a hide – was ridged and wondrously marked with white polka dots, like an enormous harlequin.

All this while our group was swimming like mad to keep up with him, and several found a free ride irresistible. They climbed aboard. His dorsal fin provided an easy purchase, as did the leading edge of his head just above his mouth. I pulled away to video the whole picture: a Brobdingnagian giant festooned with Lilliputians. He didn't seem alarmed, but his patience was obvi-ously taxed. He headed down into the depths, leaving the hitch-hikers behind.

Back aboard, the laughter and exuberant chatter had hardly begun when the radio crackled again: "Whale shark astern, approximately 1,000 meters." We were still dripping when the "Go! Go! Go!" sent us over the side again. With small variations this exhausting, high adrenaline pace continued, without a stop for lunch. The purpose was, of course, to take advantage of the plane during the four hours that it was with us. By the time it had departed, we had dived 12 times with 12 whale sharks. That was the first day. Before the week was out the number would be 62.

An attitude developed that none of us would have thought possible. We were whale-sharked out.

We learned quite a bit about the behavior of whale sharks. There were some small ones. Small is, of course, relative. They were from 20 to 25 feet long, and they were shy. The big ones were far more tolerant of us. The small ones often took off for the bottom at first sight of our approach. We learned very soon that the animals accepted our presence for longer periods of time if we did not touch them. In fact, snorkelers could hover around a whale shark for hours at the surface. The cacophony of scuba bubbles, and especially the contact required for riding, sooner or later caused them to depart from our presence.

We had encounters in clear blue oceanic waters on just one day. That was splendid photography. And we discovered on a number of occasions, when some of us followed the animals down into the murky depths, that both we and the whale sharks bottomed out at about 130 feet. With our small-capacity tanks, our stays at that depth were short with the time further shortened by the hard swimming and breathing required to keep up with the animals. But when they were set against the bottom as a reference point, the great beasts appeared even more magnificent.

I wouldn't dare tell you that we became bored with whale sharks. We did, however, begin to take time to explore the marine environment around the coral heads inside the lagoon formed by the Ningaloo Reef. The lagoon afforded safe and calm anchorage for us at night. The coral heads (the Australians call them bommies) had as fine a concentration of marine life as I have ever encountered in tropical waters. At dusk one evening, when we had landed on a beach that was backed by great sand dunes, we were drawn to a sudden spate of bird activity down the beach. We arrived in time to shoo the birds away and save the lives of an army of baby turtles that had just hatched and were hot-footing it for the sea. On the last day, we explored the cavernous recesses under the great steel navy pier built by the military at Exmouth. The marine life there was so prolific that we could have spent the entire week diving there every day without exhausting the photographic options.

The Vastness of the Sea

There is a chapter in *Moby Dick* entitled "The Vastness of the Sea." In it the cabin boy, Pip, in a moment of panic jumps out of one of the whaleboats being towed at express speed by a harpooned sperm whale. The whalers called that a "Nantucket sleigh ride." The boy had jumped once before, causing the men to abort the hunt in order to turn about to pick him up. This time, to teach him a lesson, they leave him behind. Many hours pass before they return to pick him up. In that interval he goes mad. The terrible vulnerability, fragility, helplessness of that small body in that vast ocean, the horror in his imagination of what may arise from the deep, the loss of all visual contact with ship or fellow humans without the security of defined boundaries, plunged his simple mind into other dimensions from which he never returned.

At this writing I am advised by the Bridge Officer of this magnificent 748-foot ocean-going palace that there are over three miles of water under our keel. We are over the abyssal plain, just across the equator on the Rhumbline track from Honolulu to Apia, western Samoa in the South Pacific Ocean. For five days, traveling at a speed of 17 to 20 knots, the view has been of open ocean. There have been no other ships, no whales, no air trails – just the "lonely sea and the sky," as John Masefield called it.

I have never been so aware of the vastness of the sea and the need we have to carry our terrestrial shells with us when we venture forth into any of the vast oceans that dominate our planet and are, indeed, the engine that makes life possible.

Ron and Val Taylor, the ultimate children of the sea, told me that these cruises are great fun. For years they have periodically been guest speakers on parts of round-the-world cruises. I am on the beautiful old Holland America Line *SS Rotterdam*, en route to Australia and my own annual great white shark tour. Every delight and diversion for the entertainment of man is offered aboard this cholesterol express. The food is so abundant and the cuisine so superb that every meal is an invitation to disaster. There are five restaurants aboard to choose from. When we lived together as a family in the out islands of French Polynesia years ago and subsisted on rather meager rations, I used to entertain the kids with imaginative descriptions of the menu on a great luxury ocean liner. It was a game we played. It took our minds off the canned corned beef and tubers of one sort or another that were our regular diet. Now that the real thing is presented to me I dare not take advantage of it lest my arteries clog up and I drop dead at the table.

To get back to the vastness of the sea, let me recount something I did way back in the early 1950s when I was taking my boat across the Tongue of the Ocean to Nassau. I hadn't found a crewman to make the trip with me from Ft. Lauderdale to Nassau and so I was alone at the time. Sailing east you come off the banks at the northwest channel above Andros Island and quite suddenly go from a 30-foot depth to 6,000 feet of water under your keel. Tongue of the Ocean is a deep trench that separates New Providence Island from Andros. On the Nassau side its wall was the first I ever dived on, accompanied by all the fear that rides with inexperience. At the time that I am recalling and not long after, I was over the deep blue of the trench; I stopped the engines and let *Zingaro* lose her headway. There was no wind. The water was what the Bahamians called oily glass calm. Compelled by some perverse need to prove I know not what, I proceeded to do something that had lurked in the back of my mind for a long while. I put the dive ladder over the side and slipped into the water with mask and fins. I charged up my lungs and then finned straight down toward the 6,000-foot-deep bottom as far as my ability to clear my ears would let me go – that was probably no deeper than 60 feet. I was more completely alone than I had ever been in my life. The endless, margin-less blue of void enveloped me on all sides. The sense of vulnerability, apprehension, and fear was all-pervasive. As I ascended, I fixed my sight on the deep below me. My imagination pictured a huge shark or giant squid or whatever lurked in that benthic house of horrors. Of course, nothing materialized. My boat, my haven, had drifted hardly a foot. I clambered aboard with the greatest sense of relief and satisfaction that I have ever known. I had forced myself to carry out an act that was totally contrary to my most basic instincts. It was very like handling your first sea snake even though you know that others have proved it may be done safely. It was also done with the memory of what had happened to Pip.

I recall that experience now as this great ship, this relative peapod in the vastness of the sea, pushes through the ocean swells of the South

Pacific, a mere speck on the surface of a water column three miles deep. Perhaps to banish those ghosts of the past generated by an unbridled imagination, I will bury my fear of having to be carried off the boat in a cargo net and submit to the gong that announces high tea being served in the Ritz Carlton Lounge. There I will make a kamikaze attack on the pastry cart and replace my concern with the vastness of the sea with some attention to the expansion of my waist.

Stone Carver from the Sea

*A profile of a young artist
by his father.*

If his mother were not as virtuous as Caesar's wife, I might suspect that he had been sired by Michelangelo. Certainly the genes that imbued him with the spirit and compelling drive of a creative artist did not come from his father. I know, because I don't even have the eye to whittle a stick. Perhaps he got it from Poseidon, the old earth-shaker, because Gar Waterman was introduced into the sea as a child, dived and worked with me in the sea from the time he was eight, and was as surely smitten with love for the sea as were his brother and sister.

The genes were kicking around somewhere. His brother, Gordy, became a successful cameraman with an artistic-enough eye to win two Emmys. His sister designed her own children's clothes, created something she called Sea Sheets on which she drew bizarre marine creatures, and is in demand as a marine muralist. But it was Gar who fell in love with stone and taught himself to re-create in marble from all over the world the forms and rhythms that he carried with him from his diving experiences.

A secondary school in New England that he attended in his last two years of high school had an inspired art department and a superb metal-working studio that any college would envy. The school was Phillips Academy in Andover, Massachusetts. Gar's great-grandfather attended it during the Civil War.

Classic education ruled the schoolroom in those days: An art teacher would have been ridden out of town on a rail. But in the 1970s, the latent artistic talent in a young man found ample nourishment and flowered. His metal sculpture won top prize in its class.

At Dartmouth College, Gar majored in French. At that time a hobby that delighted him hardly presented itself as a viable or promising career.

At the same time – if the truth were known – he had acquired enough French when we lived in Tahiti to sail through that major discipline with all the attendant liberal arts courses. There were no academic credits for artworks created as a hobby and not within the discipline of an art course. So Gar pursued a hobby at the Dartmouth craft shop, working with wood and bronze. The hobby evolved into a compelling force that transcended all other avenues of lifework that his education might have led him into. He also started experimenting with marble. At the end of his four years at Dartmouth, he was awarded the Marcus Hieman Award for creative art, the highest award given by Dartmouth for work in that field.

Pietrasanta, Italy is the marble sculpture center of the world. The small village in the northern province of Tuscany lies in the shadow of a great mountain of white stone, the famous Carrara marble. The quarries that provided Michelangelo with the stone for his work are still operating today. Pietrasanta and its neighboring town of Carrara support hundreds of ateliers, vast commercial yards that cut the facings for buildings from massive blocks of white stone and small work yards to which all who wish to seriously work with marble must come. And they come from all over the world, rich and famous established sculptors and the young, poor, and aspiring.

Gar spent seven seasons in Pietrasanta, renting his corner of space in one of the yards, learning his trade and developing his own unique style. The struggling young artist, very limited in funds, could find pieces of the finest marble, the dross from larger works, available at reasonable cost. So he learned to work with the beautifully textured and colored marbles that make classic sculpture so sumptuous and elegant: green marble from Argentina, blue from Brazil, delicate pink from Portugal, and rich, variable shades from Turkey, Iran, and Spain. And always, of course, the pristine, snow white marble from the home quarries.

Each spring Gar returned to the States, his rough work following in huge crates by ocean freight. In a shed in Peter Benchley's backyard and under a shelter by the sea where we go in the summer, Gar finished his works – long, tedious, infinitely patient handwork with abrasives and water, for which there is no substitute. After his seven-year apprenticeship in Italy, he came home to establish his own studio in New England. He brought with him enough raw stone to work into his lovely sea forms and fluid, graceful designs for several years.

He has had a number of fine commissions, enough to keep his head above water. But that fickle strumpet, fame, and with it a following and coterie of patrons is still over the horizon. It may never come. The odds against great success for young artists, no matter how fine their work, are discouraging, even in more encouraging economic times. I have learned from my son that a true artist lives to create, to shape with his hands what he sees with his inner eye. It is truly more important to feed his soul than to fatten his purse. Other people's thoughts are irrelevant. His own certainty of taste and true creative form is unassailable to him. That may not be a practical market philosophy and the corporeal body may subsist on a lean diet at times, but the spirit is richly fed. W. Somerset Maugham wrote in his biographical novel about Gauguin, *The Moon and Sixpence,* "Beauty is something wonderful and strange that an artist fashions out of the chaos of the world in the torment of his soul. And when he has made it, it is not given to all to know it. To recognize it you must repeat the adventure of the artist. It is a melody that he sings to you."

For Gar, the melody in his work most often has in it the timeless, restless rhythm, grace, and power of the sea.

The Lost Treasure of the Incas

In *The Wind in the Willows* Kenneth Graham wrote: "…when the cup has been drained and the play has been played, sit down by your quiet river with a store of goodly memories for company." Well, I hope to drain the cup of many more rum punches and roll off the duckboard for play in the oceans of the Lord before I hang up my fins. However, the storehouse of memories has been building for some years, and some are already fun to pull off the shelf.

To reach Isla Isabela you fly to Mazatlan, halfway down the long western coast of Mexico and opposite the tip of the Baja Peninsula across the Sea of Cortez. You may continue by boat, south along the coast for 180 miles on a course that will intersect with a tiny island 50 miles off the coast. How did I ever hit upon such an insignificant fly-speck on the map of the eastern Pacific? Way back in the primal age of skin diving, when *Skin Diver* magazine was dominated by trophy pictures of the hunt, the great sea bass and jewfish appeared on almost every other page, strung up on scaffolds like giant sausages. The proud hunters garnished the displays with their bent spears. Four or five of these behemoths, weighing anywhere from 250 to 600 pounds each, had been taken in one hunt off Isla Isabela. Looking back, that scene and the others like it that were so popular then seem wanton and grotesque now. However, most of us thought the whole business of big game hunting was wonderfully macho.

That picture came to mind some years later in 1967 when Peter Gimbel and I were location hunting for *Blue Water, White Death*. I reasoned that big fish probably meant big sharks and set out for Isla Isabela. Peter headed for South Africa, which proved more fruitful for our plans.

I invited my friend Al Giddings to join me. He was 100 percent up for the adventure. He had plenty of experience with Mexican travel and Sea of Cortez diving and so worked out the logistics. He was also my choice for a diving buddy in unknown waters with big animals. Al was built like a Mack truck, intelligently fearless, and one of the most experienced divers in California. How could I go wrong?

I cannot recall when or how the notion was seeded into my easily fevered mind that the legendary Lost Treasure of the Incas was said to lie at the bottom of a volcanic lake on the very island that was our destination. It may well have come from the captain of the boat we had hired. Although he was as furtive and raffish as the late Leo Carrillo, and his eyes failed to meet the listener's directly at any time, this listener trusted him implicitly. I passed this stunning intelligence onto Al. For an answer, he rolled his eyeballs and whistled, leaving me to interpret his answer however I might.

It was an overnight run to the island which rose out of the dawn horizon like the crown of a derby. At a distance, what looked like fleas around a dog's head enlarged into boobies and other sea birds as we approached the island. A volcanic crater dominated the scene and composed at least 85 percent of the island's surface. At the southeastern side, a sand spit and crescent beach formed a skirt at the base of the steeply rising cone.

With heroic restraint I put off retrieving the treasure from the crater lake and attended to the business of diving around the island and looking for big sharks. The result of this reconnaissance was decidedly negative. A massive plankton bloom had reduced visibility to about ten feet. In the gloom, some massive forms were more a felt presence than visible objects. Neither Al nor I was enthusiastic about encountering a shark of any size or species under those conditions. We agreed that treasure hunting was far more appealing and the order of the day.

We landed on the beach and were warmly greeted by a small company of Mexican fishermen. They had established a camp of ramshackle shelters at the top of the beach. It was manifestly apparent that they were shark fishermen. The objects of their industry were gutted, split, and drying on the beach below the camp. As we advanced through this field of corpses, billions of flies rose in black clouds, adding an audio impact to the stench. We worked through this nauseating force field and started up the side of the cone, lugging our scuba gear with us. Stunted, warped trees, hardly higher than bushes, bordered the rough path to the rim. Our ascent disturbed several hundred sea birds that were roosting in the trees. They rose reluctantly with a cacophony of squawks only when we were immediately upon them. Obviously they were unused to human disturbance. I thought, in fact, that such intrusion had probably not occurred since Inca slaves schlepped the massive chests of gold and jewels up that very slope.

The view from the top was spectacular. The crater, about 50 yards across, was filled almost to the rim with water. And the water was a stunning opalescent green. In the noon-day sun it shone like dull emerald: a flawless green bowl, a perfect repository for the treasure of a nation. Some of our crew and a gaggle of fishermen had followed us. Now they watched with expressions of fear and doubt as Al and I first waded out into the water.

That first advance was not encouraging. We sank up to our knees in glutinous muck, extracting our feet with horrible sucking sounds and releasing a stench that reminded me of my experiments with my first kid's chemistry set. We agreed that it might be prudent to leave our tanks behind at first and work our way out over the shallows with no more weight than mask, fins, and snorkel. That way we were quickly waterborne and past the clutching muck.

We finned out to the approximate middle of the lake. I glanced back at our company on the shore. Two of the fishermen were crossing themselves. All seemed mute with apprehension. Obviously the audacity of our adventure filled them with fear. I was not encouraged by the fact that we could see nothing below us as we snorkeled out. Al announced, "I'm going down to see what's there," and started deep breathing to prime himself for the dive. For some reason I was more than willing to have him make the first dive. He disappeared into the green gloom. Facedown and staring at that impenetrable wall, I awaited his return. A full minute, even though most divers think they can easily hold their breath that long, seems like an eternity when you're watching and waiting. Al, who was a prodigious breath-hold diver, stayed down about 90 seconds. He reappeared, rising out of the water like a Polaris missile and shouting with his expelled breath, "Wow! You won't believe it!"

"What? What was it?" I found myself shouting, even though we were close enough to touch. "What did you see?"

He regained his breath and, rolling his eyes heavenward for divine confirmation, continued, "I went down about 20 feet and hit a thermal layer. That first part has zero visibility; but when you pass through that layer it opens up to – I don't know – maybe 100-foot visibility. And what's down there is…well, you've got to see for yourself. You won't believe it."

I awaited no further explanation. Before he had finished that teaser, I was hyperventilating, upended, and started down. He spoke the truth – the visibility was zero. I pushed on, keen for the opening vista. Strangely the water became darker and darker, and very suddenly all light vanished. Yet I found myself still descending, my progress increasingly slowed by some invisible force. At some point, I suppose, I realized that I had not just reached the bottom. I was IN the bottom, and I had pretty damn well better get out of there. It took some doing to break free of that viscous mass. To say the least, I was much relieved when I could at least see a vague cast of light and so find my way out of whatever I was in. On the way up I think I had already guessed the composition of that bottom and knew that my good old friend Al knew it too. His uncontrolled and despicable behavior when I reached the surface confirmed it. He was laughing so hard that he almost did himself in by drowning right there. I had penetrated the upper layers of perhaps a thousand years of bird shit. It was so outrageous that I had to laugh myself. At least, I had far less hair to wash it out of than Al. There was no more talk of treasure.

My travails were not over. On our way down we passed through the fishermen's camp. They were preparing their evening meal. Tortillas were being cooked on the top of a gas drum that had been turned into a stove. The shell of a turtle, freshly caught, served as a trencher. Gurry still clung to the inside of the shell in which they were stirring the potent mélange that would fill the tortillas. Peppers, fish scraps, herbs, and some other unidentifiable (and unmentionable) ingredients could be seen floating in this cauldron of Kickapoo Joy Juice. With the generous hospitality that I have found in fishermen all over the world, they invited us to share their meal. I felt it would be discourteous to refuse and replied, "*Si.*" That and *gracias* were the extent of my Spanish. Al hissed in my ear, "Don't do it."

"But Al, think of this as hands across the border – good fellowship. It's all they have, and they want to share their humble meal with us. Think of it as diplomacy."

He repeated himself, "Don't do it."

NAFTA was still years away. I considered this a major détente and besides, I was hungry. So I stepped in where angels fear to tread and made a great show of lip-smacking and savoring the appalling gastronomic bomb they handed me. To my surprise it was entirely palatable. I accepted another. Al couldn't watch. Perhaps it was all worth it for the smiles and good will the very act of acceptance engendered. Then again, the price was quite horrible. Less than a half hour away from the island and on our way home, a thermonuclear explosion went off in my gut. All my orifices erupted. Al redeemed himself. Not only did he not laugh, he had a goodly supply of Lomotil, which I popped like a suicide pops sleeping pills.

My memory bank has brought forth the experience with bats in Ceylon, bird poop at Isla Isabela, and my own unrestrained effluvia in the aftermath of the lethal tortillas. With that I am finished with my murky recollections and promise to go on to broad sunlit uplands of diving experiences in the next round. Did I ever tell you about the time I dynamited a giant jewfish out of his cave? I'll bet you can hardly wait.

Neither Friend Nor Monster

Over the ages the human attitude toward nature has swung like a pendulum from contempt to respect to familiarity. In the same way, our approach to the shark has seesawed from an age-old fear mingled with contempt for this legendary monster to a time of respect and now to familiarity. Perhaps we have gone too far in this last direction. There have been shark-related accidents and there will be more. I believe it's time to pull back and reestablish an attitude of greater respect.

We have come a very long way from the 1950s when the availability of the Aqualung started a diving revolution. At that time of diving's infancy, experience with sharks in their environment was still very limited. Curiosity was still tempered by fear. Sharks were the enemy, a palpable threat. A Florida diver with the ironic name Scott Slaughter achieved Rambo-like notoriety by actually hunting sharks with a device he himself had developed, the bang stick. His success in single "combat" with these monsters was viewed as heroic. I myself went forth to my filming in tropical waters with a bang stick. The shark dart was developed and much favored by divers anticipating gladiatorial combat. I subscribed to several types and favored the Shark Dart, which was attached to your weight belt in a sheath. These darts were stainless steel stilettos, hollow like a hypodermic needle and just as sharp at the point. In the handle was a CO_2 cartridge. The diver, armed with this equalizer, anticipated dodging the attack of the shark and, as it blundered by, sticking it in the belly with a deft upthrust. On impact, the CO_2 would be released into the belly of the slavering brute, who would then expand like a Zeppelin and blow to the surface. I anticipated my own daring part in this scenario with great relish.

As recently as the late 1960s, when we were shooting *Blue Water, White Death*, we all carried bang sticks when we were working around sharks. That was, of course, a benchmark experience with sharks in open ocean. Valerie Taylor, who is today one of the world's leading proponents of shark conservation, was prompted to destroy one of the oceanic whitetip sharks we were working with off South Africa. These sharks never threatened us, but the act of destroying one with the bang stick was considered good action for the film.

Ultimately, bang sticks came to be recognized as a greater threat to the divers than to the sharks. Manufacturers rightly feared liability suits, and the deadly tools disappeared from the market. As growing numbers of divers returned from their tours with pictures of sharks and tales of shark encounters with which to titillate their neighbors and office colleagues, the desire to see a shark underwater and, even better, to return with a picture or a video sequence of this age-old predator began to dominate the attitude of a majority of divers. Remember, we divers are, in the opinion of the public, a small cadre of adventurers. Surviving a mad killer on the Long Island Railroad doesn't hold a candle to photographic proof of your holding the thin red line when confronting a shark. And so we arrive at the current vogue for hand-feeding sharks. It was as inevitable as trainers putting their heads into the mouths of killer whales to astound the audiences at ocean aquaria. As the competition for the diving dollar became increasingly intense, dive operators outdid one another in novel feats of daring with sharks. It was discovered long ago that sharks very quickly responded to being fed in any location that was once established. Like Pavlov's dogs, they would respond to the sound of a boat's approach and the anchor going down and be there at the dinner table, napkins tucked in, when the divers descended. And certainly the feeding was dramatic.

One of the first to develop this exercise as a routine was the dive resort of Stella Maris in the Bahamas. Peter Benchley, Sylvia Earle, and I went there in the early 1980s. Ten or 12 bull sharks came in on cue and were fed with fish offered to them at the end of a spear. I recall there was a long wait for them to overcome their own shyness and fear before one and then another would take the baits. It was great grist for the camera mill and continues to be. Recently, in the production of *The Man Who Loves Sharks* for the Discovery Channel, Howard Hall and I catalyzed the best of the shark action by setting up feeding exercises (one of which got out of control and scared us both). In a tour that I host to Truk Lagoon, a routine shark-feeding performance has now been added to the wreck diving. Until very recently the wrecks themselves were enough for a fabulous Truk Lagoon experience.

There are literally scores of such activities led by dive guides for their guests in tropical waters around the world today. In the Maldive Islands a dive operator started feeding the gray reef sharks at the edge of a pass. His confidence in in the behavior of the sharks progressed to feeding them with a fish held in his mouth. Even his beautiful daughter was pressed into the act and ultimately was encouraged by his Scandinavian clientele to do her feeding performance topless. As far as I know, the father has not lost his nose and the daughter still has both breasts. Other shark feeders are more prudent and now wear chainmail suits. However, these are not fool proof against injury. Some time not long ago, Valerie Taylor was doing a hand-feed exercise for her husband's camera when a large silvertip shark briefly took her head in its mouth and managed to deposit some of its teeth in her neck where the chain mail hood didn't quite meet with the suit.

And this brings me to my final thought. The shark-feeding syndrome has such broad currency these days that I fear the activity has engendered a too-casual attitude toward the shark. Divers who started with a healthy fear (let's call it a healthy respect) of the animal are wooed by its grace and control and its apparent shyness in the presence of humans.

Despite the common opinion that sharks are unpredictable, they have proven very predictable. Their behavior within the shark-feeding exercise is steady and under control. However, the margin of safety is very thin indeed. One small mistake in the conduct or appearance of the human element in this banquet can be the catalyst for a sudden, nightmarish accident.

There have already been accidents, and there will be more. The electrician working with 220 volts hundreds of times need only make one mistake. Human beings are fallible. The shark's response to instinct is constant and immutable.

A classic example of this was communicated to me recently. Last September I was with Bob and Dinah Halstead on their New Guinea dive boat, *Telita*. They are among the most experienced and intelligent dive guides you will find today. They initiated a shark-feeding program with silvertips, an addition to their repertoire of dive activities which became very popular. In time they advanced their intimacy with the sharks by letting the sharks take the baits directly from their hands. This might very well have continued without accident indefinitely. Dinah then made a mistake which only became apparent after the fact. She bound white reinforcing tape around both knees of her wetsuit to protect her knees from contact with the coral. In a routine exhibit, with ten guests watching and photographing, she was hand-holding the baitfish when one of the silvertips closing in for the feed made its move, its attention caught by the flash of white from the knees. Its jaws closed on her bent leg. The lower jaw cut into the calf, the upper jaw into the thigh. It released and turned around for another attack, taking less than three seconds to do so. Dinah's own defense reflex may have saved her life or limb. She thrust her Nikonos camera into the wide-open mouth of the shark. That action deflected its attack. It turned away again, spitting out the camera. The entire action spanned less than eight seconds, (this will be very sobering to many divers who have watched the leisurely movements of sharks when they are cruising about). Bob Halstead and another diver were close by and formed a protective cordon for Dinah as they escorted her to the surface. One of the guests, Eric Wittenburg, was rolling his Sony Hi-8 and so documented the attack, a rare bit of footage indeed. Dinah came through with two prominent scars on her leg, but was otherwise unscathed. She was very lucky, and she knows it.

In hindsight, Dinah knew exactly what had happened, and she spoke with me about it. There was no rancor in her reflection. She and Valerie are both far too intelligent to attribute anthropomorphic malevolence to sharks. I share with them the awareness that the onus is on us, the humans making excursions into the sharks' environment, to look after ourselves. The sister ship of the *Telita*, the *Tiata*, now works the northern part of New Guinea and continues the silvertip feeding. However, the captain, Kevin Baldwin, has prudently discontinued the hand-feeding. The baits are placed at a distance and the guests watch and photograph from a safe margin. When I attended that performance, the big silvertips were handsome, graceful, and exciting. They very well knew the difference between the baits and the observers.

The point I wish to make is that these fascinating animals are neither monsters nor friends. Their instinct is to feed. They are generally wary of humans. Even the great white, the "big boy," is wary when the human diver is not associated with food or mistaken for food (e.g., the white knee patches on Dinah and the generous feeding activity going on around Valerie with too many sharks to keep track of). Most of the shark-feeding performances are safe, with the odds strongly in favor of the divers involved. While these activities have done much to dispel the age-old fears, they have led to complacency and carelessness, which is the flipside of respect and regard for potential danger.

The shark's instincts were shaped over 300 million years ago. Its course is clearly programmed. Our instincts, on the other hand, are both young and easily eroded by familiarity. Let us use our intelligence to sustain a prudent, careful relationship with the shark.

Encounter with a Dragon

Once while diving in New Guinea, I had a real encounter with an honest, full-blown, scaly, and horrible-to-see dragon. The circumstances have made it very possibly a once-in-a-lifetime experience.

I was diving with Bob and Dinah Halstead and a dive tour group on their famous boat, the *Telita*. In the late afternoon, that time of golden, weakening sun and evening calm, we were almost at our anchorage for the night, close by a village on one of a cluster of small islands off the southeastern tip of Papua New Guinea in what is called the Milne Bay area. Bob was the first to see the great beast. He was checking the shore from the starboard door of the wheelhouse when he saw what appeared to be a log, floating motionless just 20 yards off the beach that adjoined the village. Bob could scarce believe his eyes, and I soon learned why. "It's a crocodile!" he yelled. "A saltwater crocodile, and he's after that dog on the beach!" The *Telita's* deck and wheelhouse are quite high off the water. We all stampeded to the starboard side for a look at the creature – any creature – that would provoke such a reaction of high-voltage alarm and excitement from such a seasoned skipper and diver as Bob. From the distance between us it still looked like a log. Then I recalled the documentary on the giant African crocodiles I had seen. They, too, floated like logs, watching their prey with only the two brow elevations of their eyes above water. Bob explained his excitement. "In all the years I have been diving I have never seen a croc like that in clear water. This is a rare chance to get some pictures." He turned to me. "Are you game?" The eyes of the guests, taking all this in, shifted from the distant croc to the "living legend" just addressed by Bob. This was the man who Peter Benchley had once said (facetiously, to be sure) "did not know the meaning of fear." It was already too late for me to slip away to my cabin and hide under the bunk. I heard myself responding – as if from another planet – "You bet! Let's go."

Now the road to disaster has often been paved by the fatal triumph of pride or fear of others' opinion over sane judgment. As I was swept along toward the abyss by willing hands, I recalled that all I knew about salt-water crocodiles was that they ate more people every year than great white sharks and Fiji cannibals combined. Furthermore, I had the notion that they might never have been filmed in clear water, probably because no one in his right mind would attempt it.

Meanwhile, Bob and I were in the water with with two still cameras and me pushing my video housing well ahead of me like a battering ram. And then there wasn't any more time to think. All senses strained for the first visual contact. We frequently surfaced to check with the people on the boat and be guided by their arm-waving directions. They had assembled on the top deck of the *Telita*, enthusiastically cheering us on like Roman spectators at gladiatorial games. We had no time to appreciate their warm support.

And then he was there, just a dark line at the limit of visibility, assuming sharp definition as we closed the distance. That first visual contact was as exciting as my first encounter with a great white shark almost 25 years ago. I started rolling my Hi-8 tape, watching the animal grow until he filled the frame of the viewfinder. At the same time I kept one eye on the open field, alert to his first reaction to our presence. I say "he," but in fact we had no way to determine the sex of the beast; and it hardly mattered. This animal, from seven to eight feet long, was all armored scale, powerfully muscled and badder than old King Kong. Oh, he knew we were there. Our bubbles seemed to us to thunder louder than ever, advertising our presence as flagrantly as an elephant in a flock of sheep. His only motion was to let his head sink just enough so that his eye was below the surface. The movement was almost imperceptible, no more than an inch either way. Of major significance to me was the fact that he didn't show any immediate inclination to eat us. I was conscious of the click and whine of Bob's motor drive and so was assured that he was right next to me. Should the beast attack, I would have at least a 50-50 chance of escape and even to come away with a sensational sequence of a celebrated diver being carried away in the jaws of a monster.

I let myself drift closer, hoping to fill the wide-angle frame with just the head of the croc. The sense of protection and of brashness that one has when a camera is between you and a dangerous marine animal is completely irrational, especially when the camera and housing aren't even as big as a catcher's mitt. You may also lose your sense of distance. I did. The animal slowly turned so that it was facing open water instead of the beach, and in so doing its tail brushed the dome port of my housing. Had he turned the other way, his nose would have collided with the camera. As it turned out, the video view of his armored tail going by at macro range is enough to make St. George run in the other direction.

At this point his baleful, yellow eye remained underwater – watchful, waiting. His powerful webbed feet hung limp, and his massive jaws parted slightly. The teeth are formidable – brown, conical, and larger in proportion to the jaw than a whale's or a dolphin's. When the jaws are entirely shut, some of the teeth are still visible. There is nothing pleasant about this animal. He abided our strange presence for perhaps another half minute.

Then, I suppose, some primitive instinct was generated in that primordial, predatory brain that prompted him to give way to two strange animals almost as large as he was. With a lashing motion of his tail and without apparent use of his feet – very much like a giant polliwog – he disappeared into the haze of the deep water. I kept shooting for a moment after he was well out of sight, caught up with the momentum of the splendid encounter. I turned to look at Bob. He was checking the settings of both cameras, no doubt with that sense of dread we all know that we may have blown the big one. For action like that there is only one take. There is no rehearsal. Obviously, his settings were right. He made the V sign and danced as much of a jig as one may jig under water.

My full satisfaction at having nailed the scene came with the gratifying alacrity that accompanies video shooting. I was still dripping when I pulled the Sony TR-101 out of the Amphibico housing. Ah! Dry! Next, I plugged into the monitor, fumbling with my own measure of dread and anticipation for the look-see. The boat's peanut gallery crowded in behind. And there he was, in all of his monstrous, horrible, wonderful form.

Aside from achieving that unique footage, there was the satisfying sense for both Bob and me of having put ourselves in harm's way and come off clean. It is something of a rush. We agreed that we would likely draw back from approaching a 20-foot saltwater croc in the same manner again. We thought that strange animals like ourselves, almost as big as the predator, would not trigger the instinct to attack in him. But we really didn't know, and that's what made the experience so exciting.

I'm reminded of something Winston Churchill said as he reminisced about his experiences in the Boer War: "Nothing in life is so exhilarating as to be shot at without result."

Sharks: A Three-Part Odyssey

The dive boat was loaded to capacity. Laughter, good-natured chaffing, and bad jokes highlighted the holiday spirit of this typical group of divers. Norine Rouse and I were the old timers. We were both in our seventies. It is possible that we were the only guests among the 20 that morning who had had any experience with sharks.

I. WALKER'S CAY

If there was any nervousness among the others, it might have been detected by the over-frequent testing of their purge buttons as they displayed their expertise in preparing their equipment. There is something satisfyingly macho about the bold metallic sound of the regulator attaching to the tank stem. Conversely, there is something humiliating about doing it wrong. Thirty-odd years ago I already bore a reputation as a veteran diver and was even considered a fish of some achievement in the small pool that was underwater film-making. I was on location with Howard Hall and Marty Snyderman. They are both Hall of Famers today. They were then youngsters out of that womb of diving giants, the San Diego Diving Locker. They watched me put my regulator on backwards and later get ready to jump in without my fins. Far from suspecting that I was senile before my time or brain-damaged from an ill-spent infancy, they humbly thought I had brought with me from the east coast advanced technologies not yet arrived in California.

This morning I finally got it right. We were heading out of the marina at Walker's Cay. This small island at the top of the Abaco chain is the northern-most island in the Bahamas. It is a world-class sport fishing resort. The marina's slips were filled with probably 50-million-dollars-worth of high-tech, high-towered, high-polished big game sport fishing boats. They bristled with a porcupine carapace of fishing rods. One sport fisherman had 12 rods displayed, all mounted in their sockets on the aft edge of the flying bridge and surrounding a fighting chair big enough for the King of Tonga. I was impressed.

Walker's Cay is a fairly late comer in the ranks of unique, very special dive centers. It has always had fine diving. Almost 40 years ago, when I had my own dive boat, I spent some days at Walker's Cay. I depended on my own compressor and tanks. Those days we were into spearfishing as well as movie making. I will never forget my time there, because it was in the reefs north of the Cay that I sustained one of the few outright shark attacks in all the years I have worked with sharks. Now, as we pulled away from the dock, I recalled that time. Elgin Ciampi and I were working together. We were mustard-keen to film sharks. They were hard to come by and rarely filmed back then. They represented the epitome of danger and daring for a diver and were "hot stuff" for a filmmaker. For that matter, they still are. But then, mystery and fear dominated the attitude toward sharks. Shark-infested waters, man-eaters, blood-thirsty predators and implacable enemy of divers and swimmers who ventured into their domain – those were the thoughts associated with sharks.

The attack was classic. Elgin Ciampi had the camera. I set up a spearfishing scent. I loved spearfishing. We all did. We were breath-hold divers and usually used Hawaiian slings, simple tube-like cylinders with surgical rubber tubing that you stretched back to fire a steel spear shaft slingshot fashion. That morning I was using an Arbelete, a speargun with twin rubbers and a line attached to the spear. It was fired with a trigger. I nailed a fine, fat hogfish in about 30 feet of water and started up for air. The hogfish on the spear trailed behind. I was watching the seaward side of the reef and saw the shark coming toward me at flank speed. It was a small tiger shark, easily identified by his broad head and tiger stripes. By small I mean about six feet (tigers can grow to more than 20 feet). He was on me before I reached the surface, paused a fraction of a second at my legs, and turned slightly to accommodate the bite. I yanked up my legs and thrust at his head with the stock of the speargun. He simultaneously seized the gun in his mouth and savaged the metal shaft. That was not to his liking, obviously. He turned and swam away as rapidly as he had approached. When he returned – if he did – I was no longer there. I had done a Jesus-on-the-waters retreat to the dinghy and scrambled in, colliding with Gene doing the same thing.

I call it a classic attack. The shark had been in the vicinity all the time. The wounded fish was the dinner bell. The spearfisherman was the first object that came into view associated with the wounded fish. Spearfishing would be the catalyst for many attacks in tropical waters, adding to the evil reputation of the shark.

I had been actually listening for the sound of the camera as the attack occurred and instinctively knew that Gene had not caught the action. The same thing happens to hunters. Had I been watching that drama, I might very well have seized up, too. But it would have been a wild and wonderful action shot.

Gary Adkinson put Walker's Cay diving on the map and today directs the diving activity there. He developed the totally extraordinary shark feeding activity that now attracts countless divers a year. Twenty minutes from the dock we reached a sand arena half the size of a football field and 40 feet deep. It was bordered by massive coral formations. On arrival, the boat did several turns about the area, noisily revving its engines. This was, Gary explained to me, the shark version of Pavlov's famous dinner bell.

Gary briefed the guests, instructing them to form a half circle on the bottom and not be alarmed if a few sharks appeared. When they were settled on the bottom and the adrenaline was flowing freely, Gary, watching from the surface, positioned the boat and gave the signal for the lowering of the bait. Now I have attended many small shark feeding exercises over the years, but they always involved a small clutch of dead fish strung together. I had never seen anything like the form in which the bait was prepared for the Walker's Cay event. At the marina there is a special cleaning house where the game fish that are brought in daily by the sport fishermen are gutted and cleaned. The offal is accumulated in a drum that holds about 100 pounds. It is then taken to the freezing locker next door; a reinforcing rod with an eye at the top and bottom is inserted into the mass which then freezes around it. This frozen mass of guts and heads and trimmings formed the bait ball that was lowered over the side at the center of the half circle of guests. A weight anchored it to the bottom. A buoy suspended it eight feet off the bottom.

I dropped over with the bait and watched from the surface as the dinner guests arrived. Picture a crowd making their way from the parking lot to the stadium for a big game. I had been told what to expect. I was still so rattled by what I saw that I almost forgot to shoot. The blacktip reef sharks, well-formed, robust five-to-six-footers, were already arriving for the feast – not in pairs; not in tens. They came from all directions by the scores, the number rapidly exceeding a hundred. They passed between and around the guests, paying no attention to them. The divers paid plenty of attention to the sharks, their heads swiveling like compass needles in a storm. There was no feeding frenzy other than that by the ill-mannered yellowtails and the rowdy jacks, who set upon the feast with no attempt at grace.

The sharks took their time. One or two at a time pushed through the small fry to tear off a piece. The excitement and the pace picked up when one or more sharks contested the mouthful being carried off by the banqueter. It reminded me much of seagulls harrying one another in mid-air. The gourmand, with the offal hanging from the corner of his mouth, could finally be seen retreating toward the surface, trailed by a gaggle of scrap-seeking jacks.

As far as the divers were concerned, with familiarity came imprudence if not contempt. Gary had directed that the divers should keep their distance from the bait mass. Within minutes, most had succumbed to photography frenzy. I had a field day, almost colliding with the animals head-on as they ripped off their portions with violently shaking heads. I could see Norine in her version of Seventh Heaven.

Before the bait was dispersed, about 150 sharks, 98 percent being black-tip reef sharks, were on the scene. Nurse sharks made up the rest. Gary told me that very occasionally tiger sharks and a single hammerhead have shown up but have scorned the bait. At those rare times, the smaller sharks departed the arena until the big boys were gone. During the summer months, over 200 sharks make the scene at times.

You can imagine the chatter on the boat after the dive. And for once, there could hardly be any hyperbole in the recounting of their experiences when the divers returned to their home towns and offices. There have been no accidents. The experience is repeated several times a week, weather permitting, as routinely as a ride at Disneyland. The dreaded nemesis of my first days of diving has become the popular attraction for legions of divers today.

II. Grand Bahama

Cruising southeast from Walker's Cay over the shallow sand plateau called the Grand Bahama Bank, we reached the island of Grand Bahama at the edge of the Gulf Stream. Freeport was created in the 1950s as a duty-free trade center. From that beginning, a thriving tourist industry has evolved. The skyline, as we entered the channel, is now one of high-rise luxury hotels. Marinas, luxury bistros, oases for all ranges of purses, gift shops, and a veritable gill net of tourist lures form a gauntlet for any advance from the docks to the quiet streets beyond. At one end of the crowded marina, a formidable fleet of dive boats nestles at its own finger piers. Overlooking this small armada are the buildings of UNEXSO, the Underwater Explorers Society, one of the oldest and most prestigious sport diving organizations in the western hemisphere.

Chris Allison has the stature and cultivated address of a Shakespearian actor. Tall and elegant with a touch of gray in his well-trimmed mustache, he is superbly articulate. He is the manager of UNEXSO's large operation and equal to the prestige of the organization. His welcome was without restraint. All facets of UNEXSO's varied dive activities were open to us. They included the special shark-feeding developed by Ben Rose.

Ben has been with UNEXSO since its beginning. The remarkable rapport that characterizes his association with the sharks he feeds has emerged from the thousands of hours he has spent over the years working with them. He has extended the parameters of intimacy far beyond the range one might imagine possible for man and the apex predator in the sea.

The site for Ben's shark feeding is about a half hour away from the UNEXSO dock. It is a beautiful sand area 30 feet deep, an arena that is punctuated by coral heads with handsome forests of gorgonians. At the edge of the arena is a decompression chamber, dumped there some years back to mark the site and to provide a protective barrier against which the dive guests can array themselves to watch the show. On the way out, Ben dons the chain mail suit that will cover him from head to toe like a medieval warrior. An assistant, who will watch over the guests, is similarly shark-proofed. In the classroom briefing that precedes every dive, Ben explains that the only people hurt in this activity over the years have, very occasionally, been the people feeding the sharks. And on those very rare occasions, it has always been an untoward movement by the feeder that has been the catalyst to the accident. He does not use the word attack.

The shark suit weighs 14 pounds. Ben wears double tanks plus weights and so is well anchored to the bottom some 15 feet from the line of guests. The bait of whole mackerel is in a three-foot-long black tube with a diaphragm opening. Ben accesses the baits by thrusting his hand into the tube and can hold the bait out of sight until he is ready to bring it out and pass it to his choice of shark.

As at Walker's Cay, the arrival of the boat has become the dinner bell for the sharks. They are ready and waiting, along with a number of amber-jacks, large groupers and the usual gaggle of hungry yellowtails. The sharks are bigger than the average ones at Walker's Cay. They are referred to as Caribbean reef sharks, most being about five to six feet in length. Set off among them are some distinctly larger ones, seven- to eight-feet-long with well-rounded, robust bodies. The entire assembly moved in an ordered and leisurely traffic circle around Ben, all in the same direction. The larger sharks formed the inner part of the circle. The groupers, jacks, and others formed the perimeter. Ben let them circle for some while without any feeding activity. The order and patience that created the pace never changed. Perhaps a touch of impatience might have vibrated through the watching guests as we waited for the feeding to start. Then it happened. If you weren't watching carefully, you might not have seen the start of the most amazing man/animal relationship any of us had ever witnessed. I was watching closely and shooting only a few feet away from Ben. As one of the big sharks swung by in his circular pattern, Ben very gently took the great head in his hands and steered the nose into contact with his own midriff. The eight-foot, robust animal remained motionless as Ben gently massaged its head. His hands moved over the gills and eyes and closed mouth with wonderfully gentle finesse. If the shark could have purred, it would have. The nictitating membrane covered its eyes like a nap-time shade. I thought it one of the most beautiful sights I had ever been privileged to witness. The two remained together, an enchanted tableau, for about 30 seconds. I held my breath and at one point had to look around my eyepiece to confirm what I was seeing through the lens. Then with a gentle shrug, the shark broke away and joined the circle pattern again.

The feeding was simply done with no apparent pattern of choice. At varied times Ben would extract a fish from the tube and hold it out to a passing shark. There seemed to be no favorites, although the younger ones had most of the handouts. The older, larger sharks were always the ones chosen for the massage. All accepted it with obvious pleasure. Only once was there a break in the orderly pattern. As Ben commenced the massage with one of his regulars, a somewhat younger shark shoved into the midriff position, nudging the first one out. Ben accommodated the second one without chastising him for his behavior.

We made two dives with Ben during our time there. Our fascination with the spectacle never diminished. In my mind's eye, for all my remaining years, one of the most beautiful, magical images will be that of Ben communicating with the great shark through his fingers and his gentle touch. I do not really expect to ever again encounter such a level of rapport between a man and an animal that is not credited with any understanding related to intelligence.

III. NEW PROVIDENCE

The final leg of the Bahamian shark-feeding triptych took us south by southeast to New Providence Island. We followed the Berry Islands southward to their very tip, where we found snug harbor for the night. The next morning we made the two-and-a-half-hour crossing of the Tongue of the

Ocean, that abyssal trench that cuts like the Grand Canyon between Nassau and Andros, and then reached the western end of Nassau, Lyford Cay, by lunchtime on that same day.

Just around the corner from Lyford Cay at the southwestern end of Nassau is a neat little dock area carved out of the limestone collar that rings the island. The entry to it was created by cutting a passage through the coral. There is a well-constructed dock with a compound of buildings that composes the Stuart Cove West Island Dive activity. We were expected. Stuart Cove, a deeply tanned, athletically trim young man greeted us. His hair was bleached full blond by the sun, and his smile was ready and warm. This was Stuart Cove. We felt welcome. Once again all facilities were open to us.

Our own dock lines were barely secured before we transferred to one of Stuart's dive boats and headed out the cut for his own shark arena. His wife, Michelle, accompanied us. A lithe, beautiful young lady with long hair and a smile that could launch a thousand ships, she was much into the shark-feeding process and already a central part of the action. Stuart has developed a shark experience that is in three parts, two of which are entirely unique. Under his watchful eye, Michelle fed a gaggle of Caribbean reef sharks much as Ben had. She wore chain mail protection on her hands and arms and offered the baits on the end of a short spear to the circling sharks. The sharks, some in excess of six feet, circled in the same orderly manner we had seen before. A persistent nurse shark provided comic relief by repeatedly trying to stick his nose into the bait box. He finally succeeded: upsetting the bait box, throwing the ordered feeding routine into chaos and escaping with a fat mackerel in his mouth. Michelle and Stuart have not yet developed the massage technique that highlighted Ben's performance, but – as I will describe shortly – they have achieved a control of other open-water sharks that is even more spectacular.

One of the two unique encounters that is now routine for the Coves takes place at the edge of the Tongue of the Ocean. The guests are invited to an open-water encounter with the sharks. The boat anchors near the edge of the 40-foot-deep reef where it drops off into the abyss. The drop is a sheer cliff face. The view is of oceanic blue, straight out and straight down. The surface fractures the light so that long rays, shifting and undulating, reach into the depths. It is all somewhat unnerving, even for experienced divers. The diver feels naked, stripped of all security, and unpleasantly vulnerable when he (or she), with just a few strokes of the fins, swims away from the edge and out over the six-mile-deep chasm. And the sharks are waiting there for the divers. They, too, respond to the arrival of the boat and have long since associated it with food. The feeding will take place later, about 50 yards in from the edge in a little sand arena bordered by coral heads. This encounter, with no immediate feeding, is a stage for meeting the sharks "in the wild." It matters not that the sharks are the Coves' regulars and all polite banqueters. For the guests, they emerge from the blue. The experience perfectly simulates the classic shark encounter that dominates the expectation of almost all ocean divers today. That expectation may be touched with apprehension or with keen anticipation. It is always dramatic. It is also wonderfully photogenic and has, of course, a sense of wildness, even menace, that does not exist in the circus-like atmosphere of the shark feeding.

I could hear camera shutters clicking like castanets. With me were several old friends: the two publishers of *Ocean Realm*, Charlene deJori and Cheryl Schorp, Ruthie Petzold, a professional and much-published underwater photographer; Mopsie Lovejoy, the sponsor and host of my expedition; and the crew from our boat, the *Babirusa*.

From the feeding site Stuart set his course west, over the edge of the reef and then over the abyss that is the Tongue of the Ocean. I didn't purposefully save the best for last in this account. It truly happened this way.

The day was splendid. In years past, when we lived in the Bahamas and I had my own dive boat business there from 1954-57, the weather was always at its best from May on through the summer.

Twelve miles out in the middle of the great trench is a sea buoy. It is as big as a small boat and was placed there years ago and anchored to the bottom more than a mile below by the navy. Like all floating objects in open oceanic waters, this buoy attracts pelagic animals, sharks and dolphins (dorado) primarily. Stuart was one of the first to dive by the buoy. He tried hand-feeding the silky sharks, the species that frequents that place in the greatest numbers, and found that they were as amenable and well-mannered as the Caribbean reef sharks. Now the arrival of any boat is as certain a dinner bell as the classic signal was to Pavlov's dogs. You may see them, dark brown bodies almost at the surface by the dive platform and as far down the water column as the eye can reach into that pellucid, deep blue water.

Before we entered that world of sharks, Stuart briefed us on a phenomenon called tonic immobility. The term was new to all of us. In a medical dictionary it is defined as, "A state of continuous or prolonged muscular contraction." We were told that this state may be achieved in sharks by twisting their tails. On hearing this we covertly glanced at one another and there was some rolling of eyeballs. Stuart went on to explain that when, by the tail twist, the shark is turned onto its back, it succumbs to a state of anesthesia. It is out for the count. He never did explain how he made this discovery without losing a leg. Somehow it reminded me of the question, who is going to bell the cat? And with that briefing, we jumped into the ocean, rather like jumping into an open elevator shaft at the top of a mile-high building, I thought.

And, indeed, the sharks – all silkies – were well-behaved. They circled in an orderly manner, taking the baits that Stuart and Michelle released to them. We had not been with them for more than two or three minutes when Stuart called my attention to one of the sharks with a large stainless steel hook embedded in its jaw. With the usual diver's pantomime he indicated that the tail-twisting would now be demonstrated. I started shooting and recorded a man/shark interaction more wild and wonderful than any I could ever have imagined before.

As silky in question passed by Michelle, she turned with it, grabbed its tail, and with one strong twist, turned it onto its back. If a shark could look surprised, that one would surely have done so. The flip was followed by a couple of feeble twitches, after which the shark hung limply, supported at the tail and middle by Michele. Stuart produced a pair of pliers – doesn't every diver just happen to have pliers in his vest pocket? – and, firmly grasping the unresisting shark by the head, proceeded with one hand to work the hook out of its jaw with the pliers. This might be likened to the extraction of a wisdom tooth in a human without benefit of anesthesia. The shark never twitched. The operation took about 30 seconds. Doctor nodded to anesthetist. She twisted the tail right-side-up. With just a momentary hesitation – the "where-am-I" reaction – the shark took off and once again joined the leisurely circling traffic.

I recently had an operation for which the bill from the anesthesiologist was well over $1000. Just think: she might have twisted my foot and accomplished the same purpose. But then, I would certainly have known where I was all the time.

Dr. William Morton, a dentist, is credited with introducing the medical world to anesthesia in the operating theater. When the anesthesia, which was ether, was demonstrated at the Massachusetts General Hospital in 1846, the surgeon turned to the gallery of doctors and exclaimed: "Gentlemen, this is no humbug!" Had I been able to emit more than a "blub, blub" underwater, I would have said the same to Stuart and Michelle.

Whether they are polite guests at your dinner table or you, by long and unhappy chance, become part of their (the sharks') menu, they are formidable, fascinating animals. Queequeg, the harpooner in *Moby Dick* summed it up: "Queequeg not care what god mad'm shark, wedder Feejee god or Nantucket god; but de god dat made shark must be one dam Ingin."

Hanky Panky on a Live-Aboard

Patrick O'Brian, writing about the British Navy in Napoleon's time, called them "scrubs." Victorian writers reveled in the dastardly doings of "cads" and "rotters." In this era of female emancipation, "male chauvinist pig" is much favored. I, personally, still enjoy the children's book reference to "bad chaps." In general all these terms are used to describe men who do not subscribe to gentlemanly standards, men of ill will, men who are not straight shooters. None of these terms apply to women, even if they are the sort who make lamp shades from the skins of tattooed prisoners or press a multi-million-dollar malpractice suit against a hospital at which their trip into a CAT scanner extinguished their power to read the future in a crystal ball. "Bitch" seems to be the catch-all term for that sort.

What does all this have to do with live-aboard dive boats, you may ask? For the most part nothing. Divers are a wholesome lot, a congenial company attracted to one another by their shared enthusiasm for diving and photography. People who eschew the casino, discotheques, restaurants, and wine stewards of dive resorts in favor of a physically healthy regimen of five dives a day, eat, and sleep are not apt to be bad chaps. On live-aboards the sidewalks are usually rolled up by ten p.m., and the sound of rhythmic breathing is heard through the boat.

However, every so often (but not very often) the daily routine of dive, eat, and sleep is disrupted by unsavory happenings. The cause is usually the infiltration into this pure environment of a bad chap.

Now it happens that I find myself on live-aboards for almost one-third of each year. It is fortunate that I enjoy diving, never become jaded with ferreting out macro animals with my video lens, and also enjoy meeting others of like mind and making new friends. The curse of the Flying Dutchman is not upon me. These trips can be much of a sameness, so the activities of a bad chap or the diversion of an obnoxious lady diver

(I will not use the word "bitch" again. We have always had female dogs in our family and they have been much loved.) can lend an element of spice to a trip and provide the grist for juicy gossip.

Many years ago on the good ship *Nudibranch* (ships' names and places as well as characters are entirely fictional), I set off with a new group to a popular dive location in the Caribbean. A newly married couple was among the guests. The gentleman early indicated that he might be a bad chap. He bellied up to the topside bar and started belting down scotches long before the sun had even approached the yardarm. Now this is most unusual behavior on a live-aboard. Not only do guests not drink alcoholic beverages during the day, most are entirely abstemious. If they do take a drink, it is apt to be beer or wine at the end of the day with no night dive planned. Hard liquor hardly ever makes an appearance. So we watched this strange customer with sideways glances.

By evening he was well soused and his voice strident. Bellicose accounts of his experiences in "Nam" dominated his attempts at being accepted by the group. His new bride began distancing herself from him. I thought I saw a look of impending disaster in her eyes.

The explosion came after most of us had already turned in. I thought an earthquake had overtaken us. Sledgehammer blows were being rained upon one of the cabin doors. It was the newlyweds' cabin. It was right across from mine, and the bride had locked herself in. Shouts of "Open the friggin' door" were punctuated with "You're dead meat," this last delivered at the screaming pitch of a dictator's tirade.

The owner of the ship happened to be aboard – a man of imposing girth and well-developed muscles. He was joined by the captain, who was also no faint heart, and the two appeared on the scene in less than a minute. With the speed and skill of professional bouncers, they picked up the self-confessed Nam veteran, hustled him up the stairs and onto the deck, and advised him that if he entered the cabin area of the boat again that night, they would throw him ashore and let him sleep it off on the beach. At that particular location the shore was a mosquito-ridden, snake-infested mangrove swamp. This had a remarkable sobering effect.

Nor did we hear another peep from him about Nam. His wife cut him dead next day; just completely ignored him. To his great credit and possible salvation, he eschewed the bar and conspicuously drank Cokes directly from the can. For the rest of the trip he was as good as gold. But his cabin door stayed locked each night, and he slept on a padded seat in the main lounge. No bets were placed on the survival of that marriage.

I recall another strange and unsavory happening on another boat, the *Navasink* on another sea and in another year. There is something unnerving and shocking about a cry for help from either man or woman. On a live-aboard dive boat, such a distress cry brings a rush for the rail and the liferings.

One evening, just before dinner, when most of our 16-guest complement were hanging out in the main salon, our chops moistened with the good smells from the galley, a lady's cry for help shattered our quiet talk and brought most to their feet. The distress call had come from the deck below, the cabin deck; and that made the situation even more alarming. The captain and two of the gentlemen guests made for the stairs and quickly vanished below. We looked at one another, eyebrows arched and faces expressing total ignorance of what might be happening. Within three minutes the captain and gentlemen reappeared, escorting a single lady who was clutching her pillow and a bundle of personal effects.

In the salon…silence, eyes turned away as if studying fingernails but irresistibly drawn back to the passing parade. She was escorted to another cabin area where, we soon learned, she would share a cabin with a single lady.

Dinner was forgotten. Rampant curiosity, fueled by a delicious sense of scandal, clutched at our self-control; and that exploded as soon as the escorts reappeared and two lady guests hurried to look after their sister diver in distress. The escorts were besieged with questions from all sides. They savored the delay in answering. We learned that the lady in distress had been restrained from leaving the cabin she shared with her male friend. It seems that he, having sponsored her diving holiday, supposed that certain favors were owed to him. It had been obvious to us that since coming aboard, the lady had increasingly rejected the blandishments of her suitor. We all concluded that when he blocked her escape from their cabin he had been bent on robbing her of her chaste treasure. In the nick of time, and before that fate worse than death could happen, the lady had been rescued.

The ladies pursed their lips and clucked: "Well! Did you ever!" The men trembled with righteousness and hissed, "The cad! The rotter!"

In fact, there was no small degree of interest touched with envy in all this "tut tutting." When the gentleman, now reduced to "bad chap," had come aboard with his lady friend, it was noticed – especially by the men – that the lady had a pneumatic figure of heroic proportions. And when, on the first day of diving, she appeared in a diaphanous swimsuit, "Eyes popped like champagne corks and strong men sobbed aloud." I quote from the late S. J. Perelman.

The wounded lady was much looked after. I myself, motivated by compassion and outrage that such a lovely lady should be so ill-used, felt compelled to hug her with a show of brotherly concern. Her frustrated captor hung around for another day. All of us avoided eye contact with him. The following morning, one full day before our tour was to end and before we were up, he had himself taken ashore and caught the first flight out of the island.

And that reminds me of an account I read in a book entitled *The Edwardians*. During that era the great country houses were the scene of lavish, long-weekend house parties. The hostesses were well briefed on the affairs going on among their friends. They aided and abetted these affairs by arranging for the lovers to attend the weekend without their spouses. At the end of an evening, when all had turned in and the long corridors were dark and quiet, the gentleman lover would slip out of his room and make his way to another door outside of which, by prearrangement, the lady had left some object to lead the way – perhaps a pair of slippers or a spent rose or a ribbon. The author of the book recounts how her uncle found the agreed-upon object outside the bedroom door, slipped into the darkened room, and with an exuberant cry of "cock-a-doodle-doo!" whipped off his robe and jumped upon the bed. At which point the bedside light was turned on and the young man found himself staring into the faces of the Bishop of Worcester and his wife. The author concludes, "My uncle was gone before breakfast the next morning."

And finally, on a live-aboard in the Red Sea, a cruel joke was played on me. Since no "bad chaps" were involved and I was the target of the joke, I need not hide the identity of the boat and the place. The beautiful yacht *FantaSea II* was our boat and the occasion was one of my own tours. I had loudly voiced my frustration over having encountered no Spanish dancer nudibranchs, the glorious, deep red, ten-inch-long nudibranch found in those waters. I taunted the crew: "Where are your vaunted Spanish dancers? What's happened to the Red Sea? We've been robbed!" etc.

Now, it is on night dives that one is most likely to encounter these gorgeous animals. Divers will know that on night dives the divers usually spread out about the reef. When a diver encounters something of interest he waggles his light about, signaling the find to others. In just such a circumstance I found myself far apart and alone when I noticed the waggling light some distance away and immediately headed for it. As I approached, I saw the entire group gathered in a circle, and in the glow of their lights I could already see the red, undulating movements of a huge Spanish dancer.

"Oh, those good people are sharing their find," I thought. Occasionally, the rogue diver will keep a find to himself for an exclusive – a dastardly and selfish act fortunately seldom encountered. So my heart was filled with a sense of goodwill and consideration for my diving friends even as I approached the scene.

I came in shooting, my Hi-8 aimed and firing away as the circle parted for me. The light was perfect, the creature wonderfully active as it descended to the reef. But wait! Something was not quite right. The color was right, the movements were right, but the animal did have a very unusual shape.

I pulled my eye away from the viewfinder, though still shooting, and had a hard look around the side of my housing. I stopped shooting and focused on the pair of bright red ladies' underpants as they settled on the reef. Then I noticed the cloud of bubbles coming out of each diver's mask, not rhythmic exhalation, but laughter…joyous, cruel, devastating laughter. I was the butt of an elaborate joke, using the cook's panties as the bait. My own harsh, abusive treatment of my guests had been revenged by all.

That very night I planted a powerful limpet on the bottom of the *Fantasea II*. Safely ashore in the ship's dinghy, I watched with satisfaction the ship and all the wretched people in it dissolve in a ball of flame.

So, through hanky panky, bad chaps, and witless pranksters are the live-aboard dive tours made entertaining…but not very often. You're mostly stuck with all that splendid diving and Lucullan feasts and the company of "good chaps," ladies and gentlemen both.

NOTE: *Similarity of characters or events in these stories to any living persons is entirely coincidental. At the same time, the accounts are roughly based on true happenings.*

How Not to Run a Dive Boat

In the fall of 1954 I arrived in the Bahamas with my boat, *Zingaro*. I had helped to build the boat at a small boatyard in East Blue Hill, Maine, near where we lived on the coast. The books by Hans Hass and Jacques Cousteau and the latter's articles in *National Geographic* magazine had fired my imagination and spurred my resolve to build a boat specifically for diving, take it to the tropics, and during the winter months, when my blueberry land shut down, try my hand at charter boating. I knew nothing much about such a business and had never owned or operated a motor vessel in my life. It was a brash move from the secure business of blueberry farming that I had developed over a period of four years. I could not know then that it would change the course of my life.

It did not start well and came close to alienating me from my brother for the rest of our lives. The following is what happened.

I suppose my brother Bill and I got on no better or worse than most older and younger brothers. I thought perhaps to mend our frayed relations by inviting him and his wife, Ali, to help me take my boat on her maiden voyage from Maine to the Bahamas. A nice long trip on a small boat is just the thing to aggravate and amplify any small differences or incompatibility two persons might have. But I didn't know that.

Bill was, in fact, an experienced boat handler. He had cruised with his friends and had been a captain in the Army Corps of Engineers during the war, actually specializing in the handling of landing craft. He had much to offer on our trip, and I had much to learn. I wanted none of it. It was MY boat, I was captain, and I wanted to run my show. Least of all was I prepared to suffer the superiority of my older brother.

We ran south with easy Indian Summer weather, leaving New England behind us, the promise of the south sustaining our spirits despite increasing incidents of bickering over who should be in authority and my reluctance to take any advice from my "pompous" brother. The novelty of owning and commanding this brand new 40-foot, twin-engined, specially-built dive boat filled me with pride, the kind that so often leads to a fall.

By the time we reached the entry to the inland waterway at Brielle, New Jersey, just five days into the trip, my brother and I were almost stalking one another with belaying pins. Only the mediation of his gentle wife, Ali, forestalled the inevitable. And the inevitable caught up with us at Brielle.

We swept through the inlet with an incoming tide and soon came within view of the Brielle Yacht Club. We intended to dock there for the night. As we came abreast of the club, an officer in white ducks and yachting jacket with insignia motioned me to an open finger pier. Now the finger piers projected from the shore at right angles, and the tidal current, which had now assumed the speed of a mill race, was sweeping through them. I angled *Zingaro* between two of the piers, thinking to maneuver into the open slot to which I had been directed. Bill had taken a position at the end of the bow pulpit to toss a line to an attendant. Ali was on the flying bridge with me. The stage was set. I had learned nothing about the use of spring lines that enable a boat to pivot in the middle of a current that is carrying it sideways. And sideways I went, so fast that before my wits could save me – and they were paralyzed already – my six-foot pulpit had tangled with the rugged pulpit of another boat docked down current. Bill shouted: "Throw it into reverse, you fool!" For once I took my brother's hated advice, and seizing both levers, put the boat into reverse and gunned the engines at the same time. As I watched with horror, almost hypnotized by the scene, my pulpit pulled away from its fastenings and sank into the fetid dock water with my brother on it. As the boat roared out into mid-stream I had a picture of him hanging on to the struts of the other boat's pulpit, trying to climb out of the water. Ali's eyes seemed to be starting from her head, her mouth open with shock.

Observers could be seen now on the yacht club dock, slapping their foreheads. Some wretched misfits were slapping their sides and laughing. I was too shocked to feel the weight of humiliation that I would carry with me for a long while.

We were motioned to bring the boat to the main yacht club dock usually reserved for large yachts. I managed the docking and had secured the lines about the time Bill appeared, dripping wet, disheveled, and ominously silent. That evening at supper he broke the oppressive silence that hung over us like a smothering blanket with an ultimatum. Either I relinquished full command of the boat and turned it over to him, or he and Ali would jump ship the following morning.

With that, I called my wife, Susy, long-distance where she was staying with her parents and our children in Scranton, Pennsylvania, and asked if she could join me to take the boat the rest of the way to the Bahamas. She could and did, and Bill and Ali left the following morning, wishing me well but doubting it.

Ah, the spring line. How was I to know? The proper use of it was not to sink in with this somewhat retarded, lubberly, and green captain until he – that is, I – survived another humiliating ordeal.

I did reach Nassau with only minor travails, my pride in my fine new boat somewhat deflated by the wreckage of the harpooning pulpit lashed to the cabin trunk. The pulpit was put back where it should be at the local boatyard, and I found a berth at Nassau Yacht Haven in one of the dreaded finger pier slots. I miraculously managed to get the *Zingaro* in and out of my slot without mishap for some weeks without the efficacious use of a spring line (how, I can't imagine), but that ignorance finally caught up with me and at the worst possible time.

A Hollywood production team arrived in Nassau to shoot scenes for a soon-to-be-forgotten film called *Flame of the Islands*. The island, back in 1954, was still just emerging from relative isolation and was very parochial. It was in a tizzy over the glamour of having Hollywood on its turf. The flame of the island was none other than Yvonne De Carlo. She is little remembered today (except as Lily Munster from the *Munsters* TV show), but then she had some prominence in films that had exotic cabaret scenes and nests of spies in Mediterranean sinkholes. The male star was Jim Arness, for whom fame came later in the top-rated television series, *Gunsmoke*.

Through a fortuitous connection with the Director of Public Relations for the island, a gentleman I had shamelessly cultivated, I was contracted to ferry the stars and their attendants each morning from Yacht Haven across the harbor to Hog Island (today more attractively called Paradise Island). I attempted to help Ms. De Carlo aboard when she arrived at the dock. A worm would have gotten more attention. She shrank from my hand and avoided even noticing me. Jim Arness proved not only less aloof, but friendly and interested in the boat. Indeed, we became friends over a period of days, and he and his beautiful wife were our guests for dinner.

At any rate, with this precious cargo aboard and puffed up with conceit as I noticed the envious gawks of other captains on the dock, I had my crewman, Ishmael, cast off the lines, and I backed smartly out of my slot – smarter than I had intended with the tide running with me. Before I could turn in the narrow space between the piers, my propellers fouled the bow anchor line of a boat aft of me. I was, of course, horrified. Any conceit-puffing deflated like a punctured tire. Fortunately, my panic was not as paralyzing as it had been at Brielle.

I won't bore you with details of how I extricated myself from this appalling blunder; however, it did require my diving over the side, cutting the tangled anchor line (for which I would pay dearly later), and getting clear of the docks a half hour later. Jim Arness helped and was genuinely interested in the whole misadventure. Ms. De Carlo stayed in the cabin, sipping coffee, and failed to notice or even care what was happening outside. I was grateful for that.

During the three years in which I operated out of Nassau, I got to know the reefs intimately. I grounded on them from time to time and also ran out of water several times when low tides caught me with my keel down on the sandbanks. Those occurrences were fairly routine and happened to the best of us. But the inauspicious start I had made in charter boating identified me as a scrub, a term used in the 18th century British Navy for ignorant deck hands.

My brother Bill and I now laugh about it all. He has mellowed. I am a little wiser. But Ms. De Carlo, if she hasn't gone to that great cabaret in the sky by now, must moon over the memory of the dashing captain in the Bahamas, whom she failed to take advantage of while she had a chance.

Jacqui

An article in *Ocean Realm* about barracuda and the speed with which they attack their prey put me in mind of an experience we had when we were filming *The Deep*. And that in turn brought my memory back to Jacqui Bisset, a most happy segment in my memory bank.

You may recall in the course of the plot for that adventure story by Peter Benchley that Nick Nolte and Jacqui Bisset play the parts of a young couple vacationing in Bermuda. There are drugs, treasure, a murderous but cultivated bad chap, played by Lou Gossett, and a good guy lighthouse keeper, played by the late Robert Shaw. However, before these heavies appear in the story, Nolte and Bisset are enjoying a diving holiday on a wreck. The hard-used but still picturesque wreck of the *Rhone* provided the location.

Before I proceed to the heart of the story, let me comment on the production team. Al Giddings, Chuck Nicklin, and I did the underwater camera work, very ably directed by Al Giddings. We were supported by an underwater crew of as many as 16 divers on a single shoot: light holders, cable tenders, safetymen, a continuity girl, and the senior director for the entire film, Peter Yates. The continuity girl, whose job it was to record every detail of the set and the costumes, was Geri Murphy, then a young girl on her first diving job. She later achieved fame as the principal photographer and writer for *Skin Diver* magazine. This juggernaut was on location about 30 feet deep on a section of the wreck. The action involved Nolte taking pictures of Bisset with his Nikonos while Bisset was feeding the yellowtails and a single eight-inch coney that was in the scramble. Jacqui had a plastic bag from which she drew scraps of minced conch.

Three cameras were running, catching the scene from different angles, and all eyes were on the action. Suddenly, where the coney had been there was only a puff of scales. The yellowtails had scattered a split second earlier and now returned to feed. Bisset was unaware of anything having happened; and so were all the rest of us except Nick Nolte. Now let me tell you what happened.

Another pair of eyes had been watching the feeding exercise from a distance of about 25 yards. The eyes belonged to a barracuda, about a four-footer, who hung out in the shadow of some wreckage and was a well-known resident to regular divers on the wreck. With the instinct of a superb predator he had – even from the distance – observed the vulnerability of the coney as it dropped all caution to concentrate on the feed. Nolte was on the long axis of the attack and saw it happen – and of course babbled excitedly about it when we surfaced. Would the attack show up on the 35mm film? We had to wait 48 hours to find out. That's the time it took for the dailies to be flown to New York, processed, work-printed, and the print returned by special messenger for screening by the director, producer, actors, and camera staff.

And there it was, a silver blur on just three frames of the film. Thirty-five millimeter film passes through the camera at a speed of 24 frames a second. That gave us all pause for thought and almost caused Jacqui Bisset to swoon.

What was Jacqui Bisset like as a person? Every male in the production crew was secretly in love with her. She was terrific! She had our admiration, our friendship, and perhaps most significant, our respect. And when she emerged from the water in that wet t-shirt, strong men sobbed aloud. However, it was not her opulent bosom or healthy good looks that drew us to her. It was her cheerful adjustment to the long, hard working hours, six a.m. breakfast to ten p.m. when the screening of the dailies finished. It was her dogged, and successful, resolve to overcome her fear of the sea and the underwater world. She had never dived before and took a crash course in the use of scuba less than a week before we commenced shooting. Her first open-water dive was on location before the cameras, surrounded by safety divers. She discovered, in that clear Caribbean water, that beauty was manifest and danger nonexistent, and so she began to relax and enjoy the experience. She ultimately came on like a tiger, urging us to let her do all her underwater scenes herself. Her double, Jackie Kilbride, had an easy time of it. Jacqui B. also had a splendid sense of humor and enjoyed talking and laughing with the crew. And there was something about her bearing that was ineffably ladylike, a sense of quality.

We became good friends. Her boyfriend, who visited with her during the weekends in Bermuda, trusted me. I rather wondered if that was a back-handed compliment. We dined together when he was there and Jacqui and I made a dinner twosome one evening each working week at the Southampton Princess Hotel, where we all stayed. I was probably the least macho and most conservative of any in the production. You may guess that our friendship puzzled many, credited me enormously, and pleased me to no end.

There was one action part of the script that we fortunately assigned to the double. It involved the heroine, while diving along the bottom by the hull of the wreck, spotting something that glittered just inside a hole in the side of the hull. She is carrying a short stick, the end of which is secured to her wrist. She pokes the stick into the hole, hoping to pull out the object. Something inside seizes the stick and pulls it into the hole, dragging the heroine with it. She fetches up against the hole, is pinned there struggling desperately and finally disengages her wrist from the stick. The scene was meant to be a shocker, the action wild, the audience's first indication that "something" bad and powerful was inside the wreck.

Now inside the wreck there was, indeed, something powerful. It was George Marler, the Tortola divemaster and senior diver in the area. When the stick entered the hole, George was cued to grab it and pull. He braced his feet, bent at the knees for leverage, grabbed the stick and put everything he had into the pull. On the other side, the double, Jackie Kilbride, was smashed against the iron hull with such force that her shoulder was nearly dislocated. Her struggle was fueled with real pain and desperation. Three cameras rolled. The scene did not require a retake; and obviously a retake was impossible. The double was out of commission for days, her arm in a sling, and the scene was an example of art imitating life all too well. The violence of the scene was such that it couldn't have been faked. In hindsight Jacqui B. was happy that we had insisted on her not doing the scene herself.

In the shooting script, Jacqui B. would be filmed emerging from this dive by the stern of the small boat she and Nick Nolte were using. This was to be filmed both at water level and from the support ship, which was next to the dive boat. Al and Chuck and I decided to shoot the scene half-in, half-out. To do that we mounted the underwater housings for the big 35mm Arriflexes on small inflatable mats. By inflating the mats carefully, the dome ports of the camera were bisected by the water surface. The scene was set. Twenty or more crew watched from the crew boat, cameras rolled as Jacqui popped up by the ladder. The take was proceeding perfectly when an object floated into view between the cameras and Jacqui. We stopped rolling. The director yelled, but Jacqui turned to see what had spoiled the scene and we all stared incredulously as a huge turd floated by. Nolte collapsed with laughter. Jacqui turned away, hanging on to the ladder, her body shaking with laughter. We were caught between outrage and the disgusting humor of the intrusion. The director was only outraged and bellowed, "Who flushed that head down below? I'll crucify him!"

In time the story did the rounds of the production bunch and probably most of the island. The scene was successfully shot again, sans turd and Jacqui went on to the now-famous wet t-shirt scene; and that was not played by the double.

The Man Who Loves Shrimp

Shrimp did not help me put my children through college. Sharks did. Way back when my three nippers were college age, I was teamed up with Peter Benchley, busy shooting programs for the *American Sportsman* show. Sharks were in demand. They were "box office, show biz." Ninety-five percent of the shows that I shot with Peter focused on sharks. Consequently, they paid our way those days. I was heard to say one time that I had a love affair with sharks because they put my children through college. When the Discovery Channel decided to do an hour special about me and the family, they asked me to send them a list of possible titles for the show. I drew heavily on the classics, puffed up like a swollen tick with erudite conceit, drawing on Frost, Shakespeare, and a gaggle of Romantic poets. At the end of the list of about 20 entries I threw in *The Man Who Loves Sharks*. That, of course, was the winner. Understandably, the Discovery Channel already had its own love affair with sharks.

I really don't love sharks. Frost might have said, "Something there is that doesn't love a shark." That superb and ancient predator neither gives nor receives love. He just bites and eats and manages to survive for a few hundred million years. On the other hand, I do love shrimp. I sob with anticipation at the prospect of eating them. These days I seek them out and focus on a few dozen for every shark that may happen before my lens. That doesn't mean that I avert my gaze and turn off my camera with a bored yawn when a whale shark – or any other shark, for that matter – happens by. But macro has replaced behemoth angle for me. On a wreck or reef or in the muck, I now look for shrimp. And when your eye (better if you are not Polyphemus and actually have two) becomes attuned to these omnipresent but elusive little animals, a world of shrimp opens before you. In these septuagenarian years, when many have one foot in the grave and the other on a banana peel, I find myself keen as mustard for each dive. I used to busy myself with a new translation of Homer from the original Greek when others went diving. Now I am the first on the duck board, pulsating with excitement, visions of long white antennae, translucent bodies, insect-like legs dancing in my eyes. On fortune's cap I am now the very button, thanks to shrimp.

Periclimenes pedersoni is a little translucent blue-and-white shrimp, about as big as the end joint of your thumb, at times a little larger. It is a great favorite of Caribbean, Bahamian, and Florida divers and is also the special friend of all photographers. When you see a grouper motionless on the bottom, its mouth wide open in a capacious yawn and a look of foolish ecstasy on its face, there is apt to be a Pederson shrimp (or a goby) in its mouth. Such is the spaced-out effect of this shrimp on its host that you may often aim your camera right into the mouth of the grouper and video one or more of the shrimp cleaning the gills and teeth of the host. This is, of course, a classic example of symbiosis. The shrimp pigs out on the microscopic parasites and dead tissue that encumber the host. The host gets a shave and a haircut.

Pederson shrimp were first noticed by an old friend of mine, Harry Pederson, from McAllen, Texas. He was a baby and wedding photographer by trade and a marine naturalist and underwater photographer by hobby. We both dived around Nassau in the early 1950s. He was the first to notice the little shrimp and determine that it always lived in the company of the corkscrew anemone, *Bartholomea annulata*. I have found as many as 20 in the company of the anemone. Two are more likely.

Have a close look at the anemone and you will see one or two pairs of red-and-white barber pole antennae extended through the tentacles. You will seldom see the animals to whom the antennae are attached. They are stocky, blood red, and pugnacious. They are always in pairs and derive their name, pistol shrimp, *Alpheus armatus*, from the explosive pistol shot sound they make when annoyed. Each has a pair of lobster claws, one being twice the size of the other. It is the snapping shut of that claw that makes the startling sound.

The only way you will get to see the full shrimp is by luring it out with a bait. Dee Scarr teed that up for me one time under the Kralendijk pier at Bonaire. The succulent odor of the fish bait enticed the pistol shrimp into following the scent all the way out of the anemone as the bait was slowly withdrawn, leading it on. I have heard that at least one marine scofflaw and thoroughly bad chap pulled the anemone and the coral lump to which it was attached off the bottom and overturned it. This deprived the pistol shrimp of all security as well as home sweet home. The two were as naked and vulnerable as Darth Vader without his brain cap. Only an out-and-out rotter would stoop to such strong-arm tactics to get the picture. Should I ever meet the scoundrel I will horse-whip him out of the club.

You need only leaf through a book on marine invertebrates to become aware of the great number and variety of shrimp. In a lifetime of diving, I have probably only encountered one or two percent of their number. I will just mention a few that are my favorites and two species that are associated with some unusual happenings.

Familiar to all divers on both sides of the U.S. is the great barber pole shrimp, *Stenopus hispidus*. It generally hides in the coral during the day, showing only a pair of its six long white antennae. They, like many shrimp, come out into the open at night. They are big shrimp. I've seen them six inches long. They are red-and-white candy-striped, and their antennae are almost twice the length of their bodies. If you can fill your macro frame with one, you will have a handsome face-on picture. It will be defending itself from the approach of your lens with its two long, white-tipped claws; both are also twice its body length.

On the reefs of the Caribbean and in the waters of that hemisphere, you will easily encounter an anemone with thick yellow tentacles tipped with purple, *Condylactis gigantea*. If you look carefully, you may be lucky enough to see one of the most handsome little shrimp in any ocean of the world. Its name: *Periclimenes yucatanicus*. By whatever common name that may be given to it (and I know of none), it is heavy-bodied and gloriously patterned with tan-and-white segments and a fanlike tail with disks of blue set upon it. It clings to the tentacles of its host as they sway in the current and scrambles about from stalk to stalk like a cricket in a wheat field.

I have frequently encountered a similar shrimp, equally magnificent and with much the same structure, living with an anemone in the western Pacific. Its name: *Periclimenes brevicarpalis*. It is golden brown with bold white sections, a snow white head, and purple dots along its legs. If you are into macro video and still shooting, encounters with these gorgeous animals that appear full-frame in your picture are far more exciting to me than a shot of a shark passing by. And I have had so many takes of sharks savaging baits right in front of the camera or pushing their noses into the mesh protection of a cage, that I would swap a dozen such shots for one fine take of a mantis shrimp emerging from its hole.

In New Guinea, diving with Dinah Halstead, I turned over a common sea cucumber and found hiding under it a red-and-white, heavily armored shrimp that quickly scrambled to the other side of its host to avoid my presence. This was the emperor shrimp, *Periclimenes imperator*. It finally gave up its hide-and-seek behavior and went about its business. I pressed so close with my macro video system that the crunching sounds of its eating were picked up by the mike.

An account of my shrimp encounters over the years would put me to sleep before I got through the first half-dozen. However, two encounters were so dramatic and bizarre that they are worth recounting.

As I write this, I am actually sitting over the wreck on which – in search of an elusive night-time shrimp – I had one of the scariest experiences in my years of diving. It was also about the most feckless act an experienced diver might lead himself into.

The wreck of the *Sankisan Maru*, a 367-foot Japanese freighter, lies in 80 feet of water in Truk Lagoon. It was, of course, just one of the many Japanese ships that were sunk in 1944 by the air task force of Admiral Spruance. The attack, called Operation Hailstorm, seeded the lagoon with so many wrecks that Truk Lagoon is today the most famous wreck-diving location in the world.

The previous season, on my annual trip to Truk Lagoon, I had explored the forecastle of this wreck and noticed a dark opening in the midship bulkhead. It provided entrance to an open hatch and a ladder that stretched down into blackness. The opening was so small that my ability to fit through with my tank was questionable. I was alone. The black pit below was an unknown. All factors combined to make a solo exploration of that place entirely unreasonable. So I proceeded to try it. I had often seen a handsome but particularly shy red shrimp with glittering golden eyes scurry for cover into dark recesses when exposed to my lights. I had identified it as *Rhynchocinetes hiatti*, and I wanted a clear shot at that animal. So a measure of shrimp lust exerted its siren song in this instance.

I just barely managed to squeeze through the hole, pulling my video camera and lights in after me, and let myself descend into the black abyss. I grounded out on a soft, silty bottom no more than ten feet down and turned on my lights. Through the swirl of rust brown silt loosened by my descent, I made out an iron bulkhead alive with the red shrimp I had only glimpsed before. It was Shrimp City, and the lights were the attack warning siren that panicked the populace. As they madly dashed for cover I tried to focus and shoot, but the fog of silt had disastrously thickened. My light, of course, created intense backscatter, making it virtually impossible to focus sharply on any one of the fleeing animals. On top of this confused and frustrating condition, both lights began to fail. They didn't take their time about it. There was no grace period. What I had taken for a yellowing cast to the lights, caused by the silt, had been rapidly failing batteries. With my first rational thought in that operation, an inner voice cried, "Let's get out of here!"

I had turned around on the bottom. The silt fog was now so thick that the opening through which I had come, already in an upper dark passage, had vanished. The lights died completely. I could feel one of the bulkheads; but which one? I was totally blind with not even the dimmest glow of outer light indicating the escape route. And I was ALONE. No one knew I was in there.

I won't protract the event. The fact that it's not my ghost writing this account will assure you that I did finally grope my way to the outlet. Know that the thoughts I turned toward myself in that Stygian pit were composed of self-loathing for my stupidity, fear that pressed on my will not to panic, and a horrible recall of circumstances like this into which divers had led themselves and from thence gone to their deaths.

On this trip I returned to that forbidding place. This time a buddy accompanied me. This time my batteries were fully charged, and this time I removed my fins and let myself down slowly. Shrimp City panicked again; but this time I nailed the little guys with my macro zoom and brought home the bacon without bordering on a heart attack in the process.

The other signal experience is equally bizarre but entirely joyous. It involved a pair of cleaner shrimp called scarlet ladies, *Lysmata amboinensis*. They are graceful and one-and-a-half inches long. Their backs are red, with a wide white stripe down the middle from head to tail. On their bottoms they are orange-brown. They are always in pairs. I have encountered them in the Caribbean and the Bahamas and then, just last year, on a reef in Fijian waters.

I was a guest on a splendid motor sailor, the *Nai'a*. The owner, Rob Barrel, and his delightful companion Cat Holloway, treated me to the happiest and most unlikely experience I have ever had with shrimp. They led me to a coral rise and onto a crevasse, where to my astonishment Cat lay down on the bottom with her face inches away from the opening. As I watched, she removed her regulator mouthpiece, opened her mouth wide, and waited. A pair of scarlet ladies jumped aboard her chin and on into her mouth. They busied themselves cleaning her teeth and gums and lips until she could no longer hold her breath. They exited with the wave of exhaled air.

I, of course, tried it myself and documented Cat's oral hygiene session. Surprisingly, the sensation of having those animals in your mouth was not unpleasant. Had it been, I would still feel obliged to give them something in return, having dined on thousands of their family over the years. I know a place in Palau that always has scarlet ladies in residence. On my next Palau trip I shall forego application of dental floss for some days before making my way to their lair and paying my debt.

Night

Night. A black night with few if any stars showing in the great vault of darkness that is an envelope around this ship. I am on the top deck of the *Bay Islands Aggressor* off a little island between the Honduras main-land and the island of Roatan. I asked that the lights on the top deck be turned off. The glow of my laptop intrudes on the darkness, a little beacon of twentieth century technology in this isolated corner of the world. All the others have gone night diving. It would be fatuous to even pretend that I have seen it all; but the Caribbean is a little old hat if you've been diving around the world for a lifetime.

There are still macro wonders. I captured several bizarre, totally unlikely macro critters on tape the other evening. Dan, the captain, and an old hand in this marine turf spotted for me. He found every animal that I shot. I know what to look for and where to look but lack the patient scrutiny required for spotting a finger-size goby on a sea whip. A nudibranch no larger than half the end joint of your little finger filled the frame of the camera. It had lacelike frills, the wedding garment for a Third World princess. A crab, no larger than your thumbnail clung to a long, hairy gorgonian, a miniature tarantula with horrible mandibles, reaching out like dreadful tongs to snatch microscopic plankton from inside its hunting space.

This evening I eschewed the night dive and gave no excuses for it. I am happy to have reached that stage in my diving career that requires no excuses for skipping a dive.

Right now, in this place, the fine Honduran cigar drawing easily and burning evenly and a tolerable cognac on the little top-deck table provides a near perfect hedonist's indulgence. The time, the place, the total peace, and apartness from suburbia enables the mind to track time and open to creative thoughts – especially to awareness of the moment. At home in Lawrenceville, New Jersey, I live in a quiet neighborhood – a happy, appealing American suburbia. Children and dogs liven the daytime appealingly. At night those welcome diversions – just outside my ground-floor office window – are gone; asleep. However, I am only one block from a busy road between Princeton and Trenton. Trucks rumble by into the long, late watches of the night. In the sky above, the great aerial carriers make their approach to Newark Airport when the wind is northeast. We are used to it. It is what city dwellers call "gray sound." Here, suspended in the night, the darkness unbroken save for a discrete anchor light high up and behind me, the glow of my laptop and the brief flare of my cigar end, the darkness folds me into it, a welcome cloak.

There is not even a whisper of a breeze. The sea is "oily-glass calm," as my Bahamian crewman, Ishmael, used to refer to it. Ages and ages ago, when I was a charterboatman in the Bahamas with my own dive boat, I used to occasionally put the hook down in little coves in the Exumas and the Berry Islands. Often there was no habitation within miles: no other boats, no air traffic, no sensory contact with the outside world at all. The *Aggressor* does have the continuing sound of a generator, night and day. But this is so omnipresent that it passes into one's subconscious. It does not intrude into this enchanted night. There was no generator on my old dive boat. When I occasionally cruised alone, taking Ishmael with me for crew, that dignified and wise old gentleman and I would chat quietly on the flying bridge after dinner. Then he would turn in, leaving me alone with the total night.

I remember those quiet, deliciously alone nights, as I will this one, with greater sensual recall and pleasure than any of my most spectacular dives. This sort of isolation is not for everyone. My children have to have "tunes," night and day. The ears of an entire generation in our Western world are covered with earphones, their bodies and minds seemingly refreshed by the music of their time. Public places are suffused with what I call "nothing music." It is possible that most of us are not at home with ourselves or able to generate a satisfying mood from silence.

The spell is broken. The first pair of night divers has returned. I can hear their voices, crowding one another with their enthusiasm and desire to share: "Did you see the color display put on by that squid!?" "Right under the boat, a gorgeous nudibranch!" "What was that weird beastie you were shooting over by …?" "I didn't see any sea wasps, but I sure as hell thought about them!"

I close my laptop, my mind abruptly pulled back into the real time and place. My cigar arcs over the side and into the sea, now covered with the expanding arc of ripples from the surfacing divers.

One last look at the stars, big as moons on this hot, still night. One last thought, some part of the evening's mood still holding onto me: I recall a line from Ernle Bradford's *Ulysses Found*. He was speculating on the restlessness of that heroic mariner after he had returned to Ithaca, trashed the suitors, and taken the loyal Penelope to bed again. He wrote: "I do not believe that he was content. One night they slid the black ship down into the water and unloosed the mooring rope from the pierced stone. They turned the eyes of the ship toward the west and, sitting all in order, they smote the gray sea-water."

Monster

There aren't many monsters left around these days, unless you regularly read the *National Enquirer* or *The Globe,* or one of those other delightfully entertaining sheets that are always available in the free library by the checkout counter at supermarkets. Well, we had a real-life monster encounter while diving with the *Palau Aggressor.*

We were sitting about the lounge of that estimable live-aboard that day, waiting for the conch horn to announce chow down. One of the guests, a diver named Barbara Dowell, plugged her camcorder into the lounge monitor for what we thought would be a routine screening of her dive.

She announced, with studied understatement, "I think I've discovered a monster."

Had she averred being abused by a dugong, she couldn't have commanded our attention more dramatically. We all shifted toward the monitor for a good look. I certainly didn't know what to expect but was willing to play along. Maybe a decorator crab with an anemone on its back.

She didn't fast forward. She let the tape play as she shot it, the usual replay of anemones with clownfish, sweet lips being cleaned…ho hum, abundantly available subjects, but well shot. She knew how to handle her Hi-8 system.

Then it appeared. We all simultaneously moved closer. A face that only a mother could love appeared full-frame, peering malevolently from a hole in the sand. The hole was rimmed with small stones, a proper den for a monster. The face, with fat lips, dog nose, and a fine line of small teeth just visible, reminded me of Statler and Waldorf of Muppets fame. A single, evil-looking incisor projected from the center of its upper jaw. One eye, visible from the side angle, was dull white, opaque, and chillingly horrible, like the opaline that special effects men create over the eyes of evil extraterrestrials.

Barbara was thoroughly gratified by the effect this horror had on her audience. One lady, a porcine, unstable, highly nervous, and unlikely diver, clutched her husband's arm as her knees sagged and gasped, "Oh, Henry!"

Eyeballs bulged; everyone exclaimed at once:

"What is it?"

"Jesus Christ!"

"I've never seen anything like that!"

"Mother of Jesus! Where did you find it?"

The explosion of chatter merged into a cacophony of amazement. This certainly was about as close to an unknown monster appearance as I had encountered in a long time diving.

An intrepid dive buddy on the shoot began to gently – very gently – pull away the sand behind the head, hoping to expose more of the body. He was immediately accorded hero status for raw, wild courage. The removal of sand did, indeed, expose about an inch and a half of eel-like body, rust red on top, with square scales.

The animal tolerated this exposure very briefly, and then withdrew into the sand, just as smoothly as a rod sinking into deep mud. The hero was not inclined to try digging after it.

That night a group of intrepid adventurers, led by Barbara, returned to the site. Monster was there again, in good order and unperturbed by the paparazzi at his front door. It again returned to the security of its sub-sand abode when attempts to uncover it exceeded discretion.

At the first screening, the *Aggressor's* resident fish expert, Hector, was called in to identify the horrible thing from the depths. Hector was once a professional fish collector. He has an eagle eye for spotting macro life and has never been stumped with an identification. Now amazement sat on his brow. He wrinkled his forehead, puckered his lips and a hiss of disbelief accompanied a shaking of his head. Hector was stumped. A legend was shattered, a new one born.

I had a pretty good idea about the family to which monster might belong. It was certainly an eel; and it lived under the sand, probably lurking at the opening of its hole with just its head visible, ready to dart out and grab hapless travelers and pilgrims passing by. I had been shown just such an eel by Dee Scarr under the Kralendijk Pier in Bonaire. The one there, used to being hand-fed by Dee, would dart out of the mud to its full four-foot length, seize the bait from her hand, and, in the wink of an eye, retreat into the sand with it. Ultimately she showed it to Paul Humann, the famous fish identification book author, and he included it in his *Reef Fish Identification* (2nd edition) that includes the Caribbean. He identified a similar monster as a "Spotted Spoon-Nosed Eel."

Later, ashore on Palau, two local professional divers recognized the animal; they had encountered it and others in the ship's channel right outside of the harbor. They did not have a name for it. But in one of the fish books on the boat, *Fishes of the Great Barrier Reef and Coral Sea*, we finally found an eel with identical face and head features. It is named the Crocodile Snake Eel. However, the monster in the picture is entirely white.

So our monster turned out to be only another eel, no more offensive than his brethren and certainly not a new species. But in the magic of the moment he was our real, honest t' Goshen monster, and we all shuddered with excitement and loved it.

Creatures of the Night

There is a dive activity on the Kona coast of Hawaii's Big Island that has – at this writing – failed to attract a deluge of customers. The reason? The activity scares people. It violates our most deeply rooted fears of exposure – vulnerability – to "monsters" that live in the ocean deep.

Years ago, when I was a charter boatman with my own dive boat in the Bahamas, I tested that fear. On a passage from the Little Bahama Banks to Nassau, the course takes a boat over a fearsome 6000 feet deep ocean abyss called The Tongue of the Ocean. I was alone, having failed to find a crewman to accompany me from Ft. Lauderdale to Nassau. The time was mid-day. The sea was flat-calm. I had it in mind to let my boat drift, while I went over the side and did a free dive with mask and fins as deep as I could go. The thought of doing that had entered my mind like a virus. It pecked at my shell. It haunted a region that nagged at the back of my mind. Certainly, an element of reason existed alongside the challenge. My reason assured me that "nothing down there would get me."

I won't string out the story. I did go over the side, hyperventilated, and finned down into the deep blue toward a bottom 6,000 feet away. The dive lasted no more than a minute and a half at the most. I reached a level 5,940 feet above the bottom. I forced myself to linger, peering downward along the sun shafts that converged to points far down in the darkening blue. I power-finned back up, and reached the ladder on my boat. That done, I found myself refreshed both in body and mind. I had slain the self-imposed dragon. I need never do anything like that again. Or so I thought.

Forty-one years later I found myself drifting 60 feet down over a 6,000-foot-deep abyss in the dead of night. I did have company, and it was company I trusted. Here's how it came about: Through some gossip or publication – I can't recall when and how – I heard about a lady dive operator with a company called Ocean Drifters. She worked with her own boat off the Kona coast on the Big Island of Hawaii. She took divers out at night to drift with lights over the ocean deep.

Now the Hawaiian Islands are all volcanic peaks that rise from the ocean floor. Not far out from the shore the bottom plunges to abyssal depths. These are the same waters in which Chris Newbert took his stunning picture of a pelagic octopus as he himself drifted through the night waters off the Kona coast. He did those drift dives alone. By doing so he achieved instant and heroic stature in the diving community as a man who didn't know the meaning of fear.

I got an address for Bonnie and initiated a correspondence. I had achieved enough currency as a camera person and moviemaker for Bonnie to know who I was. Her response was enthusiastic and wonderfully generous. She not only invited me to stop by on my travels for some drift dives with her, but supported the invitation with a bag of Kona coffee beans, grown and roasted by her own family. I was hooked. I would do anything for a batch of Kona coffee; I would even sublimate my sense of self-preservation and prudence to eagerly embrace the prospect of drifting through the dark of night over a black void inhabited by giant squid, oceanic whitetip sharks, and other supposed "bad chaps" and – especially – by the unknown.

Bonnie Carini proved to be as enthusiastic and full of energy as our correspondence had promised. Her family house, a quarter of a mile above the Kona coast, looks out upon a glorious expanse of sea. It is set in a verdant tropical garden of coffee trees, giant ferns, and exotic plants. The house is shaded by a giant avocado tree. Her father-in-law, a retired Yale professor, and his wife spend half of each year in that splendid fragrant environment. Bonnie's husband is a golf pro. Her daughter, Larena, now 14, took to the water like a dolphin when she was only a few months old. She and her mother are children of the sea.

Some years ago Bonnie became interested in what she calls the "ocean drifters." They are the zooplankton, a diverse and often spectacular base of the great food chain in the sea. During her daytime dives in the open ocean off Kona, she had encountered strange and wonderful drifting organisms near the surface. She had read about the drifters and knew that at nighttime they rose from deeper water – bizarre, transparent animals that hunted through the night, casting their nets of tendrils to capture food in the broth of near-microscopic phytoplankton through which they drifted. Bonnie developed a system by which divers might join the drifting parade 60 feet down at nighttime.

Here was a target area for my documentary video work, a door to a new and mysterious chamber of the sea. As far as I knew, very little had been done by way of visually recording such encounters. I found the prospect appealing. I also liked the real sense of adventure. In my mind's eye, I clothed the activity with an aura of risk, danger and utter vulnerability. I was, in fact, back where I had started when the idea of doing the solo dive over The Tongue of the Ocean challenged my willpower. Through my mind also ran the conversation between Stein and Jim, in Conrad's *Lord Jim*. Stein said to the shy Jim, whose life was immersed in escape from reality: "The way is to the destructive element submit yourself, and with the exertions of your hands and feet in the water make the deep, deep sea keep you up." I scheduled a four-day stopover in Hawaii on my way back from one of my Palau/Truk tours. The die was cast.

Bonnie Carini turned out to be a slender, fit lady of 37 years with a wild halo of sun-bleached blond hair and a smile as bright as the Hawaiian sun. The generous, warm welcome by her entire family was, as thousands of "haoles" from the mainland have discovered, characteristic of the Hawaiian Islanders. I was drawn into the family as easily as a long-lost relative.

Bonnie's own boat was undergoing repairs. In anticipation of our night drifts, she had chartered the 26-foot work boat of her old friend, Captain Pat Cunningham, a weatherworn fisherman for whom the waters of the Kona coast had been a love and a hunting ground for the great marlin for most of a lifetime.

At dusk on my second evening, we loaded our gear aboard the *Stryker* at a little cove near Bonnie's house. With the last of a golden sunset darkening to deep red, the *Stryker* was backed down the ramp into the sea. An outrigger canoe, stroked by six paddles, passed us, inbound, as we cleared the harbor with the last of the day's light.

There are two deep bottom steps a boat passes over moving straight out from the coast. The fathometer recorded our passage over those steps; five minutes with 200 feet under us; then the fathom line on the glowing instrument dropped to 600 feet for 15 more minutes before the ocean floor abruptly vanished off the graph, plunging downward beyond its range. The indication was only electronic. The gut feel was of falling from the rim of the Grand Canyon. We stopped the engine and commenced our drift over a water column more than a mile deep. It is along this edge that the sport fishermen hunt for the giant marlin, the thousand-pound leviathans.

No time to think about what was down there. Bonnie became a whirlwind of preparation, carefully preparing the down line and the four leads that would extend from it. Her system is entirely practical. A 30-foot down line is attached to the boat. At the bottom of the line are four 30-foot leads. The end of each clip is secured to the diver's buoyancy vest. Thus four divers may drift 60 feet down with the boat, which is also drifting above them. The leads allow independent movement for each diver to chase whatever drifting organism he may wish to focus on. It also assures Bonnie that her guests will not disappear into the dark beyond or chase some pelagic prize deeper than the lead permits. A 300-watt underwater light just under the surface by the boat floodlights the arena and, Bonnie explained, serves to attract the night drifters from deeper water. A vision of Peter Benchley's giant squid was quickly squashed as it flitted past my mind.

Bonnie was all efficiency, a calming stay to the apprehensions we kept under our hats. In addition to Bonnie and Captain Pat were Bonnie's brother, Louis, just back from China and soon to leave for graduate studies at Columbia. Rob Barrel and Catherine Holloway, operators of the splendid live-aboard dive yacht, Nai'a – and old friends – were visiting on business from Fiji. There was room on a fourth lead for one of them each of the two night drifts I had planned. Catherine (called Cat) was on this first night.

I was shooting video with a pair of video lights. Cat and Bonnie had still cameras with strobes. Louis carried with him the latest shark repeller, the Shark Pod, a device that broadcasts an electronic pulse when activated. Ron and Val Taylor had thoroughly tested it and found it worked well even with the great white, if the animal was not already feeding. We did not intend to feed. However, the big, beefy oceanic whitetips frequent those deep waters and can be quite nosy. The device, attached to Louis' tank and one fin, was primarily psychological insurance.

As introducers are fond of saying, "and without further ado" we were over the side, down to the end of our tethers, clipped on, and each on our own.

The light from above penetrated the intense darkness about us for little more than the circumference of our extended tethers. A scattering of suspended material, like motes of dust, reflected the light. Within less than five minutes – and so gradually that the change was hardly perceptible – I became aware of a quantum increase in that scattering, now punctuated by the appearance of large, transparent, but entirely visible animals that drifted and pulsed through the increasing broth of life.

I started shooting. The lightning flashes of the strobes picked up. The others, like myself, were so caught up in chasing down the ocean drifters and concentrating on framing them for the takes, that there wasn't time to pass even a thought about lurking monsters. I was fascinated, totally taken up with the challenge of focusing on those ephemeral macro beasties. On eye contact, inches away and illuminated by my video light from below or from the side, they were gorgeous, delicate, complexly designed space ships.

Siphonophores, transparent ectoplasmic cubes, pulsed through the water. Iridescent red and green lateral veins pulsed through their bodies. Flagelli, near-microscopic hairs, waved rhythmically, providing propulsion.

A salp chain, sometimes called a colonial salp, drifted by like a necklace of glasslike cells, each the size of my thumbnail. I later learned that each cell contains a notochord, forerunner of the vertebrae that would millions of years later support the primates. I greeted my ancestor with a 15-second run of the tape.

The broth was thickening, composed of mysid shrimp, phytoplankton, and larval zooplankton, these last too small to see. Almost all of the larger animals were transparent. One, about an inch and a half long, had twin disks, like Mickey Mouse ears, attached to a larval lobster. Another carried within it a fish, three-eighths of an inch long. As I rolled my camera, it backed out of an open end and darted out of frame.

At last, something I recognized and wanted no part of. A box jelly appeared in my lights. I maneuvered out of its path and ran my camera and lights along the 15-foot length of its nematocyst-charged tentacles trailing past as it pulsed by. This was not the box jelly with four short tentacles so feared in Australia. Bonnie confirmed, however, to our relief, that it was a fairly innocuous species.

A series of raps on a tank drew my attention to Bonnie. She pointed to a pair of squid, each about 12 inches long, fighting over a scrap of fish she had torn up and released as we drifted. Their arms were meshed as they grappled for the bait, then flew apart, leaving a small cloud of ink where they had been. Shortly after that encounter, my lights picked up another solid form among the drifting phantoms. It was a tiny dark red seahorse, no more than two inches long. We converged on it, like paparazzi, strobes flashing. Later, when we surfaced, Bonnie told me she had never encountered one in a night drift.

The time space between encounters shortened until one had to selectively choose the most exotic and interesting animals. That first night perhaps the most exotic and certainly the most predatory of the macro animals was a large drifter with a body that looked like an electronic circuit board, a grid composed of lines of glowing beads. Attached to this four-by-eight-inch rectangle was a tail so long that it extended beyond the length of my tether. I lighted it as far as I could reach. As I rolled tape, myriad slivers erupted like teeth from a comb on either side of the tail spreading a hair-like net. In that jungle of hunter and prey, that net must have been as deadly as a fine-mesh gillnet before a school of herring.

I might mention that documenting the ocean drifters with video is somewhat more difficult than doing it with a still camera with framer and strobe. Then again, some of the animals are too widely spread with their tails and tendrils to fit into a framer. With video you have two moving objects: yourself and the target, and nothing to anchor yourself. I often found it efficacious to abandon the viewing port and observe the animal from the side, placing him almost next to my dome port and counting on autofocus and the depth-of-field with a wide-angle dome port at point-blank range.

Our second night was, with some notable newcomers, a repeat of the first. However, one of the newcomers was so unexpected and startling that the encounter dominated the dive.

This time Rob Barrel and Bonnie's daughter, Larena, made up two of the four divers. As on the first night, conditions were ideal: calm sea and easy current. Toward the end of the dive that night we were in somewhat of a tangle. Having pursued our various courses in all directions as the targets dictated, the tethers were criss-crossed again and again. Rob told me later that he was watching Bonnie when something collided with the back of his head. He thought I had blundered into him and turned around to find himself nose to nose with a 20-foot whale shark. Now Rob is a cool customer with several thousand hours of diving; but he came closer to soiling his undies, he said, than at any other time in his career. He bellowed into the water, catching my attention. I almost jumped out of my suit. I swung both my lights onto him and caught the scene as he passed through our light sphere, returned for another pass, and finally turned upward to arrive on the surface by the boat, almost frightening the captain out of his wits.

I will go back for more and avail myself of Bonnie's unique and entirely wonderful night drifts. There's nothing pecking at my shell any more. The phantoms are dispersed, and the sea, as usual, provides as fine an adventure and experience as we may have on this wondrous planet.

My Son, the Manta Rider

Some years ago, when Peter Benchley and I were doing one or two *American Sportsman* shows each year, I was present at one of the most enchanting diver/marine animal encounters I have ever been part of.

We were in the Sea of Cortez on the old *Don José,* a wooden-hulled, trawler-type boat captained by Tim Means and hot as hell. We were on station over the Marisla Seamount (also known as El Bajo), a 60-foot-deep island of life that rose steeply from several hundred feet. At the top, it was about as large as a football field. It was an oasis rising from a benthic plain. It was home to the movements of a school of scalloped hammerheads that cruised over and around it. It also attracted manta rays – big ones – the giant Pacific mantas that can be 20 and more feet across from wing tip to wing tip. The erratic topography of the seamount provided cover for colonies of moray eels in the crevasses and cracks. Dense schools of grunts and surgeonfish swayed like a living canopy over the bottom, and handsome king angelfish moved imperiously through the crowds. It was an exciting, delightful marine community.

Howard Hall, then a young, developing underwater cameraman, was with us; and so was my son Gordy, also a budding underwater cameraman. His girlfriend, Diana Tylor, was the topside cameralady and director of photography. Now you have the infrastructure, the background to the incident, but there was one rather vital addition to the personnel: the co-star of the show, Howard Hall's wife, Michele.

Sharks were, of course, the objective. This was a shoot for a network documentary. Then, as now, "dangerous" or big marine animals were requisite grist for the documentary mill. Thus whale sharks, both big and – as supposed by the vast uninitiated public dangerous because they were sharks – were a major target for filmmakers. On this trip, hammerheads would have to do. Because their appearance is so grotesque, it was assumed that they were particularly dangerous. We discovered, as did legions of divers after us, that they were, in reality, particularly shy. They did not like bubbles. In fact, bubbles were anathema to them, and we terrestrial animals venturing into the sea were inextricably cursed with a roaring cacophony of bubbles at every breath.

Hammerhead outriders, advance scouts, might make a pass within visual range when we were diving on the seamount. But it was the big school that we wanted on film, and our bubbles were a bar to success. The schools cruised about the perimeter of the rise, hanging out in the surrounding deep water, about 60 feet down. At that distance the 50 or 60 in the schools looked like squiggling spermatozoa. We needed to descend into the school for any effective shooting. We tried, but with the first exhaled bubbles the school would fade away into deeper water like a mirage: now you saw them, now you didn't. Howard and I were the shooters. I was already so far gone in hedonistic indulgence that I could only breath-hold dive for 30 feet and then bolt for the surface with my corrupted body crying for air. Our hopes centered on Howard.

Howard Hall, not long out of that fertile divers' womb, Chuck Nicklin's Diving Locker in San Diego, was a veteran of spearfishing competitions and deep breath-hold diving; and he was still in shape. He was able to descend silently into the school and even below the school, coming back with fine, crisp silhouette takes of the whole school and with parallel shots at close range as he ascended easily and quietly through them. Without Howard, we would have returned with nothing but spermatozoa. So much for the hammerheads. The real, mind-blowing drama was going on back at the seamount and right under the boat.

While we men were off doing our macho, death-defying thing with the maneaters (and so we liked to think of it), Michele Hall suited up and indulged herself in a recreational dive down to the mount. From the surface, she had her first sight of the other co-star in this story. As she described the experience to us – taking all the wind out of our Rambo shark encounter – it was a big manta ray, hanging motionless in midwater below her, about halfway to the surface of the mount. Marty Snyderman, Howard's assistant cameraman and also one of the Diving Locker's progeny, was kneeling on the back of the manta. As Michele's distance to the manta closed, she saw that it had tangled with a gill net; the cephalic lobes that open on each side of the mouth and almost the entire leading edge of its wings were caught in a large segment of the netting. The extraordinary scene checked her descent for a moment; and in that moment Marty, already sucking on the last of his air, had to lift off the animal and make a fast ascent.

Herself a seasoned diver and already long experienced in working with marine animals, Michele did not power dive down to the beast, but let her buoyancy diminish and drifted quietly down like a spider on a gossamer web strand. As she neared the great animal, she realized it was a truly big manta, about 18 feet across. She continued her descent, alighting gently on the back of the manta; the animal remained motionless, supporting her, accepting her. Now Michele was at that time a practicing surgical nurse, very used to working carefully with patients. She set about cutting away the net, very carefully removing it from the raw intrusions it had made into the flesh. She could feel the great animal shuddering under her touch, wincing from contact with the raw, sensitive places.

In time – and there is no sense of time during such a dramatic crisis – the cruel impediments were entirely removed. With that, the manta began to move, gaining headway with a slow flexing of its wings. It did not take flight although they can take off with powerful bursts of speed when they are frightened. Instead, it took Michele for a ride, as she held on to the front of the wings. She told us of the ride as we stood about, gaping and rolling our eyes. The two new friends, patient and nurse, swooped and banked and flew easily around the seamount. She found herself on a magic carpet, a gentle flying machine for whom the pleasure of having its benefactor aboard seemed apparent. At the end of the ride – and the animal never descended so deep that Michele had to let go – the manta seemed to shrug, producing a little burst of speed that dislodged her. He (maybe it was a she; I never bothered to look) circled the rider once, perhaps to have a better look at his new friend, and then vanished into the deeper water.

Our focus was now divided between the hammerheads and this surprise winged visitor. We wasted little time in diving down to our anchor and readily encountered the giant manta. What's more, he hovered expectantly, like the first taxi in the line, virtually inviting us to hop aboard. We realized that Michele had created an Androcles-and-the-Lion syndrome with this animal. He associated human visitors with the comfort and release that Michele had provided. The human/animal relationship so engendered was, for most of us, far more dynamic and appealing than the hammerhead shark scene.

During the next two days, we all took turns riding the magic carpet. Peter Benchley and I climbed aboard together, holding on as Michele first did to the leading edge of his great wings, our bodies resting along his back. We could feel the muscles of his wings, like a powerful engine, pulse and ripple as we soared over and about the seamount. The strength in reserve was massive. The path of the ride could vary from about 40 feet to something more than 100 feet. He swooped and soared like the giant bird that he was. We had to be careful to exhale as he climbed steeply like a jet lifting off. The rides seldom lasted longer than three or four minutes, although it seemed longer. He either shrugged us off or descended to a depth at which we felt compelled to let go. It was, without a doubt, the most enchanting, exhilarating, rewarding experience I have had in my years as a diver.

I had a similar experience with a manta of equal size at San Benedicto Island some years later. There, two of my grown children, Gar and Susy, and I were all three carried easily on the back of a friendly manta. But the encounter at the Marisla seamount was the first and most cherished in my memory.

And that brings me to my son, the manta rider. Everyone in the crew wanted a chance to at least snorkel in order to observe the benevolent manta. Those who were certified divers wanted a chance for a ride. On our last day, with all principal shooting done and the manta still hanging around for riders, Gordy had his chance. He didn't know it at the time, but he also achieved a small measure of immortality. Howard Hall was there with his still camera and caught the perfect shot. Gordy had the tail of a remora in each hand. The two fish were attached firmly with their suckers to the back of the manta on either side of the head. They served as handlebars for Gordy. In the modest scope of the diving world, the picture was as famous as the Yanks raising the Stars and Stripes on Iwo Jima. It appeared in posters, in advertisements, and rated a double page in *National Geographic*. Two T-shirt companies ripped it off for their shirts and had to be brought to the line by Howard. And certainly every Waterman in this family has an eight-by-ten, or larger, on a wall. Gordy may ride on other animals in his career as a professional cameraman, but he will never do it with such style or be so well frozen in time and place.

There are environmentalists and nature lovers who object to humans consorting with wild animals like that. And, indeed, some harm may accrue by making certain animals dependent on man or so tame that hunters can easily destroy them. In the case of the mantas, I do not feel that the objection is valid. On the occasions of my own two wonderful rides on big mantas, the Sea of Cortez and San Benedicto Island, the animals so manifestly enjoyed the experience, returning over and over again to repeat it, that there could be no doubt that the touching and riding of them provided reciprocal pleasure. At San Benedicto, the splendid manta that carried Susy and Gar and me on his back came to the surface with us when our air ran out. As we boarded the Zodiac, he flapped around on the surface, watching us and appearing for all the world to invite us back with him.

In both places, the mantas that befriended us are gone. They were destroyed by gillnet fishermen. Whether it was intentional or not is a moot point; but the fishermen market the manta wings for food. The mantas can wreck large parts of the nets in their struggle to escape, but in doing so they usually enmesh themselves and die. The nets are indiscriminate. The fishermen in the Third World countries are poor, not malevolent. They fish with the most effective equipment they can afford in order to survive tomorrow. They overfish. They inexorably diminish, day by day and year by year, any legacy that might be left for their children and grand-children in the sea. And their numbers increase disastrously.

There is nothing new in these thoughts. A cartoon character of Walt Kelly's named Pogo observed: "We have met the enemy, and he is us." To the impressive credit of the Mexican government, the islands of San Benedicto and Socorro and their surrounding waters were declared a Protected Area in 1994. Other mantas have taken over and are always to be found there, but our original friends are long-gone.

I am grateful that I and all three of my children knew a time when there was a sort of marine Camelot, and those magnificent, winged giants became our friends.

Hans & Lotte Hass

A Remembrance

The book caught my eye. It was displayed in the window of a book store in Scranton, Pennsylvania. The title: *Diving To Adventure*. That book did not initiate my fascination and love affair with the sea, but it was a most potent catalyst in propelling me to cast my lot with a career of diving.

The author was Hans Hass. The time was 1950. I had mustered out of the Navy, finished college, married my sweetheart, returned from a long honeymoon, and was living with my wife's family in Scranton. The cigar factory my father had started was also located there. What would I do with my life? I was at sea, so to speak – and not the sea I would eventually submerge into. My father's business afforded immediate employment in the postwar job vacuum in which so many of us found ourselves. So much for background. Hans Hass and the adventure he described saved me from becoming a cigar maker. I had been breath-hold diving during the war, when I was stationed in the Canal Zone. A few of us in the squadron – mostly California boys who had also acquired the first fins, masks, and snorkels marketed by Owen Churchill and employed them "ab" and "bug" diving at home – explored the virgin tropical reefs in that area. So I was much into skin diving in the 1940s, and even did some spearfishing with a pole gun. But the adventure described by Hass and documented with black-and-white underwater still photographs so far advanced the range of exploration, daring, and excitement, that it charged me with visions of future adventures for myself. It planted a potent seed. A vague, romantic dream evolved from that book into compelling reality.

Our excursion into the sea, aided and accelerated by technology, has developed and grown so rapidly that young divers today can hardly comprehend the fact that it has happened in the course of less than one generation. Hans Hass and his early companion and wife, Lotte, are true pioneers; and they are still very much alive today. They were honored by the American Historical Diving Society at a special tribute to them in Santa Barbara. I, along with many of the most prominent figures in diving, was in attendance.

What was it Hans wrote about in *Diving To Adventure*? In 1939, as the dogs of war were being unleashed over Europe, he and a small group of fellow students and friends from the University of Vienna carried out an expedition to the tiny, sleepy, and then little-known islands of Bonaire and Curaçao in the Netherlands Antilles. They were equipped with basic skin diving equipment and crude oxygen rebreathers made by the Dräger company. The Aqualung had not yet appeared on the scene. Jacques Cousteau was unknown to the rest of the world. They were just in time to be interned by the Dutch authorities, whose government and home country had been invaded by Germany. Austria had already been annexed by Germany; so Hans and his team were enemy nationals. Happily – and to their credit – the authorities recognized that the young students posed no danger to the island and were just what they appeared to be, young people on an adventure. So Hans was allowed to set up his shore camp on the little island of Klein Bonaire.

For the tens of thousands who have dived around Klein Bonaire in recent years as it evolved into one of the most popular diving sites in the Caribbean, it would be hard to believe how pristine and well-populated with both reef and pelagic life that much-used dive area was 60 years ago. Also, today's divers, in a time when sharks are hand-fed and moray eels stroked and coddled, can hardly credit the sense of danger and the raw excitement that pervaded the truly seminal exposure to that marine environment. Only the exuberance of youth and commitment to exploration and exposure to hazard could have conceived the expedition and carried it through.

There had been other excursions into the sea by Hans before that – walking across the Danube with a shallow-water open helmet, free diving with his own underwater housing for a Leica 35mm camera on the Yugoslavian Coast in 1938, lectures before growing audiences in Germany and Austria, showing his underwater photographs, and describing his diving adventures, a sensation at that time. He terminated his studies for a law degree, committed himself to study and exploration in the sea, and never looked back. A chronicle of his achievements is well documented in Historical Diver, the publication of the American Historical Diving Society, and in a biography by Michael Jung, presently published only in German. In her book Women Pioneers In Diving, Bonnie Cardone focuses on Lotte Hass, the beautiful girl who became Hans' secretary, diving assistant, wife, and the world's first lady underwater model. The publication of eight books and the production of three theater-release feature films,

Stan Waterman

all of which played in the U.S., attest to Hans' prolific energies and enterprise. And there were breakthroughs in equipment. Remember the Hans Hass Rolleimarin, the first professional quality underwater flash camera, developed in 1950? As far back as 1951, Hans worked with the Dräger company to modify their oxygen rebreather for his work.

I can easily be carried away by an account of his accomplishments. In fact, this article is intended to be a personal observation, drawn from my personal acquaintance and friendship with Hans and Lotte. We met about 25 years ago. I can't recall the year. The place was London. The occasion, an underwater film festival held at the stately, splendid Grosvenor House and sponsored by the British Subaqua Club and *Triton* magazine (now *Diver* and Britain's premier dive journal). We were both presenters. Hans was already my idol and – as explained above – the initial catalyst to my own serious turn toward the sea. We hit it off. I found that rare, arcane anomaly in this day's social world: a gracious, courtly, well-educated gentleman, multi-lingual, renaissance in his range of interest and knowledge, tempered with humor, enthusiasm, and great affability. Among European divers, Hans Hass already stood tall, fully perceived as one of the great pioneers. In the U.S., a relatively small part of the diving community knew about him. In part, the reason was the complete dominance of Jacques Cousteau in the media, through the marketing of the first popular, practical scuba equipment, the Aqualung, the publishing of *The Silent World*, the success of the feature film of the same name, and – most especially – the launching of the television series, "The Underwater World of Jacques Cousteau." That protean, truly estimable man was launched, like a spectacular rocket, into the awareness of not only the diving world but the informed lay public around the world. The name Cousteau became synonymous with our new reach into the sea.

Deservedly, Cousteau, during his extraordinarily productive lifetime, eclipsed all others in the diving world with international recognition. His flare for showmanship was largely responsible for that broad popularity. Using the media well and associating with the National Geographic Society, he kept his name and exploits up front. There is no merit in comparing Hass to Cousteau. Together they were the paramount pioneers in their field. But now that Jacques Cousteau has departed this world, Hans Hass is being fully honored and recognized as he should have been years ago.

After Hans and I became personally acquainted, his daughter, Meta, visited with my family in Maine. That must have been in the early 1970s. She and a girlfriend, still in college together, were touring the U.S. Like her father and mother, she was cheerful, voluble, and wonderfully bright. Her studies carried on to the achievement of a Ph.D. Her marriage, strong

222

and lasting like that of her parents, produced two grandchildren for Hans and Lotte.

At the pinnacle of his diving career and his continuing study of marine animal behavior, Hans led expeditions on his own three-masted schooner, the *Xarifa*. The magnificent 165-foot sailing yacht became the field research ship for his newly formed International Institute for Submarine Research in 1951. During the 1950s, his expeditions ranged across the Atlantic to the Caribbean, the Galápagos Islands, and on through the Red Sea and the Indian Ocean to Singapore.

Having achieved the dream of any marine scientist – his own research ship and foundation with the world's oceans for his range – Hans put his diving and marine research behind and tacked onto a new course. He commenced studies for a doctorate in the field of human behavior, developing his thesis at the world-famous Max Planck Institute in Dortmund, Germany. That turn of mind, that broad reach for knowledge along with the ability to turn his energies to fresh tasks – as much as his achievements in the sea – marked Hans as a man with diverse and broad intellectual range.

My wife, Susy, and I had occasion to be in Europe and visited with Hans and Lotte in Vienna. There we discovered still another facet of these well- and full-living people. We were royally entertained with an extent of generosity and thoughtful planning that we had never experienced before (or since, for that matter). They introduced us to the glorious tradition of hospitality in that ancient city.

Not long ago, I attended a film festival and trade show at the ancient and tradition-rich city of Harrogate in northeastern England. There is a huge convention center there. Its main auditorium was filled to capacity for the presentation by their honored guests, Hans and Lotte. With the aplomb acquired from the years when he recounted his adventures and showed his slides and films in theaters around Europe, Hans gracefully and with good humor survived a false fire alarm that cleared the auditorium and interrupted his presentation for a half hour. His black-and-white film, taken of sharks in open water in the Aegean during the early 1940s, was pure archival work and brought down the house. And at a banquet with many speeches, Lotte displayed that vivacity and enthusiasm that had won Hans' heart over 50 years ago.

The ranks are thinning. Few of the real pioneers, the men and women who opened the new era of ocean exploration and research, are still with us today. Hans and Lotte Hass are among the survivors, a couple who are at the top of that pantheon, very much alive, and now very much honored throughout the diving world.

Bait Ball

The phrase "feeding frenzy" is much used and much abused. Holiday divers, returning to the attention and admiration of those land-bound mortals who have been left behind, enjoy a measure of heroism achieved with the description of feeding frenzies they have witnessed, perhaps been in the very middle of, and lived to tell about.

Feeding frenzies do occur, although very few divers are privileged to actually witness one. Most divers, if they knew what a real feeding frenzy is like, would not wish to. We had the real McCoy off Cocos Island in September of 1998. I had been waiting for such a phenomenon to unfold before my video lens for many years, most especially since I saw a remarkable documentary by Avi Klapfer of a true feeding frenzy. Avi owns the *Undersea Hunter* and the *Sea Hunter*, two fine live-aboard dive boats that operate at Cocos Island off the Pacific coast of Costa Rica. I happened to be on the *Okeanos Aggressor*, also at Cocos Island, when the long-hoped-for experience occurred.

There are ways of initiating a feeding frenzy. At one of the routine shark-feeding performances that are offered today, at which a divemaster hand-feeds a well-mannered gathering of sharks, you might cut the throat of the guest next to you, swim away, and watch the sharks pig out on him. At Cocos Island one looks for the birds. At sea, perhaps a quarter mile out, you may frequently see the air above the water broken by distant black specks. These will be boobies feeding on baitfish. At the same time, the frigate birds will hover over the melee, ready to snatch any catch away from the boobies. The frigates, unable to land on the water, are pirates living off the boobies. The birds may be hitting on a moving school of small fish. Or they may also be moving with a bait ball, in which case the schooling fish are moving in a tight ball or vortex, surrounded by pelagic predators. The schooling victims are impelled by survival instinct and mutual protection to crowd one another. An analogy might be the instinct of horses to run back into a burning barn.

At a distance, one may see dolphins at the surface. For the chance of snorkeling with these dolphins, the *Okeanos Aggressor* will drop interested guests over the side of one of the fast skiffs at the site of the action. Usually the baitfish school has moved on, being dispersed and highly mobile. With luck the dolphins may stick around, make a few passes within video or still range, and then move on themselves. A bait ball holds its position, drifting with the current. The attack on that mass by the circling "Indians" may continue throughout the day if the bait mass is dense enough. The one we lucked out on did just that.

Two professional divers were already down when I dropped over, with the birds dive-bombing all around. Jay Ireland and Georgienne Bradley were documenting the action with both stills and digital video. For them, the wild occasion was a rare and wonderful windfall. While hammerhead sharks are the big focus at Cocos Island, this scene could well make the whole week for all of us.

Sharks galore! Sharks in every sector. Sharks nearly colliding with us; sharks – as if by some predatory signal – suddenly driving into and through the bait ball from all directions. The bait ball, densely packed, immediately under a floating mess of ship's cordage, expanded into a swirling mass under the top layer. Once contacted by the shark assault, the mass convulsed, sagged, and briefly lost its tight formation, like a battle line wavering under attack. Then it reformed into an ever-whirling, powerful, cyclonic force, powerless to fight back, blindly maddened to stave off annihilation as long as possible.

Ninety-five percent of the sharks appeared to be silkies, few under six feet or over seven. A small number of Galapagos sharks shared the feast, along with rainbow runners, big black jacks, and an occasional hefty yellowfin tuna. On the perimeter of the bait ball cruised a small pod of four bottlenose dolphins. Jay and Georgienne saw them occasionally pick up a single bait fish that wandered into the open. They appeared uninterested in charging the bait ball. Instead, they circled the action in a leisurely way, perhaps enjoying it like people slowing down to eyeball an accident. It's possible that they had already eaten to surfeit before we arrived on the scene.

With almost 60 minutes of digital tape in my Sony DCR-SC100, a fresh battery, and a spanking-new Light & Motion housing that performed like a champ, I let the tape run. In such a possibly once-in-a-lifetime diving experience, you don't conserve your ammunition. So I worked as close as I could, with a wide-angle port to contain the whole matrix of action in the frame. From time to time I swung around to record the scores, literally scores, of sharks in the open water around the ball. Jay and Georgienne, concentrating on their work, hardly noticed the cruising sharks that repeatedly approached them and then swung away, inches from their bodies. It was, of course, happening to me too; but the imperative of camera people is to get the shot. Damn the torpedoes! Full speed ahead!

In this euphoria of false security I failed to notice that I had maneuvered downcurrent from the drift of the bait ball. Quite suddenly, the current carried it on top of me. With a sense of genuine alarm, I realized I was in the middle of the mass: visibility fish only. I backpedaled furiously, seeming to make no headway. Then, adding to the excitement, the sharks launched one of their gourmand forays. Their solid bodies rocketed past me, a flash of brown in the all-embracing silver cloud, coming from all directions. I flash-thought, "they can't all miss me in their blind charges;" and then, one didn't. It was a sledge-hammer blow, knocking me aside like a Mack truck might sideswipe a bicycle. I wondered if I had sustained a bite and half-expected to see blood billowing out from my wetsuit. No blood. No bite. The collision did knock the left handle off my new housing. Later, I considered the possibility of it having been the right handle: the one I was holding. And then I was out of it – in the clear, too busy to think about what happened. That would come later. Jay also found himself in the middle of the action and sustained three hits by the brown torpedoes powering through the mass. He also described the blows as like being hit by a sledgehammer and thought they were all received on his tank.

I shot the wild spectacle inside, outside, around, and up and down, grateful for the long, 60-minutes load of tape and the 90-minute battery in my digital camcorder. For more than 30 years I shot 16mm film. A magazine load lasted 12 minutes. Frustration reached epidemic proportions.

Some while after I had wrapped my coverage, Jay and Georgienne went out again, accompanied by Michael Topolovac, the president and founder of Light & Motion Industries. The rope mass had sunk. The bait school was drawn to the Zodiac. The action seethed around the inflatable skiff, right at the surface, creating a maelstrom of lashing sharks' tails, criss-crossing fins, and water boiling with the convulsions of the bait school. Into this cauldron, the divers, without getting wet and committing suicide, lowered their cameras with remote control extensions. The housings finally retired from the fray, honorably scarred with bite marks that were plainly visible on the aluminum.

In hindsight I am reminded of Conrad's words in *Lord Jim*: "To the destructive element submit yourself, and by the exertions of your hands and feet in the water, make the deep, deep sea keep you up." Whatever sustained me during the submersion into that real feeding frenzy, it was certainly not prudence. For all of us who think we are safe behind our cameras, there must be a certain kind of madness, a tunnel vision, an "out to get the shot" irrational belief that we are safe from the bullets whizzing around us.

Jaws of Death

The most ridiculous, inept, and lamentable production I have ever been party to occurred some years past. A Hollywood producer, who will remain unidentified in this narration and whom we will call "Herman," contacted me to do the underwater filming for a production to be called *Jaws of Death*.

The title implied wild adventure and the titillating flavor of hazard. The kernel of the plot was first contact with the most bloodthirsty, malevolent marine animal known to man, the killer whale. That I even lent my services to such a shoddy plot will testify to my indiscriminate lust for income. The deal: $300 per day, a princely sum back then, and $150 per day for an assistant – all plus travel expenses. I was too callow to even suggest an initial payment up front. However, in a fine fit of nepotism, I signed on my youngest son, Gar, as my assistant. He was 18 at the time, free during the summer, and much pleased with the prospect.

The producer had a track record of schlock pseudo-documentaries on such dreaded creatures as the Komodo dragon and the boa constrictor – both, in the public eye frightful menaces to explorers. Such horror/animal films, of course, go far to encourage the impression the public has of ravening beasts of prey. It mattered little or nothing to me that I would focus on the intelligent, then-little-understood orca. The name "killer whale" was enough for a Hollywood exploiter to sense success.

We joined our production boat in Vancouver. It was a 45-foot sloop with a ferro-cement hull, captained by its German owner and builder. It was his pride and joy. He ran a taut ship and was, at the outset, not enthusiastic about the exuberant hippie production manager and his girlfriend, who was signed on as cook. Both were Scientologists, favoring organically pure foods, no meats, only grains and veggies. The captain had been raised on fat wursts. The producer and his myrmidon, a porcine, pasty accountant with a wardrobe of stretch pants and tasseled loafers, were big on steaks and chops.

Gar and I and the surface cameraman could swing with the cuisine, but we all had robust appetites. The nature diet very soon became a point of contention. Not only had the cook entirely stocked the galley with her idea of food for appetites sharpened by salt air and sea, she and her boyfriend commenced a program of proselytizing for Scientology as well as sane diet. The storm clouds gathered.

We cruised north between Vancouver Island and the Canadian mainland, past Campbell River and into the Johnson Straits, northward to Port Hardy, a lumber terminus where great Douglas firs, pines, and spruce were rafted and gathered for shipping to the mills. On our way north, we had observed, with dismay, the acres of bare, scarred ground on the mountainsides that were the aftermath of clear-cutting lumber operations, in which the forest giants were mowed down by armies of chain saws.

At Port Hardy we were directed to an unused dock on a small island in the middle of the strait and assured that a resident pod of orcas would cruise up and down the strait right by our front door. The information was correct. We had hardly established ourselves at the dock before a shout drew our eyes to the great black dorsal fin of a male orca, clear and clean in the afternoon sun, breaking surface no more than 200 yards from us and followed by a rolling display of fins from the rest of the pod. The already-well-established enmity among three different factions in our team was momentarily forgotten in the promise of action the next day. The truce was short lived.

The dock to which we tied was a float that rose and fell with the tide, secured at its four corners to stout pilings by iron hoops. The tide peak and low ran between 12 and 15 feet. Secured to the dock, we rose and fell conveniently with it. A shack had been built at one of the shoreside corners of the float. It was weathered but still sound, with a good roof and rough plank floor. Herman and the pigmentless accountant (whom we shall call Sol), directly on landing and examining it, claimed it for their exclusive quarters. They carted their sleeping bags, air mattresses, and a canvas bag from which clinking-glass sounds accompanied each step across the float and into the shack. We watched this separation of boss and worker, exchanging glances and actually somewhat pleased by the move. I assumed the director and his sidekick were establishing the loneliness of command.

We had, at Port Hardy, been directed to a small village not far up the coast from our island location as a place where supplies could be had and refreshment served at a small hotel. Now our only means of transportation, other than the mother ship, was a Zodiac with a 25-horsepower outboard. Leaving us to the wholesome prospect of another dinner prepared by Mother Nature in the galley, Herman and Sol cheerily advised us not to hold dinner for them.

They were taking the Zodiac to the village for "serious production business." One of us showed them how to start the motor. Without a button to push or an ignition key to turn, they were as helpless as babes in the woods. We watched them disappear around the end of the island, and, before the sun was even over the yardarm, we thwarted the cook's inflexible regimen by attacking our own dwindling supply of refreshment.

By dark the mariners had not returned. We hoped they had been eaten by orcas. On toward midnight we were awakened by the sound of two outboard motors approaching the dock. Captain and I poked our heads out of the cabin hatch enough to watch the bosses' return. They had acquired a second boat at a small marina in the village. Available for sale was one of those wretched, tacky, ill-designed runabouts of the sort that festoon holiday lake and seaside resorts that attract city folk. As they probed about with their newly acquired powerful flashlights, we caught a glimpse of aquamarine vinyl upholstery inside a red cockpit, at the stern of which was an outboard that looked as big as an IMAX underwater housing. How these two city nerds had found their way back in the dark was beyond our comprehension. We did have a masthead riding light on, Captain's only concession for guiding them.

As we watched, they secured the Zodiac to the stern of our boat and tethered (the best word to use) their speedboat to the top of one of the pilings. The tide was high. The top of the piling was no more than five feet above the pier. They made their unsteady way to the shack. Captain and I caught one another's eye with what I recall was a very broad smile. He improved the double granny knot by which the Zodiac had been tied to the stern and we turned in.

The next morning we of the boat crew had breakfasted and were warming ourselves with second coffees on the dock by the side of the boat. There had been no stirring from within the shack. The sun was well up. We had all taken enormous satisfaction from the sight that greeted us as we first came on deck and awaited with keen expectation the first appearance of the nocturnal adventurers.

Any reader familiar with tides and floats that rise and fall will have already anticipated the astonishing and, to us – the mean-spirited and revengeful audience – the satisfying disaster that had so inexorably overtaken the pride and joy of the speedboat owners. The bow of the boat was still securely bound by the unbreakable polypropylene painter to the top of the piling. The stern was now hanging straight down with the still-ebbing tide just over the motor. All loose paraphernalia, including fishing rods and a tackle box the instant sportsmen had been induced to buy, had fallen in a most satisfying mess into the stern. The motor was completely submerged.

We waited with delicious expectation and were not disappointed. Herman and Sol emerged from the shack, yawned and stretched, and, of course, treated themselves to their first look at their shiny new acquisition.

Their mouths dropped open. Their eyeballs bulged. They were almost a parody of what we had expected. They walked hesitatingly, disbelief in their glazed faces, to the piling and stood staring at the wreckage of their newly minted dream. We sipped our coffee and watched.

In time we cut the painter. The miserable boat did have floatation material in its hull and so did not plummet to the bottom, engine first. In time, it was towed by the Zodiac back to the marina and left for resurrection. Hostility increased. Those who are stupid or ignorant – or both – must project blame for such a disaster on others. In this case, and because Herman and the young production manager had already incubated a strong aversion to one another, they actually came to blows that day on the dock. There was some flailing with ineffective roundhouse punches before we separated the combatants. This was going to be a most interesting trip.

The orcas in the Johnson Straits proved smart enough not to want any part of us. Perhaps by some occult prescience, they knew the production we were focusing on them would portray them as pathological killers with special enmity for humans.

Mind you, this ill-conceived, ridiculous production was carried out over 25 years ago or more. Orcas were not yet the pets and stars of ocean aquariums. We did not really know how they would react to divers, even though we had heard of no dangerous encounters with them. So when I dropped over the side of the Zodiac, well in front of a pod of orcas cruising down the middle of the straits, I was apprehensive. Let's be frank: I was outright scared. I was also committed to the encounter, and there was no backing out.

Gar was my assistant. I had no compunction about exposing my third-born to the chance of providing breakfast for the "killers." That, at least, might provide a chance for me to escape. I could make up a less-craven story for his mother later on.

We descended to about 30 feet, staring ahead in the direction from which they would come. They never appeared, having, of course, radar-sensed us well before any visual contact and avoided us like the plague. We could hear them, no doubt chattering about the awkward, two-legged bubblemakers in their path. Their squeaks and rasps and bizarre (to us) communication filled the watery sphere around us: non-directional, loud, and powerful. The suspense was as heavy as any sensation of that sort I have ever experienced.

Gar and I surfaced. Herman, the producer, yelled from his plastic command boat, "Did you get it?" He was outraged with our negative reply. We were happy to be alive. Yet we had taken the first physical step toward a more intelligent understanding. While still apprehensive, we were less so on the successive dives we made that day, always in the path of an advancing pod and never with success.

In fact, to complete the shoddy production, the producer some weeks later had me fly west again to dive in the Vancouver Ocean Aquarium tank with their resident orca and film a bogus scene of a kayak being overturned and the occupant attacked. The accommodating orca had been in the aquarium so long that his great dorsal fin, usually erect and almost six feet high, had collapsed and drooped limply like a deflated sausage.

There was much hanging around the dock and generally unproductive time, the production being unorganized and haphazard. I wanted to go diving and suggested to Herman that Gar and I and a young man from Vancouver, who was general grip, search for one of the big octopuses that frequent those waters. While that had nothing to do with orcas, it did promise some sort of action, being a part of the marine environment in which we were involved.

I had never encountered a big octopus but had heard about their proliferation along the Pacific coast of North America. However, I did know how to spot an octopus den.

In about 40 feet of water we located one. The giveaway is the litter of crab shells at the entrance. A peek under the ledge with an underwater light revealed several white arms with formidable suction disks extending outward. We were ready for action. Gar would hold the lights. I would be ready with the camera, and our young companion, being a local, would grab the animal and bring it to the surface. We couldn't fail. It was a tried and true exercise, routinely carried off by local divers.

I waited with my finger on the trigger of the camera. Very soon, in fact, seconds later, a frantic tentacle snaked out of the opening, followed by another. Then, without any warning, the entire animal burst out of the den. It expanded as it exited, and it was HUGE! I froze in a state of shock. This was an eight-armed Godzilla! Our designated young grabber staggered back, losing his balance, and was out of the action. Gar watched the whole disaster with eyes bulging, and the octopus took off without delay, disappearing into a crevice from which there was no way to extricate it had we wanted to. I had shot not a frame, succumbing to trigger paralysis, better known as buck fever.

We kept the account of this disgraceful encounter to ourselves and conducted the equivalent of a locker room pep talk. I convinced Gar that he had to try the grab. I had been told that if you waved the animal about, tossing it from one hand to another like a hot coal, it would become disoriented, give up, and be resigned to its fate.

Whether Gar believed this or not, he gained my undying respect by making the grab when we routed another octopus, and he actually corroborated the theory, which I only half believed myself, by juggling the beast until it turned limp and bringing it up to the Zodiac. The filming of this was surely the only genuine drama in the production other than the producer and production manager exchanging ineffective blows in a loss of tempers.

And then, there was the episode with the ling cod. I had been told by locals that ling cod could be caught with handlines and jigs at certain places along the shores of the strait. One of these places was a point at the end of the island where we were docked, just ten minutes away by Zodiac and outboard. I had a yen to catch one of the beasts, having heard that they grew to 50 pounds and more.

I purchased the required rig, checked the tide, checked out the Zodiac, and took off for the point shortly after the 4:30 a.m. summer dawn. Gar, snug in his bunk in the fo'c's'le, declined to join me. I reached the point in perfect time, skirting the shore with its chaos of giant logs thrown high onto the rocks by winter storms. A thin mist hung over the water and rose like steam among the tops of the great firs and spruce. There was a bite to the air and the splendid exhilaration one may feel when such a morning, fresh and new, in such a magnificent environment is all yours.

A great red ball of a sun was already burning off the mist as I anchored, unreeled my tough monofilament line, let the lead jig with the three hooks hit the bottom, and started the up-and-down movement that activates the jig. As I recall, I had a good bite within a couple of minutes and felt another almost immediately, jerking the line each time. The third bite was hard; my jerk set the hooks and the thrill of a great weight at the end of the four fathoms of line set my heart beating fast and my spirits soaring. All fishers will know what I mean.

Whatever I had – and I supposed it was the very fish I hoped for – did not struggle commensurate with the very considerable weight on the line. It tugged and pulled. Hand-over-hand I pulled in my mystery fish, letting the line freefall on the Zodiac bottom. And then it came into view: first as a vague form in the murky green water; then, as it came into full focus, as an enormous, grossly huge head, bigger than any I had ever seen on the Maine codfish I used to handline as a boy. It was obviously a ling cod; and it was so big that I feared I might lose it if I tried to haul it over the side of the Zodiac by the line. I had no gaff; I had no billy. I did have a paddle, and with that, holding the brute by the side of the Zodiac, I pounded it on the head to quiet its struggles. Fortunately, I was wearing mittens, which enabled me to get my free hand in its gills and so heave it over the side, where it flapped mightily and provided me with a fine sense of primitive triumph. I had never seen a cod like it. Without a scale, I could only guess its weight as between 35 and 50 pounds, maybe 40. Whatever, it was more than I could have hoped for.

That was enough for me. I pulled anchor and headed home. I reached the dock before anyone was up, offloaded my prize and, dragging it to the side of the dock, lowered it into the water with a line through its gills. I lowered it deep enough to be out of sight. As our crew emerged into the sun for their coffee on the dock, I took Gar over to the tied-off line, pulled the beast up enough for him to see, and hugely savored his astonished, "Holy smokes!!" Then I swore him to silence.

In that 43-degree water, the cod was well preserved during the day while we sallied forth on our rinky-dink production activities at the improvised whim of the producer/director, Herman. At the end of the day, it was the custom of this city fisherman to try out his expensively – and newly – acquired fishing rod with colorful lures the village hardware salesman had conned him into buying. At that time, I quietly took my own place nearby, making a great show of fishing with my hand line then galvanizing into wild action and shouting as I appeared to be struggling with something big. Gar lent a hand. I had reset the jig hooks. We put on a great show of struggling with the beast, finally landing it and subduing its fabricated struggles. Herman and his cohort watched this performance with amazement, and, without delay, pulled up their lines and put them down again at the scene of the capture.

And there they stood as the sun went down and the dinner bell rang. And there they were standing with lines down when we arose the next morning. It was the happiest, most successful ruse I have ever initiated; and it couldn't have happened to a more deserving pair.

In hindsight, the remembrance of experiences like those mitigate the reality of a misguided production by an unscrupulous, tasteless Hollywood producer. I wouldn't have missed the experience; neither would Gar. When my children were teenagers, I used to take them, one at a time, with me in the summer on expeditions and contracts like the one I have described above. Those were building blocks in the esprit that our family still has. If you have a sense of humor, either at the time or in retrospect – and we all do in my family – the course of the years and happenings and experiences can usually come up with a positive note of recollection. So it was with *Jaws of Death*.

To Feed or Not to Feed

On a dive tour aboard the *Belize Aggressor* very recently, I was witness
to a drama, a very unpleasant one. There were a number of dive boats on
the reef area off Lighthouse Key. Most were small day boats. Very often
they were without radios or – for that matter – any sort of emergency
equipment. The *Belize Aggressor* was the nearest live-aboard dive boat fully
equipped for emergencies. When a divemaster from a small boat in the
immediate area was severely bitten by a moray eel and was in critical condition, the dive boat, leaving guests in the water, pulled anchor, motored to
the stern of the *Aggressor* and delivered the stricken diver to us.

He was a native Belizean. While not yet in shock, he was severely trau-
matized. Very fortunately, we had a doctor aboard as a guest, and he was
not in the water with the other divers at the time. As the emergency bandage of toweling was removed and replaced with sterile dressing, I had a
look at the wound. I was shocked. I had never seen what a moray can do.
Two one-inch-deep grooves had been torn – not sliced – into the upper
arm. Fortunately, they were on the outside of the arm, invading only
muscle tissue. Also, we were luckily in an area developed enough for our
radio call to set in motion a medevac rescue.

After collecting its confused and somewhat panicked divers, the small
boat picked up the wounded crewman and sped away to a nearby island
that had a landing space for the rescue helicopter. Forty-five minutes later
the stricken man was in the air and headed for the hospital in Belize City.
We heard next day that he was sewn up and would survive without
complications. He was lucky.

What happened? We learned that he routinely fed the big green moray
for the entertainment of the guests. On this disastrous occasion the bag
of sardines, which he held under his arm, was not delivered fast enough
for the hungry eel. Morays have poor eyesight but excellent olfactory
senses. One may safely extrapolate: it smelled the bait and lunged for it

before the diver could set the stage for what he anticipated would be a routine feeding.

I am not sure when the handling and hand-feeding of morays started. At least 20 years ago a picture by Jim Church on the cover of *Skin Diver* magazine documented an enormous green moray draped over the arm of divemaster Wayne Hasson. Wayne was then divemaster at the old Casa Bertmar resort. The eel had earned its own celebrity status and was called Waldo. Originally, feeding by the diver had won the friendship of the eel. That is the way it always starts. Not too long after the association with Waldo had been established, I was filming Waldo and Wayne with the Peter Benchley family. The show was spectacular and – in its way – beautiful. As far as I know, Wayne never came a cropper with Waldo or his successor, Waldine.

Encouraged by the eel/diver alliance, I advised the wife of Bert Kilbride, who had a dive activity in the British Virgin Islands, to add an eel-feeding performance to her regular dive tour. She successfully did just that with a somewhat frenetic spotted moray. One day she, too, did not produce the food quickly enough. The eel was hungry and without manners. Her ear lobe must have looked like a fine piece of conch. The eel grabbed it and almost tore it off. That was the end of the feeding activity; Jacqui Kilbride did not thank me for leading her into it.

Today moray handling is old-hat. Inevitably, sharks have become the hand-feeding show. The activity proliferates in tropical diving areas all over the world. It reaches astonishing variations and levels of intimacy with the ancient and long-feared predators. At Walkers Cay in the Bahamas, Gary Atkinson has developed a shark feed-o-rama that draws as many as 200 reef sharks to a frozen block of fish parts suspended over an open sand arena. Guests with their cameras intermingle with the sharks with impunity. Also in the Bahamas, Ben Rose, wearing a chainmail protective suit, hugs and massages great seven-to-eight-foot reef sharks. They surrender to his caresses, meek as lambs. (Ben recently retired from the Undersea Explorers Club with all his limbs and digits intact.) In the Maldives, Herwarth Voightmann pushed the envelope a titillating step further (no pun intended). He had his beautiful daughter feed gray reef sharks from a fish held in her mouth...topless.

Off Key Largo recently I watched Spencer Slate's wife, Annette, a fine young slip of a lady, feed barracuda with a fish in her teeth. Spencer, of course, has done that for years. There are so many of these activities that if I touched on them all, my own thoughts about this intimacy with predators would arrive only at the end of an overlong article. Ben Rose, in his pre-show lecture to divers who watched his performance, pointed out to them that the only people who get hurt are the divers doing the feeding. "We are working with animals that are essentially wild," he said. All of the feeders, several of whom have been severely bitten on their arms, usually in close proximity to the bait, now wear chainmail gloves.

A point I wish to make should be self-evident. The sharks, the eels, the barracudas have no malice aforethought when they bite the hand that feeds them. They make mistakes. The timing may be off. The set pattern of the feeding, to which the predators may adhere time after time for hundreds of feeds, may be upset by some small deviation on the part of the feeder. A most dramatic example of this problem occurred some while back in the northern part of Papua New Guinea. Dinah and Bob Halstead, who put diving on the map with their live-aboard *Telita*, were the most respected divers in the PNG area. Dinah had developed a successful hand-feeding routine with silvertip sharks. She could not have foreseen the mistake she made when she repaired the holes in the knees of her wetsuit with white patches. At the moment of delivery to a seven-foot silvertip, the knee patch caught its eye. It missed the bait. Its jaws closed over Dinah's bent knee, severely biting both her thigh and calf. The shocking event was documented by a guest diver, shooting Hi-8 video. The drama further unfolded as the shark turned in less than three seconds with its mouth open to continue the attack. Dinah turned at the same time and shoved her Nikonos and strobe into the mouth of the attacking animal, turning it aside. Her husband, Bob, now at her side, blunted a third attack with his shark billy. Through the kindness of the videographer (Erich Wittenberg), I was able to copy that footage. I show the action in slow motion to many of the guests on the dive tours that I host. The speed of the attack is what shocks them. It is most edifying.

By "edifying," I mean this: many thousands of divers, who have witnessed the popular shark-feeding activities, have come away with revised feelings about the primordial predators. During the feeding, the sharks move so easily, so slowly, and with such grace and apparent good manners. "Why, I could turn one aside with a punch in the snout" is the concluding impression. "Predator? Fiddle de dee! They paid not the least attention to us." Thus a complacent attitude is engendered in a growing public, replacing the traditional fear of the great people-eater. I do not mind a retreat from fear, but I also see a loss of respect for an animal that divers have seen performing like the big cats at the circus. The veneer of "civilized" behavior is just that: a veneer established by conditioning and programming. The predator is still there. The Dr. Jekyll still functions with its place in the jungle at night. I do not believe that any of the predators that have allowed themselves to be approached and fed by humans become dependent on the hand-outs for their survival.

Today, just about every new diver hopes to see a shark. The shark feeding, as well as the other variations on the predator/human theme, is enormously popular. As a diver who for many years earned my bread by filming sharks for television and the movies, I like to say that sharks put my children through college. Whether the animal tamed to eat from the hand is a shark, eel, or barracuda, the diving public is enthralled with the experience of actually being in the water to witness such an exercise with safety assured.

I would wish a viewer to know that the conditions within which the performances are conducted depend entirely on food. The marine animals involved are almost universally shy. They want nothing to do with humans. Even the great white shark is unlikely to attack a human outright unless in some way the human resembles a prey that is normally available or manifests vulnerability behavior. Many of us have filmed great white sharks out of the cages in South Australia, but always on the bottom and away from where the surface feeding has been conducted. I have found them curious, interested, but not prone to all-out attack. If their curiosity closes the distance, the cage with an open door is nearby for a prudent retreat. But that is another story.

Maybe "prudence" and "respect" are the key words. The exposure to great marine animals by diver experience and through the entertainment media has done much to build a consensus for sharks. That in turn bears on legislation to protect them. Like so many controversies over humanity's relationship to the animals with which we share this planet, there are varying sides – not all good, not all bad.

Just keep in mind the words of William Blake: "What immortal hand or eye / Could frame thy fearful symmetry?" That "symmetry" may be thought of as the deep-rooted instinct in all predators. The "immortal hand or eye" imbued them with that instinct millions of years before we evolved. That imperative is still deeply rooted in them.

Reflections on Times Behind and Ahead

*N*ostalgia, in the dictionary, is defined as "homesickness." I would expand that definition to include a remembrance of times past, happy times, and usually a wish that circumstances affecting those times might return. Reality – for the most part – is that the days pass and never return. I do not expect to ever see the flounders again in my now-barren cove in Maine, or pull in great cod and pollack and haddock as we once did less than one generation ago.

The cove is called the Punch Bowl. You'll find it on marine charts of the Maine coast on the mainland across from Little Deer Isle. In the time-less rhythm of the tides, a six-foot person can walk across the middle of the cove at dead low. The water rises 12 to 15 feet with the flood. Small coves, like the Punch Bowl, are called – in the Down East vernacular – "gunk holes." The name belies the rich diverse marine environment that exists in such small coves, or did exist; and that past tense creates the nostalgia of my recollection of what used to be.

The Punch Bowl is my cove. I – and now my children – own all the land around it. I grew up there in the summers during the late 1920s and 1930s. Did I say flounders? Before breakfast, I used to hop into the dory, row out to a mooring in the cove, and, with keen anticipation and deeply satisfying excitement, bait my hook with a small piece of fresh clam. Over the side the line would play out until the sinker hit bottom. Pull up the distance between sinker and hook and wait for the bite. A minute was an unusually long wait. In a half minute, the bite would arrive, responded to with a quick tug on the line. Then, with a thrill that I can still feel in my hands, transmitted to me along that taut line, I would, hand-over-hand, with a steady, practiced rhythm, pull up and swing aboard a fat, flopping flounder. The peak thrill was the feel of that heft on the line, the strength of the struggle that forecast to me the size of my catch. If the line went slack and I knew it had been a "monster," I felt acute dismay.

At high tide I could not see the bottom. Even though I knew every inch of it as well as the floor of my own room, a sense of the unknown, a touch of mystery always attended the chance of what might be there beyond my sight. At dead low, floating just six feet over the bottom with the surface mirror calm, I could actually watch the flounders converge on my bait. High or low tide, in 15 minutes I would have a dozen or more. Then in to breakfast. Cook would clean them (those were the affluent days), and after the fresh blueberries and porridge, they would be served, crisp and brown with lemon and hash-brown potatoes.

There were also sculpins on the bottom, an ugly fish with big mouth and horns. They were bait-grabbers and often swallowed the bait and hook together. They went to feed the lobsters that we kept in a large, floating compound.

And speaking of lobsters, my father told me that when he first came to Maine in the summertime as a young man before the turn of the century, lobsters were so plentiful that you might find them among the low-tide rocks by lifting the seaweed. Lobstermen, working from their Friendship Sloops, pulled their string of pots twice a day and sold their abundant catches for 35 cents a 100 pounds. The crabs were thrown back as trash.

The bottom of the cove was alive with the bottom fish as well as big crabs, squid, and an occasional stingray. There were large patches of eelgrass interspersed by a bottom literally paved with sand dollars. Periwinkles and their big cousins, the whelks, were everywhere. If we required clams for a steamed clam dinner or to bait the 500-hook trawl that we used to set out by Marshal's Island, the men would dig two or three hodfulls in an hour at low tide.

That seemingly endless bounty from the sea continued right up to the end of the 1930s. I went away to war. The house was closed. The boats slept through four years in the dark cool of the boathouses. Far away in barracks in strange, distant parts, I dreamt of Maine. Some dreams were so vivid and real that I could feel the tugs and struggle on the flounder line. I had olfactory dreams, in which I could smell the pungent aroma of low-tide shore, mingled with spruce and pine and the windrows of seaweed that marked the high-tide line. When I returned in 1946 the flounders were all gone, and so were almost all other parts of the once wonderfully flourishing, interdependent marine ecosystem. Even the clams had played out. My cove and all the others along the coast now lived up to their names: "gunk holes."

In the 1960s, my oldest son, Gordy, and I once took our fast boat 32 miles out to sea to the isolated Mt. Desert Rock. On an otherwise barren, granite rock, less than an acre in size, there is now an abandoned Coast Guard station with lighthouse. You pick your weather and know your equipment before you venture that far offshore with a single motor and a small skiff. The tide was right. The wind was kind. The day was golden. The cod and pollack came in gangbusters. With our multi-hooked hand lines, weighted with five-pound sinkers and no more than plastic strips on the hooks, the big fish hit us before we could reach bottom. Two and three fish, from ten to 25 pounds, would weight the line so that we could hardly get it up and over the side. We had never had such fishing. We never expect to again. The gill-netters and long-liners took over. We tried several summers and returned empty-handed. That one halcyon time we returned like a Gloucester schooner from the Grand Banks in the old days. We cleaned the whole catch ourselves and fed a good part of our small village. It was on that great day that a small great white shark surfaced behind our boat, attracted by the action. He came under our 16-foot Boston Whaler, lifted the bow enough to put the fear of the sea into us, and went on his way. We decided we had enough of a catch. It was a marine Camelot. It was a golden time for growing up on the New England Coast; and it is pure gold in the memory bank.

The loss of our small, personal fishing pleasure and the rich fabric of expectation and excitement that attended putting a line over the side provide an infinitesimal view of a sad, perhaps irreversible change in the marine environment all over the ocean world. The Grand Banks, their stock of cod, haddock, and halibut once thought to be as inexhaustible as the buffalo on the Great Plains, are closed to fishing – overfished to the state of exhaustion. Commercial fish catches have diminished precipitously at all levels in the world's oceans, and the population of the great cetaceans is threatened – in some species – almost to the point of no return, despite international agreements and restrictions. The litany of abuse by an ever-increasing human population is news to no one today. Over a century ago, Wordsworth wrote: "The world is too much with us, late and soon. Getting and spending, we lay waste our powers. Little we see in Nature that is ours."

I understand that by far the most cataclysmic changes are a result of changing water temperatures. We have seen the immediate effect of such changes in the recent cycles of the El Niño and La Niña impact on parts of the world's oceans. I believe the departure of marine life along our New England coast can be accounted for by temperature change. I have seen the effect of El Niño in the Galapagos and at Cocos Island off Costa Rica. Hundreds of divers every year make the long trip to remote Cocos Island to see the great resident school of hammerhead sharks. The same dramatic encounter attracts divers to Darwin and Wolf Islands at the northernmost reach of the Galapagos. There, in water temperatures that range from the lower to mid-70s the curious but shy hammerheads come close to view the strange terrestrial animals that are viewing them. Twice in my diving an El Niño has raised the water temperatures at Cocos and in the Galapagos Islands to over 80 degrees. The hammerheads retreated to deeper, colder water. In the Galapagos, the schooling fish that sustained the great population of sea lions also vanished to colder ocean pastures. Thousands of sea lion pups died. The beaches were littered with them.

I cannot balance all the adverse factors in my mind. Global temperature increase, over-harvesting, pollution by coastal development, waste and greed (as in shark-finning), and – a very bottom line – the continued human population explosion, all lend to the demise.

Whatever the causes, I despair for generations ahead on this beleaguered planet and, at the same time, rejoice in what is still here. Half of each year I am in the sea. I am grateful for the magnificent reefs and dynamic marine environment that we still have left. And as I extend into the western Pacific, I find my excitement in the macro marine life regenerated on every trip.

I see no real conclusions nor viable remedies that I believe can affect the large, deteriorating world environmental scene. Only this: gather your nudibranchs, your pygmy seahorses, your bizarre and wonderful sea creatures while you may and while the sea still possesses such glorious abundance. Believe in and pray for the resilience of the seas and their remarkable ability to recover from gross abuse some of the time. And support those brave and determined organizations that take arms against the sea of troubles and will not cry "Uncle" to the madness of our times. They do retain a vision of hope and fight for it.

Listen to the Exhortation of the Dawn!
Look to this Day!
For it is Life, the very Life of Life.
In its brief course lie all the
Verities and Realities of your Existence;
The Bliss of Growth,
The Glory of Action,
The Splendor of Beauty;
For Yesterday is but a Dream,
And Tomorrow is only a Vision;
But Today well lived makes every
Yesterday a Dream of Happiness, and every
Tomorrow a Vision of Hope.
Look well therefore to this Day!
Such is the Salutation of the Dawn.

— SALUTATION OF THE DAWN, *from the Sanskrit*

The Heroic Man

On a recent trip a lady guest recalled having seen an extraordinary vintage documentary film about sailing around Cape Horn on one of the old square-rigged windjammers. The cameraman, shooting from high in the rigging, had recorded the struggle by the deck hands as green seas thundered across the waist of the ship and the seamen hung on for dear life. She couldn't recall the name of the daring cameraman who had documented the classic fury and danger of a round-the-horn sailing ship. I knew instantly who it was and named him. She was astounded.

"How could you possibly know and remember?" she asked. I replied, "Because he was our guest when we lived in Princeton."

His name was Irving Johnson – Captain Irving Johnson. He is no longer alive, but when he stayed overnight with us, he was very much alive: incredibly strong and clear of eye. At that time I booked a fund-raising lecture series for the Princeton Kiwanis Club. A perk was the chance to entertain the speakers at our own home and so get to know them.

When I was a boy in the 1930s, Irving Johnson was already a living legend. He had purchased a North Sea pilot schooner, named it *Yankee* and sailed around the world three times. He supported his enterprise by taking young students with him. *Yankee* was a school ship. From 11 months of hard sailing and visits to remote islands under the sun, the students returned physically hardened and skilled mariners with a new global awareness.

From the start, Capt. Johnson was a favorite of the National Geographic Society. His articles appeared regularly. His 16mm black-and-white film documentaries brought standing-room-only packed houses wherever he lectured with his films. He was the first contact with many of the most remote Pacific islands, entering lagoons through passes that had only known native sailing canoes. In the New Hebrides Islands (now called Vanuatu) he encountered a strange rite practiced by the Pentecostalists. To celebrate their entry into manhood, young boys tested and proved their courage by leaping from 100-

foot bamboo and vine towers with vines attached to their ankles. That was the progenitor of today's bungee jumping. That any survived the ordeal was astonishing. Those who did were acceptable to the village maidens. Those who didn't submit themselves to the ordeal might as well have joined a monastery. Those who landed on their heads wouldn't be concerned either way.

I never succeeded in talking my father into sending me away for a cruise with Capt. Johnson, but I tried and dreamed of it. More than 50 years later, when I was a guest speaker on a Holland American Line cruise, I finally bungee jumped from a dockside crane by the harbor in Auckland, New Zealand. By then, manhood had progressed to grandfatherhood, and the elastic give of the bungee saved me from dislocating my legs. What's more, I had already had my steady date for almost 50 years.

When, at the start of World War II, it became apparent that we would have to fight our way across the Pacific, the Navy turned to Irving Johnson for detailed information about the passes and lagoons of islands for which they had no critical information.

When Johnson stayed with us, he must have been in his seventies. He was still hard as a rock and appeared fit enough to scramble up the rigging of a great ship like a young midshipman. He entertained us by tearing a Manhattan telephone directory in half with his bare hands. The children were pop-eyed. That physical fitness saved his life when, some years later, he was climbing one of the Egyptian pyramids and survived a fall that I am told would have killed any ordinary tourist.

Those who admired and appreciated the life of adventure, true exploration, and the excoriating test of survival skills that sailing open oceans and threading a sailing ship through uncharted reefs and shoals imposes on the master of a sailing ship might say that, when Irving Johnson died, the mold was broken.

In truth, hundreds of men and women, before and since, have fit the mold well. Another whom I chanced to meet also met that mark. During World War I his name stood with Baron Manfred von Richthofen at the top of Germany's pantheon of heroes. His name: Count Felix von Luckner. Early in that war he commanded a square-rigged ship, the *Seeadler* (*Sea Eagle*) that escaped an Allied blockade of the North Sea, and, at-large in the Atlantic as a raider of sailing ships that were still in commercial service, he sank 18, causing $25 million damage to Allied shipping without a single loss of life. He was one of the last of the true knights, adhering to a code of honor. Using a ruse much used in wartime during the age of sail, he would fly British colors, create fake smoke and send a distress signal. When an Allied sailing ship approached to assist, up would run the German colors, a hidden deck gun on an elevator would emerge from the forward hold, and the signal would go out: "Surrender or we blow you out of the water." Such was his already-established reputation that the unlucky victim would readily surrender. Von Luckner would remove passengers and crew to his ship, sink the merchantman, and sail on. Ladies and officers dined with the captain and were comfortably billeted in officer country, the ladies scrupulously protected. Crew berthed with the crew of the *Seeadler*. All were allowed the freedom of the ship on the pledge that they would do nothing to hinder its activity. If there were further encounters, the prisoners were required to stay below out of sight. At the next neutral port, all were put ashore, having been kindly entertained. All returned to their homes with stories of their adventure and a high regard for the "Sea Devil."

Lowell Thomas, the late famous newscaster and author, brought Felix von Luckner to the attention of my generation with his first book, *The Sea Devil*. The book also established Lowell Thomas.

Von Luckner rounded the Horn and continued preying on Allied shipping in the Pacific. The great square-rigged raider ended her days on a reef off Mopelia, the westernmost atoll in French Polynesia, wrecked by a tidal wave. Von Luckner and his crew swam safely ashore and hid on the island. When, some weeks later, a French gunboat entered the lagoon to investigate the wreckage, the hardy Germans swam out by night, took the gunboat by surprise, set all the crew ashore and sailed away to do battle again.

During the year that I lived in French Polynesia with my family, a German divemaster, Erwin von Christian, and I hired a fishing boat to take us on an overnight sail to Mopelia Atoll from Bora Bora. There we dived on the wreckage of the *Seeadler*. Its iron parts, long overgrown by coral, were strewn about the reef for a 100 yards and more. The deck gun had been removed by the French and mounted in the town square of Papeete. A hermit, who was old and incredibly dirty, was the only inhabitant of Mopelia. We gave him tobacco and a demijohn of Algerian wine. He gave us coconuts and a nautilus shell. Satisfaction was enjoyed on both sides.

Von Luckner and his men were eventually captured by the British, interned in New Zealand and repatriated at the end of the war. Germany desperately needed a hero of Von Luckner's integrity and caliber. In retirement he founded the Youth Hostel Movement, worked with the German branch of the Boy Scouts, and married a Swedish countess. He continued to sail the world and explore with his three-masted schooner, the *Mopelia*. During the rise of the Third Reich, Hitler hoped to enlist the support and prestige of the national hero. Von Luckner refused to cooperate, fled with his wife to the U.S. and spent the war years lecturing across the country. His honor intact, he survived the second German defeat.

I had hoped to sail with him. While I was a farmer in Maine during the early 1950s, I came across a notice that Count Felix von Luckner would command a square-rigged barkentine, the *Madeleine*, to sail around the world with a young crew of paying volunteers. That started my adrenaline flowing, and this time there would be no father to stop me. The Explorers Club of New York, to which I belonged at the time, provided me with an address. A gracious letter from that splendid hero answered mine to him. He was coming to New York and would be happy to meet me.

We met in the outer reception area of Luchow's, the famous New York German restaurant. He arrived in a black bridge coat and black-visored cap without insignia. He was ramrod-straight. His handshake still had the strength gained from years of climbing the forestay of a tall ship, hand-over-hand. His wife, tall enough only to reach his shoulders, was the Swedish countess, warm and cheerful. As we did a progress through the first of the dining salons, men rose from tables to greet and salute the old warrior. The word had gone ahead with the speed of a line squall: "It's Von Luckner! The Count is here!" By the time we reached the cavernous center hall of Luchow's, the string quartet was ready. They struck up "Deutschland Über Alles." Most diners were on their feet. The applause must have overwhelmed the traffic on Fourteenth Street. The welcome was for an unstained, legendary hero.

The cruise never materialized. The promoters proved to be financially unsavory and Von Luckner withdrew. The failure of that irresistible adventure may have saved my marriage. I would have been away from my family for more than a year. We are no longer in a time when the wives of whalers paced their widows' walks for as long as three years, patiently watching the harbor for the return of their man and his ship.

The best elements in the human race will continue to generate heroic men and women too. The two I have written about were seafaring men in the last age of great tall-masted, square-rigged windjammers. Under the sea we divers have our own contemporary heroes: Hans Hass, Jacques Cousteau, Bob Ballard, Al Giddings, Howard Hall, and many others who, in my consideration, fulfill the requisites for achieving hero status. Those requisites would take them into new arenas of danger and challenge where they have acquitted themselves with courage and resolution. They emerged from those trials with integrity and inspire others to emulate their conduct and achievements.

It matters not that you may not achieve the stature of the great heroes and explorers. Those who go down to the sea in ships or with scuba have at least the seeds that may grow to exploits of heroic dimension.

Tube Sucker's Tales

Some years ago I was commissioned by the American Petroleum Institute to produce a film about their oil rigs in the Gulf of Mexico. Chevron had outraged the public with a series of nasty spills. The oil rigs needed a public relations film that would present them to the public in a favorable light. As it turned out, there was much good to report about the oil rigs. Producing a propaganda film for an industry that was considered the arch villain of the environment proved to be educational and not at all shameful. In the course of that production, I discovered that I was a "Tube Sucker."

By shameful I mean the stretching of the truth when one is paid to make a client look good and that client is actually a low-down scoundrel but paying the bills. In fact, the only shameful aspect of that shoot was the outrageous spearfishing I did with my friends from Morgan City.

All this took place about 40 years ago. Spearfishing was "In." I have a T-shirt from the Kona Photographic Society that bears the legend: "If It Moves, Shoot It." Back then we skewered big fish with spears; and under the great rig, 60 miles out into the Gulf of Mexico, there were big amberjack, humongous jewfish at the bottom 90 feet down, along with schools of big fat snappers.

It was this proliferation of marine life that was drawn to the rig that created a positive aspect to its presence there. The rig – like all the rigs – became an artificial reef. I called my finished film *The Steel Reefs*.

The first life to colonize the supports of the rig was blue-green algae. Upon that base the Crustacea began to build. I cannot recall how long our rig had been on location, but by the time we dived on it, big mollusks (the handsome oyster with curved, toothed borders, *Spondylus americanus*) dominated the armored burden of giant barnacles, coralline growths, Tubastrea, and a world of invertebrate life. The bare steel structure had become a living reef.

Large schools of spadefish cruised through the upper level. A little further down, big amberjacks – always in pairs – patrolled the sea space. Looking down through the water column, we could see the movements of schools of snappers, a fish highly prized in the market. I remember that at about 75 feet, a suspended layer of murk severely reduced visibility. At the bottom, 110 feet down, the snappers (five- to ten-pounders) were so thick that hitting one required no skill at all. And suspended over the bottom, like giant brown dirigibles, were the huge jewfish. I never had the temerity to spear one. Neither did my companions. They were veterans of spearfishing on the rigs. They knew from experience that those giants could bend a three-eighths-inch spear shaft like a pretzel, hopelessly tangle the line from spear to gun around the cross members of the rig, and smash the ambitious hunter into steel girders, breaking bones and threatening life. I was told the jewfish were as big as 500 pounds. They looked like freight cars to me.

As I mentioned at the start of this article, 40-odd years ago spear fishing was a big thing. That was the reason for our trip and the subject for my film. But that experience made me very strongly aware of the rich marine ecosystem that the rig had engendered. I learned more. While we were there, sport-fishing boats came out from the coast to fish around the rig. Much like an isolated reef on an ocean plain, the rig attracted the pelagics, and the snappers ventured out of their habitat to take the baits of the line-fishermen on the boats. A formidable sport-fishing business had evolved. Marine life, both inside and outside the rig, prospered from the presence of the steel reef. The shrimp draggers worked the bottom in close proximity to the rigs and found rich harvests there. I never learned why shrimp should proliferate near the rig.

And, of course, the rig had itself become an artificial reef. The oil companies instituted protective measures that were long-term proof against spills. Since that time there have been no notable spills at rigs even though tankers around the world have continued to have horrendous spills with dramatic damage to the environment.

But where does the name "tube sucker" come from? That was how I was addressed and labeled when I visited overnight on one of the big resident rigs. I did not take offense; I knew better. No offense was intended, but the tough crew of roughneck drillers and rig operators who were resident on the rig did not encourage any friendliness. To them I and my production team of four (I was on my second trip to the rigs) must have looked like intruding wimps from another world. Their work was dangerous and required long hours and strong bodies. Scuba diving was a sport that had nothing to do with their fight to tap the great reservoir of oil beneath the floor of the Gulf. They addressed us as, "Euw toob suckers." We were accorded slightly more respect than visiting ballet dancers. They were also interested in the Arab oil world. They referred to their Arab competitors as "Them Rag Haids."

For their endurance in that unrelenting, excoriating world of steel and sea, ghastly accidents, and isolation from the amenities of Morgan City's bars, good-time girls, or real homes and families, they lived as well as the on-rig amenities could provide. They ate like kings, with huge appetites and à la carte service from a galley on duty round-the-clock. Their cabins were air-conditioned and semiprivate. There were movies and a big-screen video viewing room. And because way back then death by lung cancer was the least of their worries, the air was as thick with tobacco smoke as a political back room.

I haven't been on a rig since. I rather expect life has changed little. The air inside may have improved and attrition on the lungs diminished. But I shall never direct the gas pump attendant to "Fill 'r up" without a remembrance of my tube sucker's visit to the land of the roughnecks.

Our film, *The Steel Reefs*, was finished in a 35mm big-screen format and actually played as a "short subject" at Radio City Music Hall in New York. My co-producer Herm Kitchen, and I went to see it. We sat way up in the "Heavens," the back of the vast balcony. It was an afternoon matinee. Only a few young couples shared the peanut gallery with us. We were immensely proud and pleased to see our work on that huge screen. But in the gloom of our surroundings, we noticed that the couples were all necking like mad. The wonders of *The Steel Reefs* were subordinated to kissing, groping. and snapping of elastics. My next production will be shot with infrared penetration of the dark in a movie house balcony – if there's one left in this century – and may even make the menu in the naughty video channels.

Like their cousins on the oil rigs, the professional hardhat divers from Merrit, Chapman & Scott did the nasty jobs of salvage and underwater construction in the zero-visibility waters of New York Harbor and its environs. Unlike them, I should never have been there. As I descended to the bottom at the entrance to New York Harbor, actually within sight of the Statue of Liberty, I knew I was over my head. My only thought was to get through the ordeal without making a total cock-up of it. It happened this way.

My father-in-law, a Pennsylvania lawyer, represented the Acker Drill Co. This prominent company had a contract to drill out the clogged outfalls of the vast Passaic Valley sewerage system. An engineering milestone in its time, almost a century ago, the outfalls dispersed the treated sewage from a large part of New Jersey. The outfalls were spaced in a pattern on the bottom of the Hudson River where the great river empties through the Narrows on its way to the sea. The outfalls had worked for years, breaking up and dispersing the sewage as a fine sludge. But as they eventually became clogged, the pressure blew out the dispersing elements, creating an open hole out of which solid waste was blown. In order to secure the drill guide over the outfall to proceed with the drilling, clearing, and repair, Acker Drill needed a visual take – a photograph – of one of the units along with measurements.

Mind you, this was 1954. Underwater photography was in its infancy. The Aqualung was, to the general public, a phenomenon. To my father-in-law, a good and generous man, I was a diver and photographer. Ergo, I would be the man for the job. With zero experience in commercial diving, I suggested 500 dollars a day plus expenses. Acker Drill also had no experience with commercial diving but must have thought that rate was a Sears Roebuck bargain. I was flown to New York City from Nassau, where I had started my dive boat business, and the next day found myself on a 40-foot cabin cruiser anchored in the narrows of the Hudson River. We were over the outfall field 60 feet below. My fellow adventurers were three men in business suits, overcoats with mufflers wrapped around their necks, and porkpie hats. A boat driver watched me with curiosity, eyed a buoy that was being intermittently dragged completely underwater, shook his head, and somehow conveyed to us that he was witness to an idiotic caper. He was.

The mufflered men huddled in the lee of the cabin trunk, watching me as I struggled into my heavy underwear and latex, Bill Barada-designed Seal Suit. Their boss had researched the conditions this January day. My acceptance of the job was based on this research. At the time we anchored, the tide would be slack. A water sample had been taken near the bottom, indicating that the water would be clear. What a cuppa tea! What an easy 500-plus! What wise, prudent interpretation of the research! I kept eyeballing the beleaguered buoy and our anchor line, taut as a bowstring. If this was slack tide, Niagara Falls would change direction. I felt sick and was already cold, but acted as calm and "in charge" as Jack Palance warming his trigger finger over a coffee cup. Through my dread premonitions ran a line from Macbeth. When he had murdered Duncan and the plot was falling apart and he wished he hadn't gotten into the mess, he said: "I am in blood stepp'd in so far that, should I wade no more, returning were as tedious as go o'er." I was ready to go over. More gear hung from my belt than an equipment ad in *Skin Diver* magazine. I had two hand lights, several calipers, and a white slate with grease pencil. A silly CO_2 inflatable plastic package that fit in the palm of my hand was clipped to my weight belt. This safety device, when squeezed in an emergency, was guaranteed to lift a locomotive from the bottom with the speed of a breaching whale. I was using a Scott Air Pack that employed a full-face mask. In that winter river temperature, I thought to keep my face warm. This professional array of sport diving equipment was completed by a 16-foot coil of light line, attached by a slipknot to some part of my rig.

I went over the side with a cavalier thumbs up. I had seen Errol Flynn make this gesture as he took off in his Sopwith Camel for a mortal combat with the Red Baron and was much impressed. That was the end of my bravado. I did reach the buoy, made a desperate grab for it, connected, and was swept under the surface with it. From then on, my actions were as mechanical and preordained as a hapless soldier going over the top in World War I. The buoy was attached to an anchor in the middle of the outfall complex.

I started pulling myself down the line, hand-over-hand. About 15 feet down, to my astonishment and relief, the wild surface current diminished to full slack. My relief was premature. The light had faded so fast that I was already in mustard-colored murk, so dense and dark that I had to feel for my light. I turned it on. Nothing appeared to happen. I held it to my face and saw that, indeed, it was working. So much for the gin-clear visibility at slack tide. The light was already of no use.

With a sense of dread that warred with my sense of obligation to fulfill my contract or at least appear to be giving my employers their money's worth, I continued my descent into the murk with a hand-over-hand death-grip on the line. I reached the bottom by penetrating it with my head by about a foot. The anchor was buried in the muck. The bottom was semi-liquid, composed of centuries of effluvium overburden that had been accumulating since Hendrik Hudson's mariners relieved themselves over the side of the *Half Moon*. I did exactly the right thing. I rested in that viscous mass and collected my thoughts. I didn't even dare think of the monstrous sharks that no doubt festooned the abyssal darkness around me. Bad sharks were much on our minds way back then. I knew I had plenty of air. As long as I remained attached to the down line, I would not stray. It was calm at the bottom, so no currents threatened my position. Ultimately, I focused on the need to spend a creditable amount of time down there. I decided to employ a search technique for which I had equipped myself with the 16 feet of line. I secured one end to the down line as far as I could reach into the mud. Then, paying it out by increments of a few feet for each circuit of its end, I would extend my search and might stumble onto one of the outfalls. Of course, I had no idea of when I had completed a full circuit. I kept one hand in front of my face, shamefully hoping that I wouldn't really encounter something in the dark – perhaps a cement bathtub with the skeletal remains of a Mafia victim.

I would like to recall virtuously that I continued this miserable performance for the full time I was at the bottom. In fact, I was so overwhelmed with the futility of it all that I pulled myself back to the down line and stayed there like a motionless carp for more minutes. I hoped a half-hour had passed. I couldn't tell. I also hoped the executive contingent in their snug cabin above me might be worried. They were.

I surfaced at the buoy. Aboard, the captain had apparently finished his newspaper and was himself rather apprehensive about the whole mad exercise. He saw me surface, actually threw a life ring which I managed to catch and hauled me the few feet back to the boat. All hands aboard, good overcoats and all, pitched in to help me into the boat. To my profound relief I very soon learned that they had become very worried about my disappearance and what I might be experiencing down there. It is likely that liability plus a good relationship with my lawyer father-in-law had engendered a growing dread. That I was safe and alive aboard the boat annulled any rancor over my not having accomplished anything while I was down there. A description of the conditions, which needed no hyperbole from me, rather clothed me in hero status. The hot coffee and brandy and sandwiches in a well-stocked hamper went far to restore my own equanimity.

Eventually, Merrit, Chapman & Scott was contracted to provide a veteran hardhat diver to do the job. I can see the grizzled veteran sitting on his stool just before the helmet was lowered over his head. Those tough, skilled men often took a long pull from a whisky bottle before they were buttoned up. They had no need for a dashing thumbs up as they disappeared underwater. Leave that to "them tube suckers" who were already over their heads when they accepted such a job in the first place.

Alien Night

No one could tell me much about her – how she foundered or what she might have been like a half century ago. She was the dark, ugly, oxidized wreck of an island trader. Even the homeliest coastal traders were once young. She must have had a lift to her bow and a freshness to her thrust making waves that the cheerful dolphins rode with squeals of delight. Her name, *Henry Bonneaud*. No half model of her hull is apt to be immortalized in a yacht club's trophy room. She was a tramp. Now she reposes in the memories of all that chanced to visit her in the dark of night. She had undergone "A sea change, into something rich and strange." She had been invested with magic.

I was diving with Rob Barrel, Cat Holloway, and guests from the Fiji live-aboard *Nai'a*. Rob had sailed her northwest from Fiji to Vanuatu for two months of exploration of dive sites along that chain of islands. We ranged north from Port Vila to Viti Levu, with its waterfall-streaked escarpment, and to the Banks Islands even farther north. It was real exploration. Even our seasoned local dive guides, Kevin and Mayumi Green, were on new turf, beyond the usual range of their dive operation on the island of Espiritu Santo. The excitement of descending to virgin sites was always an undercurrent with us. Sometimes it was requited with splendid reef life; sometimes with very modest new reefs to which we gave only a short survey.

Kevin and Mayumi know the wreck of the *Henry Bonneaud* well. It lies on the bottom off Espiritu Santo, 130 feet deep. A daytime dive will reveal only a deep, bare wreck. By night it is invaded, occupied in every compartment, hold, passage, and interstice by millions of one-inch sparklers as brilliant as stars on hot, still nights. They are flashlight fish (a species of *Photoblepharon*). So dense are their numbers that they illuminate every part of the wreck they occupy, a pulsing, sparkling life in a haunted house at the bottom of the sea.

I was the first diver down the line to the stern rail. I could vaguely discern enough of the ship's looming shape to guide myself to the after deckhouse. I became aware of a strange light emanating from a porthole. When I put my face to the open port I was shocked, most wonderfully shocked. The interior was brilliantly illuminated. A hundred lit Christmas trees could not have been more vibrant. There was a total enchantment to it all. A magic, alien presence imbued the old, sad wreck with dancing light and the sense of fairies, elves, extraterrestrial beings invading an old castle for a witches' night of revel, Walpurgesnacht, Shakespeare's Titania and her fairy maidens, Coleridge's "Kublai Khan", or perhaps a sailor's vision of Fiddler's Green. A metaphor to describe the scene may stretch your imagination to its farthest reach. In more than a half century of diving, I have seen nothing to equal the intense pleasure, the delicious charge to my senses that I experienced spying on those secret revels in the dark of the ocean bottom.

I glided along the deck, forward to the opening of the hold and on down 120 feet and more into an inner hold, drawn by the power of those lights. In the deep hold I was immersed in the light, trapped in an all-enveloping galaxy of stars. It was so strange – almost extrasensory – that it was hypnotic. The trance, ecstatic in its effect on the senses, proved as distracting and dangerous for me as it did for the other divers. All of us, prudent, careful, veteran divers as well, snapped out of our trances at the same time, looked at our computers, and were horrified to find we were well into decompression times. The line to the buoy and the waiting Zodiacs became short of hand-hold space with clusters of divers, like bee swarms or respiring grapes, hanging on in the dark from 25 feet on up. For all the divers, out of this world at 130 feet on their third or fourth dive of the day, the dread of decompression sickness hung like a black cloud of nitrogen.

But long after those pernicious little bubbles were purged from our systems, the magic of that brilliant, enchanting alien presence in the night wreck stayed with us.

Perspective

The Lembeh Strait is at the northern end of North Sulawesi which, in turn, is one of the northernmost islands in the great Indonesian Archipelago. Christians and Moslems are whacking away at one another at other points far to the southwest of North Sulawesi. Here, at the Kungkungan Bay Resort on the shore of Lembeh Strait, the only danger comes from being jaded with so much macro. After all, how many star gazers, flamboyant cuttlefish, exotic nudibranchs, fierce fire urchins that tear across the bottom like LeMans racers, and weird animals that emerge from out of the black volcanic sand like phantoms and disappear again before your eyes can you digest in one 50-minute night dive? Is it possible to become jaded with a surfeit of rare, exotic marine animals and macro goodies any one of which would just about make your day – if not your week – of underwater photography? I am ashamed to answer yes. But try to tell that to a beginning diver, fresh out of the quarry with a newly minted certification. It is all perspective.

We talked about it over our late dinner after the night dive. As may happen (to the point of tedium) with a superannuated, long-of-tooth, septuagenarian diver like myself, the "I remember when" syndrome is apt to be employed. Listeners' eyes are also apt to become glazed. Eyelids droop. I plow ahead. Veneration exacts its toll.

I grew up in the 1930s. Beebe and Barton had descended for the first time into the abyssal depths of the sea off Bermuda. Beebe's colorful descriptions of saber-toothed viperfish, gulper eels, and other "monsters" were illustrated in *National Geographic*. At the same time, I was allowed to accompany my father on fishing trips to Bimini and Cat Cay. My brother and I were advised that allowing a hand to trail in the water alongside the boat would risk an amputation by a barracuda. To fall overboard in the middle of the Gulf Stream would result in disembowelment by a shark, perhaps several sharks tearing us apart like a pack of dogs on a cat.

We believed it; so did my father. The "monsters" under the boat, seen by Beebe and Barton, would finish up the remains.

My attitude toward the sea, like that of the world's people, was more awe and fear than respect. When I first entered the world of a tropical reef, I was scared skinny. It was wartime. I was stationed with a naval air group in Panama. I was an air crewman; a radioman gunner, trained in SBD dive bombers. Today my good friend and associate Jim Church likes to tell people that I shot down four planes, but was hardly a hero. He points out that the planes were my own as I swung the twin 30-calibre machine guns too far around and shot off my own tail. Well, I have stories about Jim, too.

To get back to Panama. The year was 1944. I had the first line of skin diving equipment, shipped to me by Owen Churchill, the creator himself. They were "frog feet fins," mask, snorkel, pole spear, and – most impressive – a cork-handled knife for stabbing sharks. Several companion crewmen from California were already "ab" and "bug" divers. None of us had been in the water with barracudas and real sharks. On our first encounters, we would scramble in full rout onto the reef, over the urchins and all. We hugged the edge of the reef like ancient mariners keeping a coastline in close view. To venture into the open was perilous beyond any prudence. So it went: a supreme adventure. A triumphal march followed when we entered the ship's service with a string of fish. We exchanged our catch with the local soda fountain girls for free sodas and sundaes.

I was transferred from Panama to Texas, continuing my heroic career during which I never flew in action or fired a shot in anger. Nor did I have a chance to dive again until after the war when I was a farmer on the Maine coast. But during that land-based Texas tour at a naval air-training base, I took weekend leaves to volunteer crew on the Mexican fishing boats out of Port Aransas. The wartime manpower shortage made any volunteer hand on the nets welcome. My fascination – and excitement – in watching the bulging net retrieved with its burden of marine life from the Gulf never diminished. I wanted very much to return to the sea. College in New Hampshire, as well as my early marriage and work in a cigar factory, put all that on a back burner. Then came Maine.

We lived on the coast with ocean on three sides of what was a childhood summer home, then converted to year-round living. I became a blueberry farmer. Blueberries, wood pulp timber, and lobster fishing (plus tourism in the summer) are pretty much the choices in Maine. An electrifying news item reached us at our relatively remote village. I seem to recall that the year was 1949. A man I had never heard of, named Jacques

Cousteau, had invented a device that could take a man into the sea without breath holding. The Aqualung was born. The Cousteau name was strange to all North America. Had I received an invitation to join a rocket to the moon, I could not have been more thrilled, titillated, energized, and excited by the news. I had to have one of these devices and whatever went with them. I did finally acquire one, possibly the first in the state of Maine, along with the 25th little portable Cornelius compressor and a neck-entry "seal suit," under which one wore layers of wool underwear.

I won't go into the logistics of diving and the early equipment. I intended to focus this essay on changing attitudes toward diving and the sea. But the first dive that followed delivery of the equipment in November of 1952 was in Walkers Pond, a couple of miles from the house. My whole family, plus a gaggle of shivering neighbors and friends, attended. The crowd probably approximated the number of curious who attended the Wright Brothers' first flight at Kitty Hawk, and my bunch were just as curious and apprehensive. I waddled into the pond, swam out over my head and descended in about 15 feet of water to sit on a rock and breathe. I was in Heaven. It was a Eureka moment. There were no fish, nothing punctuated the monotony of the level mud bottom, but I was breathing under water. At that seminal point, blueberry farming lost all interest for me. Like the impulsive Toad of Toad Hall, I was enchanted, obsessed with the new device that would take me into the ocean world.

The depths beckoned. The magic goal was now 100 feet. I was like a new, feckless driver succumbing to the siren call of 100 miles per hour. What unknown perils awaited my first daring descent to that depth? First, I must find a body of water that deep. Eggemoggin Reach, right in front of our house, was only 90 feet deep. I must reach 100 feet. The prospect terrified me. Local fishermen advised me that a pond an hour away was exactly 100 feet deep. They fished there for giant trout and averred that pike, aggressive and dangerous, were thought to reach six feet, and perhaps more, also inhabited the abyssal depth of the pond.

On a Sunday, we drove with neighbors to the pond, trailing a rowboat. I had an anchor attached to a downline with a 100-foot mark on it. My wife, Susy, thought the venture entirely foolish and irresponsible. The specter of widowhood at 23 loomed large in her mind. The children whimpered with apprehension, sensing the danger of the advance into the pond's unknown. They clung to their mother's skirt. We were all tuned to disaster, including me.

In the middle of the pond, my friend Captain Bud Hawkins lowered the anchor to the exact bottom depth of 100 feet and helped me on with my tank. It was too late to wimp out. Like Macbeth, I was committed (after he had murdered his guest King Duncan, he resigned himself to the horrible, murderous future: "I am in blood stepp'd in so far that, should I wade no more retuning were as tedious as go o'er.")

I dropped over the side and looked down. The line descended out-of-sight into the horrible depth; I could see no bottom. I started down, my eye on the depth gauge, a glass thermometer-like tube with a red fluid calibrated to the mad extreme of 100 feet. At 50 feet, I could see no bottom; at 75 feet, there was still no bottom. Ninety feet – nothing but gathering gloom and murk beyond which the slavering giant pike must sense my fear-stoked emanations. Then my feet sank into the muck. Nothing but muck. If there were a trout six feet away, he would have been out of range.

The red fluid in the thermometer tube registered 100 feet. Now, if I could only reach the surface – the broad, sunlit uplands of safety, sun and air – I would never leave my wife and children again. I would not strut or be puffed up like a toad when the village heard about this feat and withdrew in awe when I entered Wardwell's General Store. I was a genuine, gold-plated, sure-as-shoot'n, hell-for-leather hero. The pond itself might in time be dedicated a shrine to that first pioneer descent with scuba. I might even open a fried clam stand there and modestly accommodate autograph seekers.

Before we moved to Maine and soon after I was discharged from the navy in 1946, I had been profoundly inspired and excited by the adventures of Hans Hass. They were set forth in his book *Diving to Adventure*. Now it would take a Cousteau article in *National Geographic* to inspire a total change of vocation. I would abandon blueberry farming, build my own dive boat at a small boatyard up the coast, and take it to the clear, tropical, shark-infested waters of the Bahamas. My life would never reverse that course. This time Susy and the children were delighted with the prospect. We had discovered that Maine winters on the coast suck.

Devil Work

I just finished reading *In the South Seas* Robert Louis Stevenson's account of his travel through the South Seas late in the 19th century. The candid, delightfully written account covers his travels on two schooners to the Marquesas, the Tuamotus, and the Gilbert Islands with residence ashore along the way. In the Marquesas, cannibalism was still practiced, although "long pig" was not a regular on the menu. However, in all the islands "Devil work" was still much a part of the local life. Stevenson recounts the cure of his wife's cold by incantations and the burning of various ground bones and herbs. He does not deride (nor does he endorse) the practices. He reports evenhandedly what he encountered. That is most commendable, I thought, and much of the reason for my enjoying and valuing his account so much.

His account of the "Devil work" opened a memory channel to an experience I had almost 40 years ago when I was on expedition in the Tuamotu Islands. As way leads on to way with those remembrances of things past, I dredged my vodka-stunted memory cells for details of that happening.

My old friend Dr. Perry Gilbert had offered me a position in an expedition to Tikehau Atoll. Tikehau is one of the hundreds of atolls – most uninhabited – that comprise the Tuamotu Archipelago, which extends west to east for 900 miles. Mururoa at the eastern end is the atoll chosen by the French for their nuclear testing. Tikehau is at the western end, a full day's travel by one of the small island trading vessels to the north of Tahiti. My trouble started on that rusting hulk that could have been featured in a Conrad novel. The passage was extremely rough, with high seas that buried the rails on either side. I foolishly ventured out on deck to watch the storm seas, lost my footing, and whacked my shin on the raised edge of the companionway. The result was a deep cut in my shin that scared my companions with its copious bleeding. Our medical kit was stowed out of reach in the hold, but our interpreter and native Tahitian guide for the trip prescribed lime juice for the wound. A tight bandage stanched the blood flow, and I hunkered down, wedged into a tight corner and immune to the wild gyrations of the ship.

We entered the pass into the Tikehau lagoon midmorning after the wild night. Arrangements had been made in advance for us to quarter in a small Seventh Day Adventist village that was adjacent to the pass. Our dunnage and supplies were ferried to the shore, as the village people gathered to watch our arrival. We waded ashore through water conspicuously polluted with offal and organic debris. Pigs rooted in the shallows. Those few feet of water that gently lapped the beach were about as septic as a sewer. Kept dry and treated with antibiotic dressings, my leg would probably have healed nicely. That slosh to the beach was its undoing; within 24 hours I would know that I was in trouble.

Dave Cave, an American expat with a rental car business in Papeete, was on our team. His wife, Leone Cave, was our interpreter and liaison with the villagers. She was something else: beautiful, dynamic, and virtually sparkling with native humor (much of it raunchy). She was half Scots, half Tahitian, born into the affluent Tahitian Bambridge family. She flirted outrageously and could outlast any man in the wild, hip-wrenching dance, the *Tamure*. She was also entirely efficient in setting up the kitchen and organizing the supplies. Perry Gilbert would make all final decisions regarding our conduct and activities, but he leaned heavily on Leone for her native savvy and wisdom. What a dynamic, kinetic lady with flashing eyes! She was more total woman than I may ever have encountered.

The villagers eyeballed our materials as we carried them ashore and set ourselves up in a spacious guest house, with beds for us all plus a kitchen established by Leone at one end with our portable butane gas stove. Several cases of the local Hinano beer came ashore; so did three large glass jeroboams of Algerian red wine. This "forbidden fruit" did not miss the keen eyes of the villagers. As Seventh Day Adventists they were a dry society. Dancing and other activities of the Devil were also forbidden.

Perry thought it diplomatic to invite the village to our place for a first night gathering to get acquainted and – through Leone – announce our planned activities. The entire village showed up: women, children, elders, every thirsty, fun-starved soul. The orange drink Fanta was available. We thought their moral strictures would confine the villagers to that nonalcoholic refreshment. Wrong! They pitched into the beer like lumberjacks in town on a Saturday night. Guitars and drums appeared. The premises turned into a terpsichorean bacchanal. I still have visions of Perry with his arms around two laughing *wahine*, caught up in the party let loose by our arrival and our forbidden refreshments.

Leone, totally in her element, was leading two men at the same time in the provocative, snake-smooth *tamure*. We learned – and should have known – that Tahitians love a party more than anything else on earth, and the Devil be damned!

At midnight Perry announced the party's end. There was no doubt that we were most welcome on Tikehau. The next morning Leone took inventory of our beer and wine. One more bash like that, and we would have to dry out ourselves. We were also aware that we had engaged in Devil work. The islanders were ready to embrace Mammon with open arms and limitless capacities for "refreshment." Perry took sober action. Leone carried a message to the village chief that we would entertain just once a week on Saturday night with a short reception with prescribed hours. Many hopeful villagers drifted by the next evening – their eyes warm with hope, tongues licking lips – and were courteously advised of the new party schedule.

By the next morning, I knew I was in trouble. In fact, the salubrious use of wine the previous night and the wild, sinuous gyrations of Leone had undoubtedly numbed the activity now proceeding as fast as a bacteria could multiply. I couldn't lift my leg without sharp pain. The area around the wound was an unhealthy, swollen red. A full-blown staph infection was going gangbusters. Our pathetic medical kit, when it was unpacked, had no antibiotics. Antiseptic cream and little more than Band-Aids made up our pharmacopoeia. I was remanded to my bunk for the day with my leg up.

From my bunk I was entertained during the day by legions of feral pigs rooting and squealing and fornicating in the trash behind our house. By the third day, the stretched skin on my shin was shiny as well as red around the open wound and did not bear touching. It had the unhealthy pallor of a swollen tick. Leone was worried; so was I. She asked if I would submit to bush medicine if we could find the local version of a witch doctor. I urged her to go for it.

The local version arrived after lunch: a disheveled old crone as septic in appearance as the waters that had incubated my infection. A snaggle of yellow fangs was revealed when her cracked lips opened to emit a cackle. Leone unwrapped the leg. The crone inspected it briefly, nodded triumphantly, and prescribed herbs found in the bush and known only to her. I was encouraged. After all, the price was right whatever happened. It is true that she had not completed Harvard Medical School, but her fee was a bottle of Hinano beer and a half-dozen cigarettes. For a bargain like that I would have tried incantations and a rattle. The Hinano was sucked up immediately to strengthen her for the herb search.

In time, she returned with a bouquet of weeds. Leone provided a cutting board and a very rusty hammer for her to pulverize the lot and moisten it with beer, for which a second bottle of Hinano was required. As she pounded the mess into a paste, I noticed that ashes from her cigarette joined the jungle poultice. Leone saw it too. Our eyes met. She winked, and we both laughed. The green mass was spread over the wound and secured with a reasonably clean dishtowel. The Devil work was done. The crone departed, possibly to put distance between herself and the patient. Leone doubted that a malpractice suit would apply in this case. We decided the leg couldn't get any worse. I took little comfort from knowing that bacteria and viruses had been around for millions of years, survived, and multiplied.

The next morning a spanking-good fever accompanied the throbbing leg. Homeopathic hope was abandoned and prudence took over. I was evacuated by outrigger canoe across the lagoon to the main village. Radio contact was made with the big, two-motor Grumman seaplane that was in the vicinity that day. They diverted, picked me up, and headed home to Papeete. The passengers on the plane, mostly tourists from the U.S., were goggle-eyed and much impressed with being part of a real "South Pacific Adventure." Stiff upper lip and Rodney Dangerfield heroics were shamefully turned on for their benefit.

In a comfortable bed at the Hotel Tahiti – my original stand – a penicillin drip put the bacteria into full retreat. While I convalesced, the Princess Champasek visited with me each afternoon, accompanied by a servant with a tea cart loaded with goodies and books. But that is another story another time. The princess, Perry Gilbert, Leone Cave, and Dewey Bergman are all gone now. They were all part of that South Sea Polynesian adventure. A lifetime of diving and filmmaking has brought with it so many friends and such fine experiences. The Seafaring Rat in *The Wind in the Willows* said as he departed his scene, "When the play has been played and the cup has been drained, come home to your river with a goodly store of memories for company." The cup hasn't quite been drained yet, and the store of memories has hardly been tapped.

The Ivory Coast Thruster Shoot

My wife, Susy, has her wing back chair for reading in the evening by the living room fireplace in our snug Lawrenceville, New Jersey house. I sit in my favorite rocker facing her and the fire. Depending on the size of my vodka scoop before dinner – usually generous to soften the world horrors on the prime-time news – with civilized wine with dinner, Morpheus may already have felled me. This evening I was still focused on *The Times*. Among the dolorous happenings upon which the media thrive was a piece on war and mayhem in the African country called the Ivory Coast. Rebels were closing in on the capitol city, Abidjan. Nothing new there as Africa and the world go these days.

The dry maple in the hearth spit and popped loud enough for me to lower the paper and check for run-away embers. My eyes took in Susy, already nodding over her book, and at the same time took in the squat, heavy stool at her feet. With the instant speed of a computer chip a memory was pulled out of storage. I had purchased that stool at a government store in Abidjan many years past. Disregarding her snooze mode I broke the evening quiet, "Susz, did I ever tell you about the hairy experience I had with Gordy diving off the Ivory Coast long ago? That's where the matriarch stool came from, and I've just been reading about bad doings on the Ivory Coast."

"You must tell me about it, dear" (resignation thinly masked her reply).

I am sure it was our oldest son Gordy's part in the adventure that gained me the patient audience.

Regretfully I have never kept a log. I particularly regret that omission now that I have begun to recount those early experiences. My guess is that the contract with Shell came in the early 1970s not long after the appearance of *Blue Water, White Death* in the theaters. I had shot and co-produced a public relations film for the American Petroleum Industry. Shell Oil Co. was prospecting for oil off the Ivory Coast. For a promotional film they needed a shot of one of the thrusters that controlled the position of the 680-foot research vessel over the hole being drilled. It had to be shot with 35mm film.

At that time I knew there were several experienced cameramen with their own 35mm underwater housings. Al Giddings, Lamar Boren, Ron

Taylor and Jordan Klein were all experienced shooters and old friends. In fact, Jordan had built the 35mm Arriflex housings we had used in *Blue Water, White Death*. All my own equipment was for 16mm shooting. Did I let the Shell people know this? Did I pitch the job to any of my more experienced old friends? Not on your life! Cupidity, avarice, meanness and plenty of deceit...thy name is Waterman. I let Shell know that I was most naturally the man for the job. I leased a 35mm housing, stocked up on Eastman color negative film and in a fine tradition of nepotism cut my own son, Gordy, in on the deal as my assistant. Thus, and in due time, the moment of truth came upon us both accompanied by unpleasant vibrations in our inner thoughts: "What are we doing here? What have we gotten ourselves into for lust of the filthy lucre?" We were under the monster 680-ft hull of the moon well drill ship with her four-point computer-automated thrusters. Any one could suck in a cow from 15 yards away. My contract called for a take of a thruster at work. That meant shooting close enough for the spinning blades to be seen clearly.

The crew chief, a tough Texan with dictatorial power over the entire operation, had to clear all activities. As a veteran hard-hat diver he disdainfully rejected us as "tube suckers." That was his classification for all scuba divers. When I requested permission for our "caper" he snarled, "You've got to be out of your mind. I ain't putting any dumb divers under the ship through the moon well. Get outa here!" He turned back to his papers.

The years have dimmed my memory of how I convinced him that we could pull it off and had been contracted by his sponsors to do the job. The permission was given like Pontius Pilate's washing his hands to distance himself from any responsibility for crucifying Christ. My recollection is still clear enough to recall that Gordy and I wished we were safe home in bed. We knew we were over our heads in a world of high-tech pros.

We entered the water through the moon well in the center of the ship. It was an open pool and entirely accessible since no drilling was going on at the time. At midships we found ourselves well away from the thrusters that were located at the port and starboard ends of the vessel. Under the shadow of the long hull they were distantly visible on the bow, silhouetted by the outside light. We searched for some object that would enable Gordy to take a couple of turns with the coil of safety line he carried. As green as we were, I knew that there was no way I would maneuver close to those giant thrusters without a safety line strong enough to resist the powerful suction.

We saw a heavy rod projecting from the hull about a foot from the hull. That would do. Gordy took a couple of turns in the line and started to play me out. I inched toward the starboard thruster. The blades were not turning. I maneuvered opposite it keeping a 15-foot distance between me and the thruster. I could easily zoom out to fill my frame with the full six-foot radius of the blades. I waited in position ready to shoot as the blades started turning. It was important to film them static first to show the speed with which they achieved thrust. Deep inside the great ship a computer made split second corrections through the four thrusters to keep the ship exactly on position. Through the moon well drilling rods could extend thousands of feet to the ocean bottom.

The blades started turning and I started shooting. The next moment I was drawn toward the thruster as if seized by a powerful hand. I will never know whether I continued shooting because my finger froze on the record trigger or because I coolly carried through the shoot. I rather suspect the former. As it happened the safety line swung me in an arc away from the thruster, depositing me in calm water by the side of the ship. I was still shooting, adrenaline fueling the whole performance. That was enough for this closet wimp. I gave Gordy the thumbs up signal. He coiled up the safety line and we emerged from the moon well trying to look as cool and professional as we really weren't.

As it turned out the take was entirely adequate. In the editing the revs of the thruster blades were incrementally slowed down. The take lasted long enough for a short cut before the camera swung out of target. I recall that I never again intruded into the world of commercial diving, being entirely content and happy to be a "tube sucker."

Sea Lions

Look to the sea lions for creature comfort, marathon nirvana, low-risk daily existence and – apparently – life in Fat City from womb to tomb.

They have always looked sleek and happy to me, even when they were rendering "My Country 'Tis of Thee" on a blow horn in the center ring of the Barnum & Bailey Circus with no more reward for their musical genius than a dead mackerel. In their natural habitat they have to be just about the most dynamically beautiful, luxuriously lazy, appealingly whiskered and self-contented animals I have had the pleasure of consorting with.

Here in the Galapagos Islands they are accessible to visitors and so used to them that you almost have to stumble over one to get a snort. An enlightened Ecuadorian government protects them as they do the entire ecosystem of the Galapagos.

North of Santa Cruz Island and close by Mosquera Island is a long sand bar, too small to rate a name, but, in its quarter-mile-length, commodious enough to provide a warm pad for thousands of sea lions. From a distance they pepper the sand like nutmeg on a junket. In the long golden light of late day that bronze-hued the sand we landed our Zodiacs. Pups – scores of them – splashed and cavorted about the boats as we stepped ashore. Their heads popped out of the water like midget whales spy hopping, their curiosity undampened by any evidence of fear. The maternal instincts of the ladies in our group were so excited by the the pups that they cooed and clucked and would surely have suckled the infants had they – the pups – allowed themselves to be picked up.

We picked our way through the bodies, hardly eliciting a nod or snort by our presence. Sleek females nursed their pups or refused to nurse them. These latter rolled from side to side as the pups scrambled back and forth over them trying to gain access to the teat. Finally either the mum or the pup would give up.

Pups no more than 18 inches long and probably about a week old flopped about pathetically squalling for their mothers. We were told that there will be no substitute mothers. Either a certain pup's mother harkens to its calls and finds it or the pup will starve. Usually maternal instinct prevails.

Overlooking each gathering of females was the master of the harem, always a much larger male, big enough to have won his exclusive control of the harem. Any intruder into his turf, whether human or bachelor sea lion is unwelcome.

We found we could only approach the big males so far before they would rear up and with ferocious, intimidating roars attack the intruder. Fortunately, these animals, so swift and acrobatic in the sea, are awkward on land. A human, fueled with high-test adrenaline, can retreat faster than they can attack.

Underwater the appeal of these lithe animals is increased a hundred fold. We dove with a group of young adults. They so obviously enjoyed the novelty of our presence that they showed off with acrobatics so smooth, supple, intricate and rapid that no human Olympic gold medalist could dream of competing. When they – and there were probably a hundred in the underwater circus – were not showing off for us they were roughhousing and playing with one another.

Someone ventured that they would most like to be reincarnated a sea lion. That set me thinking about it. At times we are inspired to such reflective utterances by watching dolphins effortlessly swimming in the bow pressure wave of the ship; or perhaps watching seabirds hang in the updraft of cliffs and swoop down in power dives to feed on the bounty of the sea. One could do worse, I thought, than to be an iguana, lazing about and toasting in the sun on the lava rock.

What neurons I have left in my brain after all these years of enjoying my martinis focused these thoughts in a few milliseconds. Then I noticed a young bull at the water's edge. There was something grotesquely wrong with him. His two tail flippers were missing. Our guide postulated that they were almost certainly bitten off by a shark.

I asked our guide, Xavier, what other natural hazards threatened these seemingly carefree animals. He related that during a severe El Niño, when the fish populations vanish, an entire area of sea lions—that means thousands of them—may starve to death. They die at sea, worn down by starvation, becoming food, themselves, for the surviving predators. Orcas prey on sea lions here in the Galapagos. Any who have seen the orcas in Patagonia hurling themselves right onto the beach to pluck off unwary pups are not likely to forget the brutal, predatory horror of the scene. Mother sea lions do, with some frequency, desert their newborn. A bull, rampaging through the herd and bent on robbing one of his harem of her chaste treasure will crush a pup that happens to be in his path or that ends up under him when he rolls over.

The litany of hazards is far more extensive, I learned. I did not begrudge this colony their time of idyllic leisure into which we intruded. At least, no teenage sea lion is going to shoot another kid in the herd because he wants his jacket.

I don't happen to believe in reincarnation; but then, I don't know any more about it than the people who do. I love watching the dolphins and birds and sea otters. The evening on the beach with the sea lions was pure enchantment. It needs no further considerations for me to be content with the experience.

The Girl on the Train

I had gone back to college after the war and was grateful for the free ride the G.I. Bill of Rights provided. Home after the war meant staying with my brother and his wife at her family home in Darien, Connecticut, or driving to Pilot Mountain, North Carolina, where my stepmother, Herta, had a farm. Mom and Dad had died early in the war. All the family I had, when I mustered out of the Navy in 1946, was my brother, Bill, and Herta.

Percy Bloch was dad's lawyer. He was wise and caring and took me under his wing. On the occasion of taking the train from Darien to weekend with Percy and his wife in their Manhattan apartment, I saw the girl on the train; and that lead to probably the most serendipitous experience of my life.

She was the handsomest girl I had ever seen. As we pulled into Grand Central Station I was standing in the vestibule by the doors of the car. She was still in the line inside the car. Honey blond hair, soft and golden, swept back from a clear, tanned face with no makeup. It needed no makeup. She was conservatively dressed with the taste that good breeding makes natural. Her body was full; her tanned legs were perfect. I had to shift my position in the crowd to observe them and watch her more closely. She exuded quality, outdoor health and grace. She had the Ingrid Bergman look. In the crook of her arm she carried a bunch of garden flowers, their stems still long.

The doors opened as the train clanged and hissed to a stop. I was swept out with the crowd. So intent was I to feast my eyes upon this splendid creature, that I hurried up the platform to the exit ramp There I took a position to the side that gave me the advantage of watching her come by. My gaze followed her to the last view of her hair as she was lost in the crowd.

All the way to the Blochs, who lived on Park Avenue, I scanned the sidewalk crowds from the cab window on the one in two million chances that I would see her again. At the same time I was overcome with a sadness and disgust for my inability to have seized the moment, boldly introduced myself and with a clever, witty sally have caught her interest. Instead – and as I always did – I succumbed to faint heart and missed the current when it served. I had an old school friend who was so self-confident and fast off the mark that girls and women, young and older, fell into his hands like ripe fruit. He entertained me with stories of his conquests. In grade school he was playing doctor with the girls before I even knew what a vagina was or looked like. As a shave tail lieutenant in the Air Force he spotted a young woman in a convertible stopped at a traffic light. He was on leave in a town near the air base. Several thousand men found dates virtually nonexistent. My friend stepped from the curb, opened the door of the car and slid in beside the woman as the light changed. She, of course, expressed outrage and insult. Before she could find a place to pull over and get him out, he had talked her into a smile. Before the day was over, he had talked his way into her bed.

He died some years ago, no doubt with a smile on his face. I listened to his stories enthralled. As though I could learn by having a seminar on his technique, I used to ply him with questions. "What exactly do you do? How do you get started? What moves do you make?" During those college years after the war I used to take him to dinner, fill him up with meat and drink and hope to learn the technique that would enable me to finally score. I never did. I still don't have it today.

The circumstance that connected me with the girl on the train was so utterly unlikely and romantic, that for once in my life I grabbed the moment. But that is still ahead.

I told Percy and Peggy Bloch about the girl and about my whole young life of missed chances. They laughed, pointed out to me what a hopeless romantic I was and what would happen to manners if we sprang upon every girl in the crowd who caught our fancy. I agreed with them; but through the weekend the vision of the girl was strong and real in my mind's eye. In the theater that evening I scanned the crowd when the lights were still on and did a reconnaissance of the intermission crowd on the foyer.

My return to Darien was scheduled for nine p.m. on the New Haven Railroad from Grand Central. I arrived at the station early and found the gate to the platform open, even though it was too early for general boarding. The cars were almost empty at that time. On a wild whim I decided to walk the length of the platform, scanning the lighted interiors of the cars as I passed. Half way along the long line of cars I saw her. She was sitting alone in an otherwise empty car. I was thunder-struck, stopped dead, my senses short-circuiting, but only for a heart beat. The serendipity of my finding her again in that great city was so unbelievable that it overwhelmed all the hesitation and fear of rebuke that always blunted my hopes. I swung into the car, walked resolutely up to the lone passenger and, smiling at the shear brass of the question, said, "Is this seat taken?"

She looked up, flashed a heart-stopping smile and slid over to make room. It was so long ago that I can't exactly recall what I said. But I think I held out my hand, introduced myself and explained that we had started the weekend at the same time. I had seen her the day before, leaving the train.

We laughed about the "crowded car" and the "Is this seat taken?" pitch. Without embarrassment we fell into easy talk. She was returning home to Westport, just two stops beyond Darien, and would return to college – as I would – the following week. She was at Smith. I was at Dartmouth. The connection was easy.

I had under my arm a rolled up chart. She asked what it was. I opened it and explained that I would join a friend that summer to cruise from New Haven to Martha's Vineyard on his 40-foot ketch. She knew boats and cruising. The ambiance was enthusiastic. The conductor called "DAARRIAN...Darien" too soon. We were still warming up and responding to one another's long, straight looks. We exchanged addresses. Manners and the sense of freedom between boys and girls have so changed, that today I would have spontaneously embraced and kissed her. We shook hands.

Some letters passed between us. I drove to two Connecticut addresses that she called home. Both were large, attractive, and affluent. I was still in college. I had acquired a Cadillac convertible to bolster my self-assurance. It was a prop that – in fact – did me no good at all. Instead of writing the girl to ask for a time when I might call on her, I counted on a surprise visit. The young prince would roll up in his deluxe carriage, impressing both girl and family. She was at home neither time.

I never saw her again. Even today, happily married for more than 50 years and with three grown children and five grandchildren, I still survey the passengers on a train or – more likely now – a plane, when I board.

A Royal Birthday Party

My 80th birthday seems to have become an on-going celebration. Indeed–considering the libidinous, voluptuarian, indulgent tenor of my life – it is remarkable that I have reached four score years. The real date, April 5, 2003, was duly celebrated in Bali at the end of my three-week Banda Sea tour. I had much to celebrate. My daughter had survived an emergency operation at a rustic (to put it gently) hospital in the town of Sorong at the western end of Irian Jaya. A report on that harrowing experience was written for *Fathoms*.

At this writing, I am the day-after survivor of a third celebration of the same birthday. Why so late? My best friend, Peter Benchley, decided to have a party for me. To that end he chartered the entire *Tahiti Aggressor*, invited me to ask some of my friends and planned to bring some of his family and friends as well. Since his son, Christopher, was not free from school until early June, the boat was chartered for the last week in June, on into early July.

For the first time in our 53 married years my good and patient wife, Susy, would go on a dive trip. For years I have earned my bread by hosting trips on live-aboard dive boats for almost half of each year. My world of diving has been as strange to Susy as her world of organic food and environmental causes has been for me. She started the first organic food store in Princeton, The Whole Earth Center. Under her direction it prospered. Management of that multi-million dollar business, grand mothering and keeping a snug harbor for me to come home to has been her energetic and productive lot. Except when I took the whole family with me to French Polynesia in 1965, we never had the time or opportunity to share an adventure together. The experience was not only a joyous revelation to her, it was nothing less than an epiphany. I had revealed that live-aboards could be "civilized." No prudent man, returning from a trip alone and met at the airport by his wife will answer affirmatively her question, "Did you have a good time?" I have always effected a dolorous face, shaken my head and allowed that once more I was lucky to escape that "hell ship" alive.

It happens that the *Tahiti Aggressor* and its clone, the *Palau Aggressor* may just be the two most comfortable, diver-friendly live-aboards in the world. My "hell ship" image was blasted. The food approached grand cuisine. The crew knocked themselves out to serve and help us in every way. Three responsible, well-trained dive guides escorted us through the passes of the Tuamotu atolls safely. No strays were caught in the ferocious tidal currents to be carried far into or out of the lagoons.

With its many rivers, diving around the island of Tahiti can encounter limited visibility. Tahiti, itself, is also so developed and crowded these days that we hardly recognized it. We couldn't even find the house we lived in when we spent a year there and in the islands 38 years ago.

One must fly to Rangiroa and from thence by small plane or boat travel to the atolls of the Tuamotu Islands. We did just that, joining the *Aggressor* at Rangiroa and motoring overnight to, Toau, Apataki and Fakarava Atolls.

Now pass diving is not for beginners or, for that matter, for seasoned divers without experienced guides. The atoll lagoons are often many square miles in size. Countless millions of gallons of lagoon water flush out with the lowering tide creating millraces with six to eight knot currents. There is no extricating yourself once you stray into the main stream. I myself have been caught as I pushed closer from the edge of the current into its full clutch in order to have a better video take of the gray reef sharks that ride the current. Once in the "destructive element" (as Conrad called it) you can only ride with it, hoping that alert skiff tenders will spot your sausage or flag above the five-foot waves when you surface a quarter of a mile into the lagoon.

There is splendid diving on the ocean side and around the corners of the passes. Clear water with fine schools of snappers, Pacific barracuda, pennant fish, gaggles of butterflyfish, and turtles feeding on the coral abound. Lone silvertip and gray reef sharks cruised up from the deep for a look at the intruders, and the guides actually located two stone fish; I mean real stone fish, not just scorpion fish. So why hit the passes at all? Sharks, of course. All divers today lust after sharks. The gray reef sharks, beautiful five to six-footers, gather by the countless hundreds in the passes. We had our finest encounter in the pass at Apataki Atoll. There, at a signal from the guides, we used our reef hooks (issued to each diver) to station ourselves as close to the current as we could get and still retreat out of it when we unhooked. Thus hooked in with a line attached to the buoyancy compensation vest both hands were free for the camera.

Howard Hall, with his enormous homemade housing for his high definition video camera was right next to me. Michele Hall, shooting stills for *National Geographic Traveler* magazine, was over my shoulder and Doug Seifert, one of the world's top shark photographers, was just beyond her. From over our heads the sharks arrived, so dense that they seemed to flow like a gray wave over us and into the trough of the pass. A wall of sharks paraded past us, ten to 12 feet away, effortlessly moving up current then reversing to flow past us again with the current. Singles veered closer, inspecting us with baleful eyes. The incoming tide should bring with it clear ocean water and so provide good visibility. Perhaps we were still a little too soon after the tide change; some of the cloudy water, vented from the lagoon, returned with the inflow. Thus only the central body of sharks moving past us had acceptable resolution for our cameras. Even denser masses of sharks created a wall of barely defined gray against the farther side of the pass. My grandchildren would call it "aaawsom!" That, I believe, is a valid description.

And how did my wife of 53 years handle the challenge? Susy is not a diver and hadn't bought a bathing suit for almost 25 years. She was inexperienced and uncertified with scuba; apprehensive, but determined. Paul Stone, the *Aggressor's* captain and an instructor as well, devoted all his spare time to getting her started. With infinite patience and care and commendably fast learning for a 74-year-old lady, he got her started. Buddying with him she was able to join us in the pass and experience the great shark parade first hand. Having survived ordeal by shark without flinching she is now puffed up like a conceited toad. The neighbors have heard no end of it. She's ready to dive the *Titanic*.

A note about the company of guests: it was an all-star cast that none of us are apt to experience again. The guests included Ron and Val Taylor, Howard and Michele Hall, Rob Barrell and Cat Holloway of the *Nai'a* in Fiji, Doug Seifert, Greg Stone and his wife from the New England Aquarium, Peter Benchley and his wife, Wendy, plus their two sons. Wendy's sister, Sally and her daughter, Drury, are both seasoned divers. All together we made up a splendid gathering with enough tall and wild stories to space out a thousand and one nights.

Who says old age is only good for cheese? I can't wait for another decade to reach 90 and go at it again.

Letters
Home

Even if you're positive-thinking, hopped up on Viagra, and your face has been lifted and stapled to make you look like a feral woodchuck, nonetheless one day you'll look like something from the lost lagoon and have the sex drive of a smoked salmon. Nature doesn't care about your golden years; it's aiming for turnover.

— Garrison Keillor

Letters From the Flying Dutchman

There are times when I feel like the legendary Flying Dutchman. There is, of course, a story about that legend. I profess that I do not know it, nor do I consider myself cursed to sail forever through all eternity without setting foot on land. Hollywood did a soon-to-be-forgotten film, very thinly based on the story. James Mason was cast as the sea-weary Dutchman. Ava Gardner a pneumatic numkin married to Mickey Rooney at the time, was the malleable hunk of pulchritude who yielded her "chaste treasure" to the sex-starved captain. Had I no shore leave for a thousand years or more, I expect I might have succumbed to Ms. Gardner's charms, not withstanding the vigilance of hubby Rooney.

There is not enough shore leave to suit me these days. When I have it, I make tracks home to New Jersey and my good wife of more than 50 years. The half of each year that I spend with live-aboard dive boats and the increasingly tedious, endless hours of air travel wear upon me; thus, the sense of unremitting travel, ever receding horizons and sails set and pulling beyond the plumbing of all the western worlds.

So much for explaining the allusion to the Flying Dutchman. In fact, there is nothing of curse about my vocation, and I would have it no other way. I still love diving. I hardly envy my contemporaries in suburban New Jersey who still commute to New York to offices in glass towers or retire to Sun City for twilight years of shuffleboard, bingo and bridge. The adventure in diving is regenerated – to varying degrees – every time I strap on my scuba, become a man/fish and drop down to the reefs and walls and, most especially, the muck.

I first encountered muck diving with Bob and Dinah Halstead in New Guinea. I have had too much of sharks, killer whales, slavering moray eels and others critters so beloved of network television programs. I am grateful to them. They put my children through college. But I now find myself drawn to the macro life of shallow-water areas that border beaches, often attended by villages and often strewn with shore debris. The submarine junkyards at the base of commercial piers afford prime macro targets. The quest is for symbiotic shrimp and crabs, no larger than your thumbnail.

Larger targets are venomous scorpionfish and stonefish, exotic pipefish and leaf fish, and nudibranchs with extravagant colors and designs. The range of macro life is endless. Thus, the excitement in the search for it is also endless.

The hot spots for these exotica are in the western Pacific, Indonesia, Bali, Papua New Guinea and the Solomon Islands. Those areas, that beckon me on like a siren song, are ever farther away from New Jersey. Thus, marathon travel is at odds with my love of home.

During these trips, that involve almost half of each year, I keep a thread of contact open with home and friends. Letters to my wife, Susy, to my friend, Peter Benchley, and to my friends, the ladies of *Ocean Realm*, are written on my laptop. They must await printing and mailing until I return to my office, weeks or even months later. In the case of my wife and home delivery, I feed them into the printer and walk them from my office to Susy's desk, a dozen steps away. They are a chronicle of my experiences, still fresh and newly minted. They also express feelings and set forth impressions that my peers might (or might not) find interesting. I do not flatter myself that the diving world thirsts for entry to my ruminations, but here are a few examples:

Aboard the *Truk Aggressor* – Last day

Dear Susz:

The week has run its course. There is, inevitably, a strong sense of déjà vu…same routine, same food, same variety of guests…something of *The Magic Mountain* effect. I did much reading, had my own cabin with a wonderfully comfortable bunk and so slept well. Two or three macro targets were special along with one good animal behavior shot: banner fish attacking a jellyfish. So went the week.

Tomorrow we fly back to Guam. I'll have an overnight at the same hotel from which I wrote you last week, then fly to Palau early next morning. There will be plenty of fine animal behavior targets there, and also that wonderfully comfortable boat. That week will also run its course; then the long road home where, because I always want most to go there, they are happy to take me in.

Love from your wandering man,

Palau/Nov. 12th…almost home. Hoorah!

Enthusiasm regenerated: the special macro port for my housing has finally come into full play. Last night I went for a night dive with our divemaster, Hector. He has absolutely uncanny perception for the macro

animals that I wouldn't see in a thousand years. A whip coral shrimp and a red gorgonian crab, no larger than your little fingernail, came up clear and large on my viewer. It was so exciting that I was as turned on as I used to be long ago with my first diving adventures. I am happy to have that happen.

I have heard you say so many times in my showing of *The Man Who Loves Sharks*: "He goes on these adventures with the enthusiasm of a little boy." Perhaps I did, long long ago. Now I come to dread the approaching time for leaving home and entertain the primary hope that I may have a cabin of my own and some measure of privacy on these cruises. I hardly expect to have any of the dives in the same old locations generate any excitement. For me the macro world provides horizons that "…fade forever and forever as I move." Papua New Guinea will be a bonanza for macro with its "muck diving" and make – almost make – that endless air travel worthwhile.

I found a Thomas Wolfe in the very-limited paper back library on the boat. Ninety-eight percent of those left by guests are dogs. That's why they are left behind. Some of the super-best-sellers I have read. Occasionally something of value is left behind. *You Can't Go Home Again* was there on a second row hidden behind the trash. Another nugget I mined from the mindless pap: *Gulliver's Travels.* Right now I have Wolfe with me, well into it for the second time. He is describing the rich, varied fabric of life at Penn Station. His description – like all of his prose – is so rich and full that it is the finest Lucullan feast in literature that I know of.

See you soon, my dearest lady. Your face in the crowd by the baggage carousels is anticipated with great joy.

ABOARD THE *TIATA*
IN THE CHANNEL BETWEEN NEW IRELAND AND NEW HANOVER ISLANDS
PAPUA NEW GUINEA
NOVEMBER 11, 1999

Dearest Susy:

Magnificent weather, calm seas and splendid diving. The group is wonderfully amiable with one another, all old friends and perhaps the best bunch I have ever had. The old *Tiata* is in beautiful shape, perfectly kept up and Kevin Baldwin, her captain and owner, in top form. And I'm coming down with a wretched cold and sore throat.

It has to be the legacy of the most tedious, tiring air travel ordeal I can recall. I was in the air a little over 24 hours with just one overnight break in Manila. I was thoroughly bagged. However, we started off with a fine first diving day, some nice stuff on tape and a splendid sleep in my own private cabin. The auspices were excellent. Then this morning I felt that first advance warning of worse to come: a scratchy throat. It evolved into a full-fledged sore throat and cold and energy loss. So I am presently beached and must pass on the night dive, all here in the most glorious diving in the world.

Rod and Jacqui have just started the same symptoms. God only knows how long it will last and how much diving I will miss. What a drag. But I've just had a cup of herb tea with honey in it and feel restorative currents moving in my worn-out machinery.

Spent half the day in my bunk, heaving myself up to greet the divers when they came up from their dives and attending all the meals, even though I have no appetite. However, I am incrementally better and may be able to dive tomorrow. When these ill winds blow I always dream of being home, snug in my own bed and taken care of by you.

Third Day Malaise

I think I'm coming out of it. I slept all afternoon and dozed on and off this morning. As usual, the foul bug got down into my chest; but I'm breathing easier and expect to dive tomorrow. Most importantly, the guests are having a fine time. The weather is beautiful. Kevin, the captain/owner, is wonderfully entertaining and the food is first class – of *Queen Mary* caliber.

I can do without the diving, having had a half-century of it. But I hate to be sick and out of the game and do love diving this area.

Out of the Woods

It was the old three-day flu. It's retreated into my chest, but my nose is open and I've had no trouble clearing. Tonight's night dive will make this a four-dive day; not bad for an old fart.

The night diving is wonderful. The water is 87 degrees, calm and clear. The critters are all out, the lights of the divers twinkling companionably all over the reef, my own light probing the terrain I slowly move over. Last night my light picked up a handsome cuttlefish within the first few minutes.

Tomorrow we dive the Japanese mini-submarine wreck, an old favorite.

EUREKA!

This day I had an epiphany I've been looking and waiting for a long while. It is easy to shoot morays. They gape at you from their holes, so patient and unaffected by your presence that you can close in to focus on their whiskers. What I look for is the presence of a cleaner shrimp or wrasse entering the mouth of the beast: the host opening wide for the service. This morning I hit the jackpot.

On the way back to the boat – and the last diver still in – I had enough air left to cruise slowly along a crevasse in the reef, searching the niches and interstices for any macro subject. Just before surfacing and right under the boat I found myself looking into the face of a whopping big green-mottled moray. His great head was framed by the entrance to his den. Flitting about his head was a blue and black cleaner wrasse. I settled down quietly, perhaps two feet away, flipped off my filter, turned on my lights and filled my monitor screen with his head. The beady blue eyes watched me unconcerned. On cue – and certainly on Actor's Equity – the capacious mouth opened wide, inviting the wrasse to engage in some oral hygiene. The little fish accommodated. The mouth opened wider. My zoom extended the focus deeper into the gaping tunnel and recorded the reckless wrasse advancing into the very gullet of the beast. I thought of Conrad's line: "To the destructive element submit yourself."

The deep penetration must have tickled the moray. He shook his head, ejected the intrepid spelunker and then invited another cleaning session.

Shooting this and seeing it clear and sharp on the monitor, a guarantee that you are nailing it, I had that wonderful, almost sublime feeling that one may have when a long hoped for action in animal behavior is unfolding before you, and is more spectacular than you dared wish.

When it was a wrap I checked all systems, hardly daring to believe that nothing was amiss, having, in the excitement of the action, too many times found too late that I was on "Standby" instead of "Record." But I hadn't screwed up. The review of the take on the big salon monitor had the guests and crew cheering. I thought – happily – that you're never too old for an experience like that to regenerate excitement and deep satisfaction. This has been a *beulah* Day!

MORE EXCITEMENT, MORE GOOD LUCK

An extraordinary fabulous shrimp! I was looking into a small cave about 85 feet down along the reef wall, playing my light against the back of the cave, when I saw a movement that directed my focus. Onto the bright image of my video monitor appeared a magnificent, hairy, brilliant shrimp about an inch long. He had a proboscis-like projection with a white lure at the end, blue and white banded legs and yellow and black hairy body. He tolerated my light and my intrusion just long enough for a fine take, then quickly disappeared into a hole behind him. It is identified as a marbled shrimp, not often seen and seldom photographed because of its shyness.

And then this evening on my night dive, my light caught the glittering red eyes of a shrimp far ahead. The eyes reflected the light so brilliantly that I could home in on them, holding them in my light beam. I came within focus range, started shooting as he moved along the sand bottom. Then, to my astonishment, he commenced burying himself in the sand. Now you see him, and now you don't; and the video take caught the full action.

I have surely been blessed.

LAST DAY

The days have passed like they did for Hans Castorp in *The Magic Mountain*. The regimen is so well balanced – eat, sleep, dive – that the days evaporate. I've been doing four dives a day for the first time in ages. We have been night diving before dinner, when darkness is full. So dinner is served about nine p.m. with wine and the usual groaning board. By ten p.m. only snores can be heard about the ship.

There has been more laughter with this good group than I can recall. All the guests are good-natured, well endowed with humor and experience. Willi and Nanny, from Spain, want us to visit them on the island of Ibiza (off the Costa del Sol). Malika and Jean-Claude want us to visit them in Geneva. Rod and Jacqui want us to visit them on Vancouver Island. All mean it. I have in mind to make the grand tour together when my diving play has been played. We'll do the rounds and these people will be real for you.

Canoes full of children gathered around the boat this morning. We could see them starting from the village while we were still at breakfast. There were mothers with small children and babies all in the same canoe. There were more small boys with their own canoes than I have ever seen. By small boys I mean four and five. Many had their own boy-size canoes, like a kid's first bike. They live in the water and on the water. They tread water with their paddles just behind the boat, watching the divers enter and return with keen interest, laughing and shouting and skylarking. They are happy and healthy. The mothers have betelnut-stained teeth and smiles. The young boys flash white-toothed smiles.

I was told by the crew that one of the boys, alone in his own canoe, was deaf and dumb. As the canoes returned to the village I heard much shrieking of laughter. The boy was splashing one of the big canoes carrying women and children. They retaliated, all having a fine time. It was a heart-warming, joyous sight. These small villages have a measure of paradise. What we don't see, of course, are the tropical diseases that plague them (along with the missionaries). But they have strong, well-formed bodies. They appear to be *Les Enfants du Paradis*.

Last dive is always 12 hours before flying to let the last of the nitrogen bubbles out of the tissues. Then back to Port Moresby, where I'll be met by the manager of a small resort on a nearby island. The *Ocean Realm* ladies recommended the resort to me and they are hosting me for the two days before my next connection out…then the long tedious haul to Manila, Guam, Hawaii, Newark and turkey time.

See you soon. What joy!

LAST DAY ASHORE

I had intended to write no more and save the events of the last two days for telling. That was before I knew what the events would be.

Because there is a two-day connection between the end of the *Tiata* tour and a flight from Port Moresby that would connect with Continental all the way home, I elected to spend the time at a small dive resort just 20 minutes from the airport. The alternative was to vegetate in a Port Moresby motel. The resort, a very simple "No Kleenex" resort with cottage rooms hard by the high-tide mark and no air conditioning, was – nonetheless – given a good rating by the *Ocean Realm* ladies and my friend, Norbert Wu. The price was right – I am being comped.

I anticipated very little in the diving, the whole shooting match being so near the wretched town of Port Moresby. The dive set up was like old times. I carried my camera and dive gear from my room to a "trolley" each morning. All was then rolled out a 150 yard-long pier to the boat at the end of the low-tide mark. The day boat was crowded, as most shore-based day boats are. One misses the comparative space and ease of diving that attends good live-aboard dive boats. The divemaster was a voluble, affable New Zealander. The native dive guide, with dread locks and a murderous face, had the unlikely name of Algernon. He also had the eyes of a submarine hawk and could spot the impossible macro "tinys" like the ones we saw in Roger Steene's book.

And they were there. I have never had such a macro bonanza. Yesterday we went right to a pygmy seahorse, a creature so small that it was only discovered a short while ago. I was prepared with my super-macro dome port. That was followed on a third afternoon dive by a dragonet, ablaze with color under my lights, four different harlequin ghost pipefish, festoons of hingeback shrimp along with scarlet ladies, mantis shrimp lurking in their holes and more. All that was in one 70 minute dive at a site called the Lion Island Muck Dive, and all in about 30 feet of water. It was the most productive single macro dive in all my years.

I had an epiphany at this unprepossessing resort. I will most happily beat the drums for the Loloata Resort, a splendid experience even though the general accommodations are very modest.

So there you have it, my dear. The wind sits in the shoulder of my sail. The long journey home starts in four hours. The thoughts of home and you at the airport will help to sustain me.

Love to you,

SEPTEMBER 10, 1999

My dearest Susy:

As I sit in a mostly empty end of this enormous airport, almost two hours before my flight, I feel like a traveler in time, belonging nowhere, unattached, soon to join another boat for another week with new people, just finished a day and what was left of a night in another strange inn.

Your fall shocked me. You and the children are really the only anchors I have in this fragmented life. We are so physically fragile, more so as we grow older. I am more aware of that than you might guess. I step carefully these days. I don't count on young balance any more and hedge my movements with handholds. If I shower in a strange bathtub with no rubber safety mat, I move with the greatest of caution.

I don't want to lose you. I dread the time when either of us becomes physically dependent, either through accident or normal aging. What will be, will be. But we must be increasingly careful…intelligently careful. It was not smart of me to heft that big wood this summer. I will be more careful. You must, too.

I love you, my dear, and feel helpless in being so far away when you have hurt yourself. I expect you have bruised yourself severely, as I did with that horrendous fall on the boat in New Guinea. However, at our ages hip injuries are classic. I do pray that you have done yourself no real injury.

May you mend well and swiftly and be wholly yourself by the time I return home. This letter will be long after the fact. It will let you know how I feel being so far away.

ABOARD THE *FIJI AGGRESSOR*
SEPTEMBER 13, 1999

I finally reached the boat at 4:30 a.m., having arrived in Nadi at 2:30 a.m. No one was there to meet me. The travel office knew nothing about the contract for a car and driver to take me to the boat in Lautoka, a half-hour away. It all finally worked out…phone calls that roused irate agents out of bed and the arms of their concubines. The crew on the boat were

up, received me with relief and saw me to my own, blessed private cabin and so to bed. I was up at seven a.m. to meet the guests, one of whom was the doctor who, with his son, was with me in Belize a few months ago. This time he had his wife with him and was fully equipped with a Light & Motion system like mine. That's good business for L&M and for me, too. One engine was down. That's why they were still here; but we are finally off today.

There's a couple on this trip, older than I am used to encountering. He is one day younger than I am, his birthday being April 6. His wife is 74 with a birthday in April as well. He's a retired CPA; she a retired anesthesiologist. They still ski together and proceed after this trip to the Solomon Islands for a week on the new *Solomon Island Aggressor*. They are full-of-beans, hard and fit as nuts and ALIVE. We talked about growing up during the Depression. They both came from Ohio farms. They had enough to eat, but no money. I did not compare my silver-spoon family circumstances. Instead, I possibly appreciate more the luck of having had a father whose prudence and enterprise saw us through the Depression with full comfort.

Aboard the *Turks & Caicos Aggressor*
August 18, 2003

Dear Nippers and Mom:

Maine is still with me, late and soon. Your love and care for that special, wonderful place, that privileged heritage, so warms my heart that all of your outrages and grievous failings are as the idle wind that passes me by. I have watched you and the Katzenjammer boys pitch in with zeal and astonishing skill to the inside work. As the son of a father who couldn't even hammer a nail (I can do little better) the skill you boys acquired and the enterprise that went with it has astounded both Mom and me to say the least. As it has turned out it has been a saving grace economically for us. I did not inherit my dad's business enterprise.

Neither Dad nor I could draw a stick figure, but you, Boonie, no longer Fatty, have from Mom the genes of an artist with splendid taste, imagination and – most of all – delightful whimsy that makes the house a most special Waterman house.

And Mum…we have all come to understand how vital your foresight has been in planning the infrastructure, the working materials that have made the new house livable. We could easily forget that you guided Phil Holt in the architectural layout of the house. You are the goddess of light. The house brings the outside to us far more than the old one did.

I feel that you wives, Mary Sue and Thea, have come to love the place as you, a loved part of the Waterman family. I am grateful to you all for pitching in to make the Punch Bowl work. If I should be eaten by a shark tomorrow or just roll over in vodka-soaked paralysis, I would go my way content that the P.B. is safe at least for our generation. Mum and I will have gone to that glass collector in the sky by the time the P.B. comes under the ownership and custody of a fourth generation. There may be five different wives with their own natural and different priorities and loyalties.

Economics may heavily and negatively impact on supporting a summer home. Our good friend, Peter Benchley, with all of his affluence was finally unwilling to support the compound much loved by Wendy's family.

But while we are alive I see the P.B. also alive and well with strong hope for sustaining it in our time. Thank you with all my heart. Your grandfather, my own dad, would have been pleased and thank you most heartily as well.

So – for a change – this is not a pontificating, excoriating broadside to my family. It is a big THANK YOU.

On Slowing Down

There is no question about it. I have slowed down. Perhaps an 80-year-old man should expect that. A measure of guilt, a dash of humiliation and a strong measure of shame accompany the slow down nonetheless.

I was extravagantly praised, eulogized and outrageously honored at the surprise birthday party for me on the *Sea Hunter*. As the others now suit up for the first dive of the day here at Cocos Island, and I announce with more certainty than I feel that "I am bagging the first dive. I'll be with my team on the blue boat for the second dive this morning."

No one gainsays me or looks embarrassed for me. They would protest that I have earned it. I darn well know that with a small measure of discipline I could have suited up and gone with them. I have known many tough old birds, local legends in their time, who were climbing on roofs, doing a man's labor for a full day when they were in their nineties. Scott Lymburner was one. He was a grizzled old timer in Sargentville, Maine, where we had our summer home.

"There's a leak in the roof. Can you come over Scott?"

"I'll be there tomorrow morning"

The reply would be received on the hand-cranked, party line phone way back in the late twenties. Forty years later Scott could be reached on the touch-tone phone. The answer, dependable and reassuring, would be the same. He would arrive in his Chevy with his helper, Mr. Billings, both grown old together. The ladder would go up to the high roof of the big two-story house. The ancient pair would climb the height – not exactly scrambling up any more – reach the roof, assess the damage and replace the shingles. Both were in their nineties.

So I could well join the four dives a day. But some of Cocos Island diving is what we call "Gorilla Diving." It requires plenty of physical strength and energy. One must pull oneself one-handed down an anchor line, a formidable ten-pound camera housing with lights in the other hand, 18 pounds of weight to counter the five-mill wet suit, the bottom 110 feet and still out-of-sight at the top and a six-knot current slanting the line as taught as a bow string. That was par for the course at the dive site called Alcyon. It was a fine dive. It also took the starch out of me and I was thoroughly fatigued after it. I just plain didn't feel like doing the next dive. So I didn't. I started spacing my dives, doing two a day and possibly a third for a night dive. Two turned out to be comfortable. I was graciously assured that this was prudent. One literate guest generously reminded me of Thoreau's words, "If a man does not keep pace with his companions, perhaps it is because he hears a different drummer. Let him step to the music which he hears, however measured or far away."

To my self-serving self I evoked Emerson's thesis, "Do your thing and I shall know thee" (somewhat vulgarized in a hippie era a century later). I like to think that I know myself. The word "lazy" comes to mind. I am not easy with it.

Let me bounce back from this self-flagellation with a kind defense of myself. I have dived these sites for so many years and documented almost all of the marine wildlife here. I am almost as jaded with this diving as I am with the wrecks of Truk Lagoon. Thus my motivation has been dulled. There are seldom any surprises. In Indonesia, diving the Lembeh Strait, the macro marine life was so prolific and variable that I did not – and would not – miss a dive. The same holds for New Guinea. The water is warm. The "muck diving" is seldom deeper than 60 feet. There is such a profusion of macro animals that you can always expect something new to show up. With that prospect and the ease of diving, four dives a day would still be routine for me. Of course there are times when this indulgent attitude kicks back at me most unhappily. Recently in the Galapagos I sat out a dive during which three great mola molas appeared before the divers' cameras, posing patiently while the shutters clicked and the tapes spun before they moved on. I have only encountered one in all my diving years. I retired to my cabin and thought of drinking hemlock.

Editors' Note

While sailing in Fijian waters aboard the Nai'a in 2002 Cat Holloway approached Ned DeLoach with a proposal: Stan Waterman was nearly ready to publish his memoirs. Would New World Publications be interested in taking on the project? Ned expressed immediate enthusiasm.

The concept matured for two years. Finally, in Houston during the 2004 Diving Equipment & Marketing Association trade show, Nancy McGee and William Warmus, sitting on opposite sides of Stan during breakfast, made the case that publication in 2005 was possible and desirable. Nancy, Waterman's business associate and manager, took the proposal to Ned and Paul Humann, owners of New World Publications that afternoon, and the result is the book you hold in your hands.

We are grateful to Stan's friends Peter Benchley and Howard Hall for writing the foreword. Thanks to Anna DeLoach for editing the photography gallery, Michael O'Connell and Eric Riesch for their layout and design expertise, Nancy DeLoach for copyediting assistance, and Patricia Driscoll and Nancy McGee for reviewing the manuscript.

— Ned DeLoach, Ken Marks and William Warmus

Photo Credits

Ned DeLoach 51; Brett Gilliam 67; Howard Hall Productions cover portrait, 43, 44, 45, 46, 48, 50, 61, 66; Cat Holloway 52, 59; Paul Humann 65; Geri Murphy 63; Alese/Morton Pechter 56; Douglas David Seifert 47; Joel Silverstein 64. All other photos from The Stan Waterman Collection.